Following Djuna

THEORIES OF REPRESENTATION AND DIFFERENCE
General Editor, Teresa de Lauretis

FOLLOWING DJUNA

Women Lovers and the Erotics of Loss

CAROLYN ALLEN

INDIANA UNIVERSITY PRESS
Bloomington and Indianapolis

The paper used in this publication meets the minimum requirements of American
National Standard for Information Sciences—Permanence of Paper for Printed
Library Materials, ANSI Z39.48-1984.

Manufactured in the United States of America

Library of Congress Cataloging-in-Publication Data
Allen, Carolyn.
Following Djuna : women lovers and the erotics of loss / Carolyn Allen.
p.   cm.
Includes bibliographical references and index.
ISBN 0-253-33023-8 (alk. paper). — ISBN 0-253-21047-x (pbk. : alk. paper)
1. Lesbians' writings, American—History and criticism. 2. American fiction—Women
authors—History and criticism. 3. English fiction—Women authors—History and criticism.
4. Lesbians' writings, English—History and criticism. 5. Erotic stories, American—History
and criticism. 6. Erotic stories, English—History and criticism. 7. Harris, Bertha, 1937- —
Criticism and interpretation. 8. Winterson, Jeanette, 1959- —Criticism and interpretation.
9. Brown, Rebecca, 1956- —Criticism and interpretation. 10. Homosexuality and
literature—History—20th century. 11. Loss (Psychology) in literature. 12. Barnes,
Djuna—Influence. 13. Lesbians in literature. 14. Women in literature. I. Title.
PS153.L46A45   1996
810.9'9206643—dc20   95-23531
1   2   3   4   5   01   00   99   98   97   96

CONTENTS

ACKNOWLEDGMENTS

As always in my life, my greatest debt is to my friends.

Marsha McCroskey first led me to read *Nightwood*. Early on, Donna Gerstenberger suggested that I shape my reading into a scholarly article; she has been an inspiration ever since. Evan Watkins generously read all my drafts with much care and a practiced eye. Mary Travers, Liz Burbank, and Jane Adam provided invaluable help with individual sections. Sue-Ellen Case sustained me long-distance in large ways and small. My other long-time friends—Jerry Allen, Judy Howard, Marilyn Hawkins, Pat Novotny, Emily Warn, Sydney Kaplan, Linda Bierds, and Yvonne Mandorf—provided encouragement and support at just the right moments. Kate Cummings continues as always to challenge my thinking and make me see things new. My love and thanks to them all.

Thanks, too, to my colleagues in the Red and Black Books Collective who give me a chance to live a political life outside of academia, and whose passion for books helps me through long days.

I am grateful for the professional leave from the University of Washington that allowed me time to complete my manuscript.

Finally, my deep appreciation to Teresa de Lauretis for her encouragement, and to Joan Catapano for her patience.

*   *   *

The first section of Part One is revised from its appearance as "The Erotics of Nora's Narrative in Djuna Barnes's *Nightwood*," *Signs* 19 (Autumn 1993):177–200. © 1993 by The University of Chicago. All rights reserved.

The second section of Part One is revised from its appearance as "Sexual Narrative in the Fiction of Djuna Barnes," in *Sexual Practice, Textual Theory*, ed. Susan J. Wolfe and Julia Penelope (Cambridge, Mass.: Basil Blackwell, 1993), pp. 184–98. A shorter version, "Writing toward *Nightwood*," appeared earlier in *Silence and Power: A Reevaluation of Djuna Barnes*, ed. Mary Lynn Broe (Carbondale: Southern Illinois University Press, 1991), pp. 54–65.

Following Djuna

Introduction

DJUNA BARNES AND BERTHA HARRIS
READING EROTICS/FOLLOWING DJUNA

In "The More Profound Nationality of Their Lesbianism," a witty and provocative tribute to lesbian Paris in the 1920s, Bertha Harris writes about Djuna Barnes with a kind of transferential love. Casting her as the subject who is supposed to know, Harris fantasizes Barnes as the woman who can help her discover her cultural history:

> I was hanging out on the corner of Patchin Place—not, under any circumstances, to catch a glimpse of e. e. cummings—but waiting for Djuna Barnes to take her afternoon walk and, with all discretion follow her—move the way she moved, turn the way she turned, hold my head like her head. As often as I could (and with discretion) I followed her and trailing her, received the silent messages about my past I needed and she could give; and never once during our exchange did I encroach upon her lordly attitude to give her my name. (77)

Harris is but one of a number of modern and contemporary women writers who have acknowledged Djuna Barnes as an influence, or whose work has been critically compared to Barnes's, or who write with thematic and stylistic preoccupations like those of Barnes. The list includes French writers such as Monique Wittig and Michèle Causse, Québécoise fiction theorist Nicole Brossard, Australian prose-poet Mary Fallon, and British and U.S. fictions writers such as Jane Bowles, Anaïs Nin, Jeanette Winterson, Rebecca Brown, Barbara Sorel, and Jane DeLynn. References to Barnes continue to show up in 1990s pop culture texts as well. Katherine V. Forrest's *Murder at the Nightwood Bar* is about to become a movie; a recent issue of *Venus Infers: A Magazine for Leather Dykes* features erotica by "Lydia Steptoe," the pseudonym under which Barnes wrote satiric sketches in the 1920s for *Charm* and *Vanity Fair.*

Bertha Harris's tribute continues: "The name she made up for me was my real name; and it was that name she used, when, in my fantasy, she would stop and take my hand to thank me for all the flowers I daily stuffed into her mailbox in Patchin Place and then tell me how it was to be a dyke in Paris, in the Twenties" (77). Harris subsequently identifies those flowers as "sweetheart roses," recounts following Barnes down Village streets, and imagines honoring *Nightwood,* Barnes's most famous text, by calling a chapter title up to her Greenwich Village apartment: "'Watchman, What of the Night?'" In short, Harris's transference to Barnes is also a seduction in which the younger woman pursues the older in a fantasy that imagines a double return of sexual attention and literary knowledge.[1]

Not surprisingly, the other "Barnesian" writers I have named focus their own work, as Harris does, on sexual and affective exchanges between women lovers. From among these writers whose work implicitly or explicitly references Barnes's lyrical prose, nonlinear form, and fascination with the psyche, I read at length Jeanette Winterson's *Written on the Body* and Rebecca Brown's *The Terrible Girls* because, like *Nightwood*'s, their narrators obsess about the loss of a lover. That obsession, in turn, creates intricate meditations on women as lovers and constructs an erotics out of the very loss that has occasioned the obsession.

The stakes in reading these exchanges are literary and theoretical, personal and political. By reviewing fictional erotics between women in novels by Harris, Barnes, Jeanette Winterson, and Rebecca Brown, I enact an erotics of reading that produces the beginnings of both a literary "tradition" and a "genealogy," familiar, if differently nuanced, terms for the complex interconnections among readers, writers, and texts. The personal and textual relations I posit between Barnes and Harris not only exemplify a tradition and genealogy in the making, but also anticipate the theoretical implications of my subsequent readings for a necessarily partial version of women's erotics beyond the text. Just as Harris's fantasy seduction of Barnes imagines sexual attention and counts on literary-cultural knowledge, so reading enactments return personal memory and unconscious investments in producing narratives that are at once sexual and epistemological. As texts written by others about women's affective and sexual exchanges, fictions in the Barnes tradition lure and inform. But as scripts requiring enactment, they also depend on readers' performances. For if, as Shoshana Felman argues, the unconscious is a kind of "unmeant knowledge," then enacting fictional scripts draws from that knowledge to produce meaning that is contingent, partial, even momentary, but always self-seductive and self-informing (Felman 1982a, 30). Thus I intend my extended readings not only to function toward the formation of a particular literary tradition, but also, and more importantly, to suggest how the texts I discuss seduce and inform in re-presenting loss, risk, excess, and retrospective desire.

I argue that fictions "following Djuna" share with Barnes's work, particularly with *Nightwood,* theoretical, thematic, and formal features that imply their intertextual, paradigmatic connection. Barnes's writing, as Catherine Stimpson notes in passing, constructs sophisticated sexual theories (Stimpson 1991, 372). In imagining the start of a Barnes tradition, I specify Stimpson's observation by reading Barnes, Harris, Winterson, and Brown with an eye toward the "theories" they construct—that is, with attention to how their representations of women's erotics in the contexts of loss contribute to personal and political knowledges in particular sociohistorical formations.

The tendency of "theory" to generalize makes it crucial to stress the racial and cultural particularity of my readings. The fictions I discuss construct erotics as textual effect between white women characters from varying economic circumstances in specific historical moments. I take up the literary fictions of four writers—Anglo/American and British—in readings that both perform and produce textual erotics that are necessarily limited by the texts on which they draw. Women's erotics in this particular paradigm of experimental novels occur in situations of obsession, loss, and inequalities of power. Their writers are more interested in opening up the "dark places," as Jeanette Winterson puts it, between women lovers than in providing escape to a world where the girl always gets—and keeps—the girl. Their endings aren't happy; their lovers don't walk unproblematically into the sunset; the threat of loss is always in the air.

As fictions of loss whose stories of desire are heightened by narrative retrospection, novels in the nascent Barnes tradition inscribe the complexity of emotional and sexual exchanges between women lovers. These psychosexual dynamics have historically not been well served by classic psychoanalytic texts. As Teresa de Lauretis points out in articulating her psychoanalytically informed theory of lesbian sexuality in *The Practice of Love,* "the major public discourses on lesbian sexuality available in this century are discourses of sexual indifference—of inversion, of masculinity complex, of lesbianism as pre-Oedipal fusion, psychosis, hysteria, bisexuality, or oscillation between masculinity and femininity—and they are all inadequate to the task" (1994, 75). Given this inadequacy, I am interested in seeing what versions of women's erotics might be produced by novels in a tradition determined in part by its retrospective inscription of loss and desire. My argument draws primarily from literary texts, but it also poses their erotics as interventions in or revisions of what de Lauretis calls the "*passionate fictions*" of psychoanalysis (3).

So far, in designating exchanges between women lovers, I have used the phrases "erotics between women" and "lesbian erotics" interchangeably. Such an equivalency is not unproblematic given ongoing debates about the definitions, parameters, and efficacy of "lesbian" as an identity position; I employ "erotics between women" to avoid reifications of "lesbian," and to enable recognition of the historical specificity of "lesbian" as a descriptive term. Most important, "erotics between women" underlines my argument's focus on relational, dyadic interchanges rather than on individual "identity" issues.[2] I intend "erotics between women" to signal the complicated sexual and emotional dynamics of desire between women, however they name themselves.

In the remainder of my introduction, Harris's transferential seduction of Barnes, especially when it plays out textually in the relation of Harris's novel *Lover* to Barnes's *Ladies Almanack,* provides a context in which to situate both "women lovers" and "erotics" as my analytic reference points for reading erotics in fiction and for enacting an erotics of reading. Harris's tribute to Barnes in "More Profound" also suggests how an erotics of reading produces a literary genealogy counter to the better-known legacy of Radclyffe Hall and *The Well of Loneliness*. *Nightwood* serves as a touchstone not only for Harris's own formation as a writer, but for my formulation of women's erotics as they are constructed by recent novels in the *Nightwood* tradition.

I

Tell me how it was to be a dyke in Paris, in the Twenties.

—Harris, "More Profound" 77

Harris begins "More Profound" by referring to her shadowing of Barnes, but she pays tribute also to erotic connections between [and among] women lovers in Paris of the 1920s more generally. In so doing she has no qualms in naming the women "lesbian," though the Barnes text she cites, *Ladies Almanack,* is much less forthright. Published in 1928, *Ladies Almanack* is a kind of comic *roman à clef* in almanac form about the "ladies" of Natalie Clifford Barney's coterie. Organized month by month, Barnes's self-proclaimed "slight satiric wigging" at once celebrates the sexual triumphs of Dame Evangeline Musset (Barney) and worries about various limitations and proclivities of her circle.[3] Harris unhesitatingly calls it an "outrageous lesbian comedy," and "for its time, a document of lesbian revolution" (81). She quotes from *Almanack*: "Lesbians are made in Heaven, Djuna Barnes seems to say; and they are the children of angels: 'This is the part about Heaven that has never been told . . . there was heard under the Dome of Heaven a great Crowing, and from the Midst, an Egg, as incredible as a thing forgotten, fell to Earth, and striking, split and hatched, and from out of it stepped one saying, 'Pardon me, I must be going!' And this was the first Woman born with a Difference. After this the Angels parted, and the Face of each was the Mother look. Why was that?'" (81). Writing as a lesbian-feminist in 1973, Harris can easily celebrate "lesbian" as an embodied (and heavenly) identity.[4] But for Barnes writing in 1928 as for many 1990s readers, "lesbian" as a celebratory identity is much more problematic.

Biographical evidence about Barnes's life is not yet complete, but suggests that she was married twice and probably had both male and female lovers, including, briefly, Barney (Lanser 1991, 164). There is no doubt, however, about the passionate intensity of her ten-year relationship with silverpoint artist Thelma Wood, to whom Barnes's novel *Ryder,* also published in 1928, is dedicated. Long after she and Thelma had parted, Barnes told one friend, "I'm not a lesbian. I just loved Thelma," but wrote to another, "I was not offended in the least to be thought lesbian—it's simply that I'm very reticent about my personal life."[5] Even apart from Barnes's biographical circumstances, her varying portrayals of "woman born with a difference" in *Ladies Almanack* unsettle any secure lesbian identity. The story of Dame Musset, who "developed in the Womb of her most gentle Mother to be a Boy" (*LA* 7) and who wears hip boots, carries a whip, and rides horses astride, parodies sexologists' theories of female inversion.[6] This origin story is offset by the equally originary account of angelic parthenogenesis that produces "the Woman born with a Difference"; moreover, both "biology-as-destiny" myths exist in tension with stories of "contingent inverts" (Ellis 1937) who come "down from the Bed of Matrimony" to take other women as lovers; in fact, some of these latter lovers in time "return to their posts" (*LA* 54). All of which is to say that in *Ladies Almanack* there is no single identity position or causal explanation for women who take women lovers.[7]

The most illuminating commentaries on "lesbian" identity in *Ladies Almanack* read Barnes as inscribing Adrienne Rich's lesbian continuum, or making no distinction between female sexuality and specifically lesbian sexuality (Lanser 1991, 161; Abraham 1991, 266). I would invoke rather than the continuum, which includes women's relationships to each other whether specifically sexual or not, something closer to Monique Wittig's "universalizing" of a lesbian point of view. Indeed, Wittig explicitly praises Barnes for universalizing the feminine rather than the masculine and thus canceling out gender difference (Wittig 1983, 64).[8] What is at issue in *Ladies Almanack* are differences not between men and women, but between lesbian sexuality and women's sexuality more generally; nevertheless, as a text by one whom Wittig calls a "minority writer," by which she means lesbian or gay, *Ladies Almanack* may be read not only as blurring distinctions between heterosexual and homosexual female desire, but as universalizing sexual connections between women and thus making them the norm.[9] That is, although there is, as both Abraham and Lanser point out, a slippage of Women generally to women with women lovers more specifically, most references to "Women" or "Ladies" in *Ladies Almanack* seem to name generally (women) but refer specifically (women with women).[10]

In part, the "universalizing" of erotic connections between women regardless of identity position is a consequence of *Ladies Almanack*'s substantial, often licentious, attention to the sexual. From Dame Musset's "Genius at bringing up by Hand" to her indestructible flickering tongue which continues to give pleasure from her funeral urn, erotics between women include specific sexual practices. There is no danger of mistaking women's deeply felt but platonic friendships for the giving and taking of sexual pleasure. In fact, "deep" is altogether the wrong generic descriptor for *Ladies Almanack*. Barnes's is a text of surfaces, both literarily, since Barnes's drawings in the style of *L'imagerie populaire* illustrate the book, and figuratively: of caricatures, of satire, and of parody. Its erotics reside in recounting Dame Musset's fame as a lover of women, her distillation as "the Consolation every Woman has at her Finger Tips," her refusal to continue pleasuring a lover who wants more, her complaints about the undersides of upholstered furniture as seen with "the Lesbian Eye" by one who spends much time rolling beneath it with her "lady" (35). "December" concludes the story of Dame Musset, dead at ninety-nine and mourned by generations of women, including some "who had not told their Husbands everything." Together they place the Urn with its living tongue, still flickering and able to satisfy, on an Altar in the Temple of Love.

Ironically, given the 1990s' reputation for sexual preoccupation, the references to lesbian sexual practices in Barnes's 1928 text are at least as explicit as any in the 1990s texts of Harris, Winterson, or Brown.[11] These contemporary texts assume sexual practices between women, but they rarely spend much time elaborating them. Instead, they concentrate on women's affective, emotional interchanges. Embedded in Dame Musset's picaresque tale are reflections on some of the affects that will become crucial to the erotics both of *Nightwood* and of the novels by Winterson and Brown. Lines such as "Love of Woman for Woman should increase Terror" (20); "Woman's is a Kiss in the Mirror" (23); "Acute Melancholy is noticeable in those who have gone a long Way into this Matter" (27); "a Woman tears her Shift for a Likeness in a shift, and Mystery that is lost to the proportion of Mystery" (57) anticipate *Nightwood*'s preoccupations, not with sexual practices but with emotional resonances between women lovers. Erotics between women, then, in the Barnes tradition from *Ladies Almanack* and *Nightwood* through *Written on the Body* and *The Terrible Girls,* signifies both sexual and affective exchanges between white women lovers, but affective relations take precedence. The precise nature of those erotics as they are produced in readings of Barnes, Harris, Winterson, and Brown is the subject of this book. Part One more explicitly defines "erotics" as a term signaling affects between women lovers in the novels. Throughout, "lesbian" works as an adjective to describe the various erotics at play in fictional productions, but it does not name a stable identity position.

Three years after her 1973 tribute to lesbian Paris, Harris published her third novel, *Lover;* when it was republished in 1993, Karla Jay remarked in her "Foreword," "the rich language, which reflects that of Djuna Barnes, makes *Lover* the perfect sequel to *Ladies Almanack* in our reprints of lesbian classics."[12] Jay's critical connection reaffirms Harris's tribute to Barnes; her reprinting of *Lover* makes possible my argument that Harris's seduction of Barnes, begun in "More Profound," continues in *Lover.* A wildly experimental and exuberant fiction of erotic connections among women, *Lover* not only recalls *Ladies Almanack*'s satiric innuendo; with its experimental form, its preoccupation with origins, and its bawdy sexual references, it also reads as an attempt to seduce Barnes the putative interpreter of Harris's cultural past, by textually topping her, so to speak. If *Ladies Almanack* "universalizes" a lesbian perspective by blurring the distinctions between women lovers and women more generally, *Lover* carries the very notion of "lesbian" beyond the hetero/homo sexual divide and the representation of women-as-couple.[13] *Ladies Almanack* concerns itself with such two-women co-nundrums as what to do when a younger woman falls in love with an older one, how to find a lover who will stay for the long term, and how a woman should best speak endearingly to her love. In some "months," these problems are taken up by ladies in pairs—Lady Buck-and-Balk and Tilly-Tweed-In-Blood (Una Troubridge and Radclyffe Hall), Nip and Tuck (Janet Flanner and Solita Solano), the two Doxies (models never identified). In still other chapters, the problems of Ladies are contrasted to those of "Maids and their Beards": various figures debate whether Women's marriages should be legalized, or whether duels would serve to settle the score when a lady strays from her love. Though its portrayals of women in couples normalize lesbian relations, the almanac never questions and indeed depends upon the very binary logic that elsewhere produces lesbians as "the other" of a heterosexual "same."

Lover captures the spirit of *Almanack,* but further politicizes it by dismantling the construction of women-in-couples and largely ignoring (hetero)sexual difference. From its opening synopsis of *Der Rosenkavalier's* multiple gender crossings, through its continual transformation of one character into another, then another, and back again, to its repeated conflicted and shifting origin stories, *Lover* complicates *Ladies Almanack's* blurring of distinctions between lesbians and other women by privileging multiple performances of what Harris calls in the introduction "sexual subversives" (xxi). There are pairs of lovers, all right, and twins, too, but the relationships between and among these couples are never stable. Samaria is Flynn's grandmother and also her lover; a young girl sitting in a swing eating candy hearts is Veronica, but Daisy claims later that she too is the girl in the swing, and Veronica wonders if the swinger couldn't also be her lover Samaria.

Lover reads as a topping of *Ladies Almanack* rather than of *Nightwood,* because it is a text of surfaces rather than depths, of actions rather than recollections. Where *Ladies Almanack* worries the fate of women who seduce, *Lover* argues that every seduction is a glorious performance. The novel's 1993 "Introduction" begins with Harris's account of her own seduction by the honeyed voice of Milton Cross. Harris shorthands the experience of this vocal seduction as "Unnatural lust couched in sumptuous harmonics." Her reading instruction for *Lover* follows shortly, linked by proximity to her own formative seduction by opera: "*Lover* should be absorbed as though it were a theatrical performance. Watch it" (xix).

It might be *Lover's* emphasis on performance in part that Wayne Koestenbaum has in mind when he calls the novel "a vaudeville version of queer theory" (1993, 18). And so it is, if by queer theory he means especially that "the sentences in *Lover* are theoretical because they suggest conduct, because they have edges, because they make the reader want to memorize and emulate them" (18). (The sentences in *Lover* are in fact infinitely more memorable and memorizable than those of most academic theory, queer or otherwise.) But because they "suggest conduct," and because seductive performances constitute the narrative, Harris's novel anticipates queer theory's current emphasis on performance and performatives, on acts rather than on object choice. But to the extent that queer theory implies a discursive "umbrella" sheltering gay, lesbian, bisexual, transgendered, and nonnormative heterosexual sexualities, *Lover's* sexual subversives don't quite fit. Veronica may masquerade as David Niven, Flynn dress as an Etonian son, and the beloved imagine herself as a drag queen named Roman, but the lovers of Harris's novel are almost exclusively women with women lovers, making it readable as a queer text of women's erotics. Further, at the same time that Harris's introduction directs readers to watch *Lover*'s performances, it also details how "*Lover* enjoys postmodernism" (xxv) and highlights the novel's interest in forgeries, fakes, aesthetics, and "deliberate plotlessness" (xxvi). Such descriptions point to the ways in which the erotics of *Lover*'s surface top those of *Ladies Almanack* and, as I suggest below, seduce the reader, rather than thematically inscribe psychic complexities between lovers as *Nightwood* may be said to do.

Lover begins appropriately with women performing center stage:

> This one was lying strapped to a table. Covered in her juices, Samaria was being pulled through the lips of her vulva. That is how Samaria met her.
> She was being pulled, yelling already, through the lips of Daisy's vulva. That is how Flynn met Daisy.
> Veronica, however, came out of nowhere, and so she used to go exclusively with Veronica. (5)

The performance of birth, with its indefinite pronouns, and blurring of mothers and daughters sets the tone for a narrative in which characters fade into one another, shift shape and occasionally gender, perform as actors, as forgers, as rope-walkers on beams of light. Other performances, from cross-dressed versions of *Hamlet,* through a movie starring the mother of one lover, to the writing of a novel called *Lover,* make *Lover* a novel both about performance (in its thematics) and performative (in that its self-referential structure about lovers and *Lover* "constitute[s] the identity it is purported to be" [Butler 1990, 25]). As one might expect from a writer who records her transference to Barnes, Harris's novel acts out resistance through repetition even as it insists on the transformational possibilities of love.[14] The novel's erotics between and among women, marked by costume changes and shape-shifting characters, constitute a performance narrative that is interwoven with, and countered by, a narrative of reproduction (as signaled, for example, by the opening birth scene quoted above) featuring repeating mothers and daughters, multiple and competing origin stories, and discourses of the womanly body. Despite the novel's attention to surfaces, motherhood in *Lover* is, as Harris says in the introduction, "the real worm in the bowl of waxed fruit" (xxvi). The repetitions of the reproductive narrative function as resistance against two related cultural formations that circulate almost as widely in the 1990s as they did in the 1970s: mothers cannot be lovers, and lesbians/"lovers" cannot be mothers. This resistant and repeated narrative of reproduction also returns and plays out the concern in *Ladies Almanack,* voiced primarily by Patience Scalpel, that Ladies by themselves might not have children. In contrast to the ambivalence of Barnes's text, *Lover* declares decisively for both mothers and lovers.

Again like *Ladies Almanack, Lover* is something of a *roman à clef.* Harris writes in her introduction that real flesh and blood hovers "at a safe distance behind *Lover*'s characters. As I wrote, I had in mind some of the most intellectually gifted, visionary, creative, and sexually subversive women of our time" (xxiv). She names Jill Johnston, Joanna Russ, Yvonne Rainier, Kate Millett, and Valerie Solanas, among others. But where *Ladies Almanack* either describes the philosophical dilemmas, or parodies the romantic clichés, or laments the characteristics of its "girl's girls," *Lover* consistently celebrates the performances of its subversives. "The real action is the action of the lover; and all else is that action disguised," says Veronica, who acts by composing the novel that is *Lover*. In this novel "all that really happened is that the lover won the beloved, and became the beloved; and the nature of all kinds of rapture, including this, is that it must clothe itself in disguise . . . the act of love a magic-lantern show, a proliferation of forgeries: which, taken all in all, seem real enough" (207–208). *Lover* follows from *Ladies Almanack* in its attention to a lesbian coterie, its celebration of the explicitly sexual, its experimental form, its dazzling language play. But its seductive topping insists on performance over description, on multiple erotic connections among women rather than between two lovers, and on creation of a "pleasure-dome . . . for sexual subversives."[15] Koestenbaum glosses the sexual explicitness of Harris's pleasure-dome: "Djuna Barnes wanted to go this far but couldn't. Bertha does it for Djuna" (18). He may underestimate the number of sexual references in the language and illustrations of *Ladies Almanack,* but he is right to point to the genealogy. Harris's fantasized seduction of Barnes in "More Profound" creates one version of an erotics between women; *Lover*'s fictional performances, in which "all that really happened is that the lover won the beloved and became the beloved," flirt with another but reject producing psychodynamic detail in favor of presenting stylish forgers and daring lovers.

A third version of women's erotics appears in the concluding moment of *Lover*'s introduction: Harris says, "I wrote *Lover* to seduce Louise Fishman. It worked" (lxxviii).[16] Textual seductions and the erotics of reading they invite inform my readings throughout this book; they are most directly addressed in my discussion of Rebecca Brown's work in Part Three.[17] One of *Lover*'s many threads follows the story of Flynn, who gives up her dream of building a brain machine in favor of falling in love; exegesis destroys, love creates. The reader of *Lover* stands in for Louise Fishman, taking the text as it looms large, being seduced by its play, its surprising turns, its new takes on the oldest story in the world. But increasingly, despite the warning posed by the novel's destruction of the brain machine, the reader responds with the critic's gesture to master, to top, to know. The loving struggle between seductive text and the reader's alternate desire to surrender and to master constitutes an erotics of reading particularly operative in the Barnes tradition because its novels experiment with literary forms and language. Nonlinear plots, parodies of such genres as the romance and the almanac, comic literalizing of cliché, and the use of set pieces as tableaux all entice but ultimately invite active participation. "I have a narrative, but you will be put to it to find it," says one of *Nightwood*'s narrators, and *Lover*'s story is even less straightforwardly presented. Ultimately, of course, story isn't the point ("all that really happened was the lover won the beloved"); acting as lover is. *Lover* as theatrical performance lures the reader as voyeuer, but because the actors and settings shift, disappear, and reappear in new guises, the reader must also participate to make the seductive scene of reading work.

By engaging its reader in Harris's seduction of Louise Fishman, *Lover* enacts an erotics of reading akin to that of Québécoise writer Nicole Brossard, who like Harris has written a tribute to Barnes, "Djuna Barnes: De Profil Moderne" (1981).[18] In a genealogical gesture further establishing Barnes's influence, Brossard begins her tribute by quoting Anaïs Nin: "'Reading *Nightwood* finally crystallized my aspiration for poetic prose in novels. . . . I am happy to pay tribute to the depth, vision, and power of *Nightwood*'" (quoted in Brossard 1981, 190). Brossard then recalls discussing Barnes, and like Harris in "More Profound," Natalie Barney, Romaine Brooks, Dolly Wilde, and others with French writer Michèle Causse,[19] who tells her: "'It is always a woman who introduces you to *Nightwood*.'" Brossard responds: "'Yes, and in most cases, she is a lesbian, as if each sentence of the novel found in her a resonance, a memory, an abyss, a tension'" (191). Later in the tribute Brossard remembers sitting on the shore reading *Nightwood*: "I can't stop reading through this lovers' month of June. Fascinated, excited, almost on the verge of writing myself, I am . . . overcome by the intimate beauty. . . . What matters to Nora where Robin is concerned matters to me where *Nightwood* is concerned: 'Robin is not in your life, you are in her dream, you'll never get out of it'" (204).

Brossard's entanglement with the novel (likened by her *Nightwood* quote to that of its lovers Nora and Robin), her excitement, her submersion in the novel's beauty repeats her earlier invocation of Barnes in *Lovhers*, a series of prose poems that constitute what her translator calls "an exploration of the erotics of reading" (Brossard 1986, 10). In the opening section of *Lovhers* she says, holding "a book by Djuna Barnes," "I can't stop reading/deliring" (a translation that does not do justice to the French pun on reading as delirium [*lire/délire*]). But she also makes delirium, as well as the unfixing of reading, explicitly sexual: "with these same mouths that know how to make a speech, ours tasting of words tasting of kisses (i don't stop reading/deliring—excitation: what arouses the unrecorded in my skin)" (20).

In the next section, the erotics of reading put in motion by the "lovhers" reading of *Nightwood* is theorized. In a scene reminiscent of one section near the beginning of Barthes's *A Lover's Discourse,* "i" sits at a sidewalk cafe without her "Absent One," reading her lover's writing (Barthes 1978, 17).[20] Like Barthes, who sees that "reading is a conductor of Desire to write" (1989, 40), Brossard connects reading to writing ("almost on the verge of writing myself"), but in the cafe scene the pleasures of her texts are also the pleasures of the specific lover and her touch: "i am telling you about my passion for reading you hidden behind these quotations. the facts are such that your project of the text and the text of the project are completed in the taste of the words, in the taste of the kiss. i know that you are real to me/therefore" (1986, 29–30).[21] I imagine Louise Fishman and Thelma Wood reading *Lover* and *Ladies Almanack* with similar passionate attention and recollection. Or perhaps, what I see is Harris and Barnes imagining such attentive and charged readings from their objects of desire who are also the objects of their immediate fictional address. Brossard speaks in *Lovhers* of how the reader imagines the writer-lover, a fantasy that captures as well how the writer of this scene desires to be imagined by her reader-lover: "i picture you obsessively in the midst of writing excessively as if nothing could stop you" (25).

But the specific scene of reading in *Lovhers* may be understood to include not only the writer-reader couple portrayed, but also the more distant reader holding the book *Lovhers* when Brossard writes: "reading the text of your project, i become aware of the extent to which our fictions intersect" (25). The fictions and memories of this outside reader intersect with those written on the page so that, as Barthes says, one reads "while looking up from the book," or more specifically, as he writes in another essay, "the pleasure of the Text is achieved . . . whenever another writing succeeds in writing fragments of our own daily lives, in short, whenever a *co-existence* occurs" (Barthes 1989, 29; 1976, 7). Wittig's account of Barnes's "literary experimentation" resonates with Barthes's description of reading in that it too calls on a specifically visual trope. Wittig argues that Barnes's reader experiences "an out-of-the-corner-of-the-eye perception" in which the field of imaginative vision is "fractured" by "universalizing" the estranged world of Barnes's characters (1983, 64). That sideways glimpse may put the straight reader into a universalized queer world, but it may also work like "reading while looking up" for the queer reader who sees from the corner of the eye familiar scenes of estrangement. Erotics between women in the Barnes tradition both depend on and produce Brossard's fictional intersections, Barthes's coexistences, and Wittig's angled glimpses. In performing them, readers project, identify, remember, imagine, fill in, and reshape. They are enticed, seduced, and controlled by the text. But like lovers who don't know their place, they also flip to take charge, to master, to direct the scene of reading. They are, in short, both the subjects and objects of textual desire.[22]

II

> We roamed the streets making up our histories
> as we went along and gradually I no longer
> saw myself as beginning and ending with *The
> Well of Loneliness:* I was shadowing Djuna
> Barnes.
>
> —Harris, "More Profound," 78

Nearly every critic who addresses Radclyffe Hall's 1928 novel, *The Well of Loneliness,* agrees that it is the most famous (or, almost equally often, infamous) lesbian novel written in English.[23] By fictionalizing early twentieth-century sexology's "female invert," *Well* produces a stereotype of the masculine lesbian that has influenced several generations of readers trying to understand their sexual feelings.[24] Hall's text is above all a novel of identity: as a polemical plea for tolerance of inversion addressed to a homophobic world, its relentless emphasis on the congenital, given nature of the invert makes it a textbook for the essentialist thinking of Krafft-Ebing and Havelock Ellis. The erotics of attraction and the subject positions of the lesbian couples in the novel are made a consequence of its attention to the plight of the homosexual in a world of "normal" people. Thus its main character, Stephen Gordon, born different, doomed by that difference to a world outside the dominant, enters into relations with Woman, who in the novel is constructed from the poles of betraying coquette to innocent virgin. If not quite the whore and the virgin, Angela and Mary stand in for Woman who either flirts with the mannish lesbian out of boredom or loves "her" with true wifely devotion. Stephen, by contrast, views "herself" as a masculine protector of her feminine loves. Only when she sees that her masculinity will not keep Mary safe from a world that abhors her kind does she sacrifice her lover so that Mary may have a protected heterosexual future.

As an invert, Stephen is neither Woman nor Man, but something closer to Gautier's "third sex." She is not quite Ulrich's "man's soul in a woman's body," but she is determined from birth as an invert who has "her" own essential nature. Her gender, as a consequence, is primarily masculine, though the text does occasionally refer to her woman's part, her gentleness. But from her name, through her identification with her father, her love of horses, her regret at not continuing the family bloodlines, to the reference to her "manhood," the text foregrounds her putative masculinity.

Since Stephen's inversion is a given from birth and not a social construction, the novel largely describes it (over and over) and concentrates on Stephen's treatment at the hands of rejecting world, embodied most fully in her mother. Thus the novel's central dynamics pit the essential invert against the social norm, so that its focus is sociological rather than psychological, despite Havelock Ellis's introductory note praising its psychological significance in its "completely faithful and uncompromising" presentation of "one particular aspect of sexual life as it exists among us to-day." His note never names Hall's topic as inversion, or homosexuality or lesbianism, so it really is about "the love that dare not speak its name." While *Well*'s reception indicates the constitutive role of literature in lesbian identity construction, the text itself is interested in a polemic against oppression whose internalization dictates the frequent self-loathing of the lesbian subject. It remains a narrative of development with little attention to lesbian erotics since it is intended as a plea for tolerance.

Harris's comment in "More Profound" recognizes at once the confining limitations and the cultural pervasiveness of the stereotype reified in Hall's novel. When Bertha pursues Djuna down the streets of Greenwich Village, she fantasizes learning an additional, alternative history of "what it was to be a dyke in Paris." In other essays of the 1970s, Harris cites not Barnes the teacher but Barnes the writer and *Nightwood* the text as sources for inspiration. In so doing, she speaks indirectly to another difference between Barnes's work and Hall's, a difference Catharine Stimpson, in her astute account of lesbian literary traditions, refers to as *Well*'s "lack of intricacy" (1982, 249). Harris identifies writers such as Barnes as "the incarnation of metaphor, paradox, dream, iconoclasm, illusion, sarcasm, wit, irony: the stuff of literature" (1979, 26). The implied stylistic contrast between accessible, straightforward linear "realism" and less-accessible intricate nonlinear figuration accounts in part both for *Well*'s extensive readership and, until recently, for *Nightwood*'s relative obscurity.[25]

In referring to "the Barnes tradition," I take my cue from Harris's explicit celebration of Barnes's writing and her recognition that Barnes provided her an additional version of identity from which to reconstruct her cultural history. But my argument follows particularly from two other features of Barnes's work that Harris points to, features that separate *Nightwood* from *The Well of Loneliness*—Barnes's attention to the psyche rather than to the social surround, and to the psyche's encounters with others: "When Djuna Barnes wrote *Nightwood* she was creating, in the silent, devouring magic of her lesbian, Robin Vote, a sleepless swimmer in the depths of all our imaginations; and her new name is Jaws—and her ancient name, Beauty" (Harris 1977, 8).[26] Robin's names speak to her identity as a character in the novel, but the power of her "devouring magic" involves her with others and finally captures her lovers; the dynamics of that capture constitute Nora's obsessive rethinking of all that has passed between them. By contrast, as I have suggested, *The Well of Loneliness* is most often a novel about singular identity. From Stephen's agonized and essentialized history follow traditions of "coming out" and "growing up" novels that focus on what it means to be "a lesbian" in any given culture or time period, how one discovers such an identity, how one tells others about that discovery, and what consequences follow from such a telling. Many of these novels, especially those of the last twenty-five years, from *Rubyfruit Jungle* to *Oranges Are Not the Only Fruit,* have expressed eventual delight and comfort in lesbian/dyke/queer girl identifications. But as Catharine Stimpson points out, even "positive" narratives maintain their connection by contrast to "the dying fall" tradition in which she situates both *Well* and *Nightwood* (1982, 244). *Nightwood*'s narrative of Robin's "devouring magic" instead constructs the emotional entanglements between Robin and Nora as lovers; unlike *Well,* it has little to offer about individual struggle with a seemingly unified subjectivity determined from birth, about family background or relation to homophobic society. Which is not to say that there isn't some agonizing about queerness in *Nightwood,* especially in the monologues of Matthew O'Connor; but Barnes's novel does not make the pains of an essentialized identity, masculine or otherwise, central. Its torments are elsewhere.

In the discussions that follow, I read fictions that imagine the workings not of individual identity but of dyadic relation between women lovers. "Fictions that imagine" refers not only to the novels of Barnes, Winterson, and Brown as texts, but also to the structure of their intricate narratives. In all of them, the "dyadic relations," sexual and emotional, are constructed by narrators looking back on their lost loves. As narratives, they are fictions imagined by the lover who now has only recollected memories. But for readers, the retrospective narrative is all there is of each story; the dynamics of power and exchange may be one-sided because narrated from a single point of view, but they mark a story of two women together nevertheless.

In suggesting a "Barnes tradition" and setting it against Radclyffe Hall's legacy, I do not intend "tradition" in the strong sense of critics such as Foster, Rule, Stimpson, Faderman, Zimmerman, Aguilar-San Juan, and others who have undertaken to set out different versions of carefully delineated "lesbian literary traditions." Instead "tradition" functions in a more limited pointing to the ways in which some of Barnes's themes and textual obsessions, preference for lyrical prose, and experimental forms are "handed down," and continue in such contemporary writers as Bertha Harris. The term also marks how these writers have acknowledged Barnes's work and/or how critical commentators have compared them to Barnes. Indeed, both Harris and Rebecca Brown have been explicitly compared to Barnes by critics, as have other contemporary writers such as Jane DeLynn, who also might be said to write in this "tradition."

Elaine Marks's still-crucial description of what she calls "lesbian intertextuality" is closer to what I mean by "tradition" than critical canon formation or studies of influence. Marks constructs a paradigm in which "we are obliged to acknowledge the inevitable presence of the Sappho model" (1979, 356). Citing French texts by both men and women, she identifies certain shifting and historically specific *topoi* (e.g., erotic connections between older and younger women, the woman writer as a lover of women, the aggressive claimer of the lesbian body) and discourses (initially *apologia*, later Amazonian myth) that carry Sappho's trace. I read in the texts of Harris, Winterson, and Brown traces of Barnes's *topoi* and figures. Marks, too, refers to Harris's "delightful essay" ("More Profound"); the impure Paris of Colette in her essay intersects the night world of Barnes in mine: intertextuality as an erotics of citation.

To invoke "tradition" and "paradigm" is to start from Barnes and read forward. It is equally the case, however, that reading directions lead back to Barnes as well as forward from her, that the work of writers such as Harris, Winterson, and Brown makes possible new and different readings of Barnes's work. My argument thus constructs not only a tradition as Marks sets it out, but also a genealogy. I intend "genealogy" to function not in Foucault's sense of an analysis of power effects in the constitution of knowledge, but in the sense captured by the Milan Women's Bookstore Collective in *Sexual Difference: A Theory of Social-Symbolic Practice*. The Collective constructs from political events between 1966 and 1986 a "genealogy," a theory of women's social relationships and the practices informing them and produced from them, based on "entrustment" through personal friendship, political struggle, and readings of women's writing. As de Lauretis points out in her introduction, the book consistently dodges "the crucial

questions of sexuality, fantasy, and the erotic" in its definition of sexual difference. Nevertheless, it creates "a symbolic community . . . that is at once discovered, invented, and constructed through feminist practices of reference and
address" (de Lauretis 1990, 17,2). Indeed, despite the rhetorical hedging about
specifically sexual exchanges between women, the Collective's opening discussion of entrustment in women's symbolic matrices focuses on Vita Sackville-West
and Virginia Woolf, and H. D. and Bryher, relationships in which sexuality and
fantasy figure significantly.

Extending the Collective's sense of a sociopolitical genealogy of address to a
genealogical erotics of reading foregrounds the obvious but too often invisible
critical truism that every "tradition" of literary "handing down" is a fiction about
the past made in the present. More important, however, just as the Collective
produces a "symbolic community" from reassessing past events, so readers produce a genealogy from recollected readings and fleeting fantasies. Harris reads
Barnes, and Marks notes Harris on Barnes; Joan Nestle compares Rebecca
Brown to Barnes on the back cover of *The Terrible Girls,* and I reread Barnes in
light of Nestle's comparison.

Reading and re-readings, then, both produce and are produced by genealogy,
tradition, and paradigm. If "poetics" signifies the formal aesthetics of texts being
read and "politics" their contextual networks of power, "erotics" points to the
working out of readerly desire in the production of a genealogy, a tradition, a
paradigm. At the same time, "erotics" intersects both with "poetics" and with
"politics" by signifying the reader's performances of textual scripts charged with
the relation of power to desire. "Erotics" differs from "erotic" both because it
names a series of reading acts and because it assumes, rather than describes,
sexual exchanges in its focus on affective, emotional dynamics. Further, it produces readings from literary fiction rather than from "erotica," a genre playing
on a different register of pleasures.

In the discussions that follow, the work of desire in literary texts, rather than
the formation of a literary tradition, takes precedence. The constellation among
women and texts with which I began this introduction—Bertha Harris's transferential tribute to Barnes, *Lover*'s topping of *Ladies Almanack,* the sexual exchanges and readerly lure of these two experimental narratives, and *Lover*'s
seduction of Louise Fishman—constitute versions of erotics between women. I
focus on women's affective exchanges in the context of specifically sexual relationships re-presented by narrators who cannot forget the lovers they have lost.
I think of my method throughout the chapters as "reading from the inside out";
that is, I intend my micro-examinations as performative. I want readers who care
about erotics between women to consider the complexities of their own emotional entanglements against those constructed by Barnes, Harris, Winterson,
and Brown.[27] Most of us have to cope with the loss of a lover at some point;
these novels, with their heightened language and intricate retrospective narrations, center the affects of loss in all its intensity.

III

> The education of the lesbian into artist into les-
> bian into scholar into dyke—was delayed until
> New York and the Phoenix Bookshop on Cor-
> nelia Street where the nice owner urged *Night-*
> *wood* on me for seventy-five cents and I met on
> the upper west side the most elegant of all
> Firbankian heroes who toured the night streets
> with me and called out at the gates of Patchin
> Place, "Watchman, What of the Night?"
>
> —Harris, "More Profound" 78

Nightwood, more than *Ladies Almanack,* is the touchstone for my readings of Winterson and Brown not only because it is Barnes's best-known text, but also because its narrative of lesbian loss inscribes the excess of desire occasioned by fictions of memory as few other novels have. "Lesbian fiction abounds with falling in love, romance, the thrill of anticipation, but not much passion, obsession, loss, or intensely painful desire," writes Bonnie Zimmerman in assessing the thematics of lesbian fictions of the seventies and eighties (1990, 105).[28] Elizabeth Wilson notes how infrequently " 'the dark side' " of lesbian relationships and " 'the ambiguities of passion, the excitement of danger' " are fictionally represented (1986, 181). Michele Roberts laments that lesbian romance cannot make space "for the exploration of 'bad' feelings, angry feelings. . . . I'd love to read a lesbian romance which tackled head-on the anger and rage that women can feel for each other, the way in which the bad mother can surface in a relationship, the way in which women can exercise power over each other" (1986, 231). The Barnes tradition, especially when it bears the thematic and stylistic traces of *Nightwood,* takes up "the dark side" of women's erotics. In fact, *Nightwood* addresses directly the surfacing of the "bad mother" and the affective exercises of power that Roberts calls for, as I discuss in Part One. More generally, because *Nightwood*'s erotics center on one lover's anguish in the face of loss and because Nora's narrative insists on obsessive retelling, rather than on sequential acting, Barnes's novel both represents affective intensity in its characters and produces intensity as reading-effect. Thus, buying *Nightwood* begins Bertha Harris's education not only as a lesbian but, as she says in "More Profound," as an artist, a scholar, and a dyke. From it she learns one version of the intricacies of women's relation as lovers, but she also takes in the artistry of its complicated retrospective narrative, and its web of scholarly references from Dante to Barney. Her identification as "dyke" rests partially on proclaiming the subversive power of *Night-wood*'s intense rendering of loss, perhaps even on its status as an outlaw text of "damnation" rather than of redemption (Stimpson 1982).

The Terrible Girls (1990) and *Written on the Body* (1992) might also be called outlaw texts with outlaw narrators. Like Nora in *Nightwood,* Brown's and Winterson's narrators focus retrospectively on loving made more acute by loss.

They care less about plot than about the circumstances and mechanisms of desire. They prefer lyric meditations of psychic interiority to mimetic representation of social interaction. They engage in fictions of memory even as they suffer the consequences of such fictions.

Unlike *Nightwood*'s, however, the narrators of *The Terrible Girls* and *Written on the Body* are named "I," and their lovers "you." This refusal to unambiguously sex either narrators or lovers makes both texts further removed than *Nightwood* from conventional laws purporting to govern readerly identification by insisting on a coherent and singular reading position. Rather, their narrative ambiguity produces instead a nonidentical reader who may take up multiple reading positions. Such a narrative strategy inscribes fictionally the fragmented and contradictory subject—here, a reading subject—of much poststructuralist theory. At the same time, and in the narrower subset of recent theorizing called queer, these ambiguous narrators and their lovers embody Harris's "sexual subversives," and what queer theory recognizes as a deliberate destablilizing of sex and gender identifications.

There is a sense in which all the texts I've mentioned are queer texts: *Ladies Almanack* addresses "girl's girls" who may also have husbands; *Lover* does the same, and its characters delight in variously gendered performances; *Nightwood* tells the story not only of Nora and Robin, but also of Robin's marriage to Felix and of Matthew's longing to be some good man's wife. The argument of my book, however, does not purport to rest on complete readings of any of these novels: Matthew's longings don't get heard; Henri, co-narrator of *The Passion*, barely appears; not all the stories in *The Terrible Girls* contribute to my reading. Instead my argument depends on micro-reading only the narratives within each text that engage affective exchanges between women as lovers. Perhaps instead of "women" I should say "women-effects" in honor of their textual construction. But because I consciously wish to blur the distinctions between the diegetic dynamics of characters "in" the novels and those of readers who look up, remembering, from the page, I have permitted myself this slippage between "characters" and "readers" in discussing intrarelational dynamics. Thinking of the multiple subject positions of both characters and readers, I use the term "lesbian" as an adjective for emotional and sexual connections between women lovers, however "queer" they might be to themselves or others. I use "lesbian" as an adjective not to institutionalize a logic of identity that would determine internally coherent and unchanging "selves," but at once to secure recognition, and to destabilize any easy sense of what acts and affects "lesbian" might describe.

I'm not claiming that the erotics in these novels constitute any sort of "universal" lesbian paradigm, any more than they make up a nonspecified (and therefore, by default, dominant) "lesbian tradition." Books in the Barnes tradition feature white, usually middle-class characters whose preoccupations are with each other.[29] The world of work barely intrudes. Communities, lesbian or otherwise, don't exist. There's much tension and much struggle, but it is psychic, not sociopolitical. Any "theory" generated from them is limited by those contexts. Since they were written at different historical moments and from different national perspectives even given their whiteness, they bear the marks of differing sociocultural "conversations." *Ladies Almanack*'s portrayal of Dame Musset, for example, depends on theories of inversion prevalent in the 1920s; *The Terrible Girls* refers obliquely to the struggle between 1970s lesbian-feminists and contemporary queer girls. Nevertheless, certain formal and thematic preoccupations run through all these texts, and these repetitions lead me to read novels in the Barnes tradition as if they produced theoretical narratives, a few of many such stories inscribing women's erotics.[30] I argue that the acts and affects of Barnesian narratives contribute theoretically, but only partially, to an understanding of women's erotics as they are enacted beyond the fictional page.

The intensity of affect produced in and by narratives of loss makes them especially germane texts for reading the complicated exchanges between women lovers. Novels such as Jewelle Gomez's *The Gilda Stories,* Sarah Schulman's *After Delores,* and Cherry Muhanji's *Her,* although thematically, structurally, and stylistically different from Barnes, all contain scenes of loss that produce versions of women's erotics because their narrators meditate on the intensity of desire and the circumstances of separation. Genres other than the novel also construct the complications of loss. Audre Lorde's *Zami,* Adrienne Rich's "Twenty-One Love Poems," Marilyn Hacker's *Love, Death and the Changing of Seasons,* some stories in Becky Birtha's *Lover's Choice,* and poems in Cheryl Clarke's *Experimental Love* and Sapphire's *American Dreams* (to suggest only several recent American examples) figure relational dynamics in the context of loss and produce erotics of their own.

In reading the erotics of novels in the Barnes tradition, I have set them in conversation with certain psychoanalytic texts, primarily of Freud, but also of Melanie Klein and Beverly Burch, since these fictions, especially Freud's, have dramatically influenced popular perceptions of women as lovers. Or, more accurately with respect to Freud, influence comes from popular fictions named "freudian," which have a life of their own, sometimes quite removed from Freud's own texts, in middle-class Euro-American cultures. I have most often posed the novels' writing of women's erotics as interventions in or extensions of these psychoanalytic fictions, given the frequently problematic inscription of female homosexuality in them. In so doing, I am mindful of Shoshana Felman's elegant formulations of the relations between psychoanalysis and literature as a dialogue "between two different bodies of language and between two different modes of knowledge" so that "involving psychoanalysis in the scene of literary analysis" is to "explore, bring to light and articulate the various (indirect) ways in which the two domains do indeed *implicate each other,* each one finding itself enlightened, informed, but also affected, displaced, by the other" (1982b, 6, 8–9, emphasis in the original).

Erotics between women in *Nightwood, The Passion, Written on the Body,* and *The Terrible Girls* intervene particularly in psychoanalytic fictions of narcissism and identification because the novels' retrospective narratives of desire rewrite "sameness" and "boundary loss," two staples of pejorative female homosexual castings. My theoretical narrative of women's erotics in *Nightwood* takes up exchanges of power between women lovers. I employ the figure of a palimpsest to stand in for multiple and shifting formations of power exchange that operate between lovers. In Barnes's novel, these formations are most often figured as "mother/child," though they sometimes also involve "wife/husband." Brown's and Winterson's novels occasionally repeat these structures and figure other couples in addition as married/unmarried, working-class/upper-class, butch/-femme, top/bottom. Throughout these texts, lovers sometimes switch places within the pairings, and the pairings themselves "show through" and layer each other in changing configurations so that there is never a static setting of the palimpsest, but a productive tension in trading the formations off against each other. I argue further (1) that the "mother/child couple" is itself a rewriting of dominant culture's insistence on formulaic prescriptions of "mothering," and (2) that the differences inscribed in such shifting formulative power exchanges defend psychically against a phobic, often constitutive "sameness" attributed to same-sex couples by the heterosexual glance. *Nightwood*'s scripting of differences between women lovers becomes, then, not "sameness" but "resemblance," a formulation that I read back into Freud's essay "On Narcissism."

Winterson's *Written on the Body* and her earlier and preliminary moves toward a women's erotics in *The Passion* also figure resemblance, but they suggest as well how mechanisms of identification work in exchanges of desire. In so doing they resonate with and revise psychoanalytic theorizings of projection and incorporation. If projective identification is less exclusively aggressive in *Written on the Body* than it is, say, in the fictions of Melanie Klein, it still invites risks of all kinds. I argue that Winterson's novels, like *Nightwood,* whose language they sometimes echo, eroticize not only resemblance but also the risks inherent in likeness between lovers—risks of loss (of self, of lover, of control), and of intimacy and vulnerability. In a double gesture, the language of the novels at once locates these erotic risks in the threat of egoistic boundary loss, and defends against that threat by posing something close to what Freud describes in *Inhibitions, Symptoms and Anxiety* as "voluntary anxiety." Anxiety also operates as a defense in the scene of reading, particularly in *Written on the Body,* since the sex of the narrator is not definitively given. Especially in the novel's middle section, in which the narrator reinvents the body of the lover in a poetics that is also a defense against loss, the ambiguous sex of "I" produces an anxiety that defends against readerly over-investment.

The Terrible Girls continues *Nightwood*'s preoccupation with power differences and anticipates the risks of identification and desire set out in Winterson's novels. Little power is exchanged in Brown's novel-in-stories; instead the retrospective narration recognizes both the attraction and the difficulties of differences reified by repetition into static patterns of dominance and submission. The narrator recounts both the power of these inequalities and her struggle against the destructive patterns they dictate. With its emphasis on differences as they structure resemblance and on the coexistence of identification and desire, the novel occasions a return to Freud, this time to "Mourning and Melancholia," where narcissism and identification are knotted together in Freud's formulation "narcissistic identification." In arguing with Freud, Brown's novel, like Barnes's before and Winterson's after, insists on erotics between women lovers not as self-absorbed narcissism, but as a fully object-oriented desire that depends on partial, passionate identification rather than on devouring incorporation.

My discussion of *The Terrible Girls* also engages specifically with reading as an erotics of "identification." Just as Bertha Harris's reading of Barnes taught her what it was to be a lesbian, an artist, a scholar, and a dyke, so other readers find that "identifying" with a text is more like performing various and contingent identifications. Reading erotics between women lovers permits, even demands, engaging a complex constellation of positions and subjectivities that both reveal and produce personal pasts and possible futures. "There is no literature that is not based on the pervasive sexuality of its time," writes Harris at the end of "More Profound." And there is no reading of that literature, no identification, no transference, no seduction that does not also call on the reader's desire to fantasize, to act out, to perform, perhaps even to know. Harris calls one such performance "the primary gesture toward the making at last of a decent literature out of the experience of a decent world." In a phantasmatic identification of my own, I imagine Brown and Winterson enacting the erotics that will come to be written in their fictions, repeating Harris's gesture of love, and "following a woman like Djuna Barnes, and all she might represent, down a single street on a particular afternoon" (88).

Part One

DJUNA BARNES
THE EROTICS OF NURTURE

1. *NIGHTWOOD:* GENDER, NARCISSISM, AND THE EROTIC
MATERNAL IN THE NARRATIVE OF NORA FLOOD

If your lesbian lover wanders out night after night looking for love but always comes home to where you keep her safe, who has the power in the relationship? And do you feel like a wife? a mother? both? neither?[1] Djuna Barnes's 1936 novel *Nightwood* does not pose these questions directly, but it does suggest the psychological complexity of emotional and sexual dynamics between women. Understanding these dynamics depends in part on reading texts in culturally, racially, and historically specific contexts; Nora's narrative of love and loss in *Nightwood* theorizes erotics between women by refiguring classic white stereotypes of lesbian desire. Barnes's text poses Nora Flood and her lover Robin Vote as an intimate couple who alternately play out (and play on) conventional hegemonic scripts for "wife and husband" and "mother and child"; *Nightwood*'s lesbian narrative thus raises many of the questions about sameness and difference, possession and jealousy, power and control, performance and essence that inform contemporary inquiries about desire between women. But the novel also intervenes in recent queer theory by skirting over gender difference to obsess at greater length about the limitations of nurturing. In what follows, I first suggest how Nora's story may be read as a narrative of lesbian erotics, then go on to argue how such an erotics critiques Freud's influential writings on narcissism and desire.

As my Introduction explains, I use the term "lesbian" to sign sexual desire between women and the term "erotics" to describe the complicated sexual and emotional dynamics of lesbian relationship in the novel. Employing "erotics" in this sense invokes the discourses of Teresa de Lauretis, Marilyn Frye, and Audre Lorde, all of whom extend the idea of "the erotic" beyond the narrowly sexual. Lorde recognizes the erotic both as "a resource . . . firmly rooted in the power of [women's] unexpressed or unrecognized feeling . . . a considered source of power and information within our lives" and as "those physical, emotional, and psychic expressions of what is deepest and strongest and richest within each of us, being shared: the passion of love, its deepest meanings" (Lorde 1985, 53, 56). Arguing against phallocentric ideas of what constitutes sexual activity, Frye suggests that lesbians weave "a web of meanings which maps emotional intensity, excitement, arousal, bodily play, orgasm, passion and relational adventure" across "a wide field of our passions and bodily pleasures" (1990, 312, 313). De Lauretis calls for theorizing a nonessentialized "'lesbian desire' that constitutes the kind of subjectivity and sexuality we experience as lesbian and want to claim as lesbians; and which therefore we need to theorize, articulate and find ways of representing, not only in its difference from heterosexual norms, its ab-normality, but also and more importantly in its own constitutive processes, its specific modalities and conditions of existence" (1991a, 256). Though writing from differing theoretical positions, all three insist on the implications of the emotional for the sexual.[2]

Such a frame is especially appropriate for *Nightwood,* where the women lovers are connected less by explicit sexual practices than by complex dynamics of power and desire. A reading of *Nightwood*'s erotics, in turn, permits theorizing not only "sexual difference within homosexuality," a move Judith Butler notes as necessary for queer theory (1993, 240), but other differences between like lovers as well. *Nightwood*'s erotics—which assume a specifically sexual relationship in the context of Nora and Robin's emotional and intellectual life—are grounded in the interplay of sameness and difference that the two women, as desiring subjects, enact through networks of power exchange. I imagine these exchange networks as a set of overlaying transparencies that taken together form a palimpsest on which traces are visible across exchanges. The dynamics of these exchanges produce and reproduce ("draw on," to borrow one of *Nightwood*'s many repeated double meanings) discourses of mothering, gender difference, and love of self in another like the self.

Throughout the novel the two women are intimately connected, even when—or more accurately, especially when—Robin's absence heightens Nora's desire. On occasion, the language supposes ideologies of gender to pose them as a feminine/masculine couple. But more frequently it scripts them as players in a dramatic struggle between mother and child. Relations of power in these seemingly conventional binaries are unstable rather than fixed; power circulates by being exchanged both within these pairings (Nora agonizes over Robin's philanderings, but in the end she draws Robin back to her) and among them (Nora has maternal control, but she defers to Robin's masculine freedom). In some moments, a single interaction, Nora's frantic search for Robin, for instance, inscribes either feminine-masculine or mother-child difference—or both. These relations of difference, within and across which power is sometimes balanced but seldom simultaneously equal, are crucial in the novel because another of its repeated formulations focuses attention on the "sameness" of the lovers. In my reading, circulations of power ensured by the palimpsest of differences counter "sameness" to produce neither narcissistic identification nor radical alterity, but a doubled subjectivity of resemblance. Nora and Robin may both be women, but their embodied similarity is only the ground for figuring difference. Furthermore, by representing its lesbian lovers as playing riffs on two of dominant culture's founding binaries, feminine/masculine and mother/child, *Nightwood* enacts the "subversive and parodic redeployment of power" rather than "the impossible fantasy of [power's] full-scale transcendence" that Judith Butler (1990, 124) calls for in lesbian practice.[3] At the same time, *Nightwood's* erotics contextualize historically the work of Butler and some other contemporary queer theorists in that the most detailed overlay in the palimpsest is not the figuring of gender so prominent in recent work on lesbian/gay/queer sexualities, but the "disfiguring" of the mother-child couple, a preoccupation of sexologists from Barnes's generation, as I argue below.[4]

Nightwood has been described by some historians of lesbian fiction and culture as a depressing story of all-consuming obsession, a work that portrays lesbian life negatively and fails to celebrate lesbian heroes (e.g., Faderman 1991, 102).[5] But lesbian erotics are only partially about conscious victories and romantic sunsets. They are also about conscious and unconscious struggle, circulations of power, failure of nerve, and fear of loss, always in the context of a hostile public. In part, the tendency of lesbian-feminist fiction to celebrate and affirm lesbian life in what Naiad Press editor Barbara Grier (quoted in DeLombard 1995, 135) calls "'yes-you're-a-lesbian-and-you're-wonderful type of books'" comes in response to the overwhelmingly negative portrayals of lesbians in straight fiction and the many failures of relationships in lesbian popular fiction of the decades before the lesbian/gay liberation movement began in the United States in the late 1960s.[6] Lesbian presses, especially those concentrating on fiction, publish mostly "genre fiction"—romances or, recently, mysteries and detective stories or erotica, presumably because that is what lesbian readers buy. A kind of tautology is involved here, however, given that lesbians buy what lesbian presses publish (perhaps, as friends recently suggested, in the hope that "this book will be the really good one," or "this will be the one where I can see my own life written out"). But seldom does genre fiction attempt to capture the complex dynamics between lesbian subjects. As an account of these complexities, *Nightwood* remains a classic.

Many lesbian writers especially honor Barnes as influential for them and often praise *Nightwood* rather than damn it. Nicole Brossard begins *Lovhers* with women who perform their desire for each other while reading "a book by Djuna Barnes" (1986, 21). She uses *Nightwood* explicitly in *Picture Theory,* where she quotes directly from the novel throughout the second titled section; Monique Wittig celebrates *Nightwood's* reworking of gender; Michèle Causse names Barnes along with Brossard and Adrienne Rich as giving ontological existence to women; Lee Lynch, like Bertha Harris before her, recalls her pilgrimage to Barnes's New York street; even writers who, like Lynch, find Barnes's characters remote from their own more economically proscribed lesbian experiences praise the brilliance of the writing.[7] At the same time, however, erotics between women in *Nightwood* position subjects who are white, middle-class North Americans and who divide their time between the United States and Europe. As is often true of Anglo-American novels of the period, the race and class positions of the characters are marked by the absence of explicit markings, as if their privileged status made it unnecessary to describe their whiteness. In contrast, the racially marked portrayal of the black character, Nikka, and the highly problematic inscription of Jewishness call attention not only to the whiteness of the lesbian narrative, but to the disturbing racialization that marks some of the novel's other narrative directions.[8] So *Nightwood*'s detailed rewriting of mother-child dynamics and its less pervasive play on gendered positions in its narrative of women lovers are both historically and culturally limited.

With these limitations in mind, *Nightwood* may be read as a theoretical fiction, or as a fiction of theory—a narrative that produces theory as well as story. These productions in the novel are multiple and suggest multiple hermeneutical possibilities. Barnes as writer is also a producer/interpreter of her own memories and imaginings; many commentators point out that her lover Thelma Wood was a model for her *Nightwood* character Robin Vote; recent readers of archival material point to her complicated family relationships and especially to her life with her grandmother as formative, making it difficult not to read those traces in *Nightwood*'s dream sequences.[9] But I have pursued another kind of reading. I will argue that Nora's retelling of her relationship with Robin is a narrative of lesbian desire and power, a narrative "found" as Nora recounts her loss of Robin. Retelling the story of her past desire, Nora desires again and in excess of her earlier passion. Nora's retrospective recasting of her relationship with Robin leads her slowly to see something that she had not seen as a participant: her own culpability in the betrayal and loss she suffers. Her discovery ultimately sends her out one last time to look for her lost lover. I will outline the interplay of likeness and difference in the erotics of Nora's double narrative, and then suggest how this narrative might function as a critique of Freud's writings on homosexuality and narcissism, writings which both incorporate and produce classic dominant culture stereotypes of a pathologized "female homosexuality."

I. Nora and Robin: *Nightwood*'s Retrospective Narrative of Desire

In each of *Nightwood*'s first four chapters, an omniscient voice introduces one of the principal characters. The lesbian story begins in Nora's chapter, "Night Watch," with a third-person narration briefly describing how Nora and Robin meet, travel, and live together despite Robin's increasingly frequent nights out, until Robin takes a new lover, Jenny Petherbridge. The events sketched by the omniscient narrator of "Night Watch" are later reinterpreted in Nora's own retelling of her story in "Go Down, Matthew." The novel's narrative structure, like the figure that best describes its erotics, is palimpsestic in that the story of Robin and Nora is told first by a third-person narrator, then reviewed and reshaped through repetition by Nora's own overlaying account to Matthew O'Connor, the novel's ebullient doctor-confessor.

As she recasts for Matthew her past life with Robin, Nora experiences more intensely her longing for her lover, so that her retrospective narrating is both about her desire and itself an act of desiring—that is, both descriptive and productive.[10] Her acts of retelling mark erotics between women as including a kind of powerful excess that finally defeats the two models suggested by Nora's talking to Matthew: the medical discourse of "the talking cure" and the religious discourse of confession. In *Nightwood*'s parodic psychoanalytic scenes, both doctor and patient speak volumes, but seldom directly to each other. Rather than cure Nora of her obsession with Robin, her meetings with Matthew convince her to seek out her lover once more. In its confessional mode, the novel reverses the traditional power of the confessor in that Matthew fails in his absolution of his "parishioner."[11]

In this doubled narrative of desire and desiring, girl meets girl, girl loses girl to another, girl retells the story of their relationship to the "doctor," stops talking in favor of searching, and finally finds the girl again. Because it is a story of obsession following a breakup, the dynamics are heightened by the difficulties of nonheterosexual loving, the fictionalizing power of memory, and the pain of lesbian loss. The outlines of the original story take only ten pages of narration.[12] These pages provide the novel's scant plot and suggest the relative balance of power that first characterizes Nora and Robin's relationship. They meet in the audience of a circus for which Nora is the sometime publicist. When Nora arrives, the clowns and animals have already begun to enter the ring, "the belly of a great mother where there was yet room to play" (54). As the animals with their "dusty eyes" parade past, "the orbit of their light" illuminates the place where Robin sits, her hands shaking as she lights her cigarette (54). The animals set the stage for the entrance of the lions with their "withheld strength"; one of them honors Robin by going down before her.

> Then as one powerful lioness came to the turn of the bars, exactly opposite the girl, she turned her furious great head with its yellow eyes afire and went down, her paws thrust through the bars and, as she regarded the girl, as if a river were falling behind impassable heat, her eyes flowed in tears that never reached the surface. At that the girl rose straight up. Nora took her hand. "Let's get out of here!" the girl said, and still holding her hand Nora took her out.
>
> In the lobby Nora said, "My name is Nora Flood," and she waited. After a pause the girl said, "I'm Robin Vote." She looked about her distractedly. "I don't want to be here." But it was all she said; she did not explain where she wished to be.
>
> She stayed with Nora until the mid-winter. Two spirits were working in her, love and anonymity. Yet they were so "haunted" of each other that separation was impossible. (54–55)

Love at first sight, so often a staple of lesbian fiction, does its work here, but unlike conventional plottings, neither the course of their courtship nor the details of their life together are narrated; attraction somehow becomes mutual need.[13] The first part of the passage conveys Nora and Robin's erotic connection through tropes of fire, heat, unshed tears, and fury. In the context of the whole novel, the passage is one in a continuing series that identifies Robin as atavistic, "a wild thing, caught in a woman's skin" (146). But in the specifics of the lesbian narrative, Robin is both the subject of power and the object of the gaze as the lion sees her and goes down. Nora signals her role as protector by taking Robin's hand and leading her out. In this scene the couple could be figured either as Nora's protective butch to Robin's fragile femme, or as Nora's protective mother to Robin's disconcerted child. The reference to the circus ring as "the belly of the great mother" suggests a mother-child dynamic, and indeed it is that coupling that most marks the erotics between Nora and Robin. The syntax of the last paragraph is also ambiguous. In the statement "they were so 'haunted' of each other," "they" may refer to the "two spirits" of love and anonymity that make Robin wander between the apartment she shares with Nora and the bars and cafes where she anonymously picks up other lovers. But at this opening point in the narration, her wanderings have not yet been described. So for the moment, "they" suggests Nora and Robin together as a sexual couple, "haunted" by one another. As the first narrated account of their relationship, the passage does not attempt to account for the sources of their desire but instead poses, however briefly, a relative balance of power between them. It also outlines the erotics that will play out as Nora retells their story: they are "haunted" by each other, alike and impossible to separate, and yet different in that one leads, one follows, one looks, and one is looked at. This tension—their similarity as same-sex lovers and their need to cross it with constructions of difference—becomes the subject of Nora's retrospective obsession. The powerful erotics of this passage continue in the subsequent narrative as Nora recalls what they were to each other. Her retelling draws figures on the palimpsest's overlays of gender and nurturing. They take their shape from dominant culture, but their outlines change in the context of lesbian performance.

II

> And I, who want power, chose a girl who
> resembles a boy.
>
> —Nora in *Nightwood* (136)

Some years ago, feminists scholars spoke with confidence about sex and gender; "sex" suggested "female or male," biologically defined; "gender" referred to socially constructed expectations of behavior or parodic performance labeled "feminine or masculine." But this distinction has never been as universal as we might hope; once the editor of a journal in a discipline other than mine changed all my uses of "sex" to "gender." Deployments of these terms has often varied according to the purposes of the writer. In a now-classic essay, Gayle Rubin stresses the connection between sex and gender by introducing the "sex/gender system" to mark the "set of arrangements by which a society transforms biological sexuality into products of human activity, and in which these transformed sexual needs are satisfied" (1978, esp. 159). Further thinking has complicated and reconfigured these terms for varying theoretical purposes. Eve Sedgwick brings sex and gender together under the rubric "gender" because she wants to avoid confusion between "sex" and "sexuality" in a discussion considering sexuality through axes other than gender (1990, 29). Writing specifically about gender in Barnes after translating *Spillway,* Wittig suggested that Barnes "cancels out the genders by making them obsolete" (1983, 64).[14] Wittig means that Barnes makes universal "the feminine," which Wittig takes to stand for both sex and gender. Barnes "makes no difference in the way she describes male and female characters"; instead she allows "the feminine" to substitute for and thus cancel not only the hegemonic universalizing "masculine," but also gender altogether (64). Wittig's argument helps place the radical nature of Barnes's work in the context of both masculinist social power and "minority" writing. But for theorizing *Nightwood*'s specifically lesbian erotics, the distinction between "sex" and "gender" is necessary; without it, the gender overlay, on which is figured one kind of power exchange in the sameness-difference relation, would be subsumed by the similar sex of the two lovers.

Judith Butler argues that the separation between sex and gender is more radically discontinuous than either Rubin or Wittig implies. In her view, both sex and gender are not only constructed but performative and unstable, and as a consequence, neither ought be construed as prediscursive or a "locus of agency" (Butler 1990, 140). The erotics of Nora's narrative assume a definition of sexuality based on the same-sex relations of the characters; a reading of other narratives in the novel, Matthew's, for example, or Robin's various other liaisons, might take up Sedgwick's interest in the fluidity of desire and contradictions of sexuality. In contrast, the gender relations of Nora and Robin emphasize the theoretical necessity of separating gender enactments from sexed bodies.[15] Still, gender difference between women in the novel is minimal. Its scarcity places *Nightwood* historically between depictions of essentialized gender such as that in *The Well of Loneliness* and accounts of playful butch/femme performance recently so prominent in lesbian writing.[16]

Nora's gender position in *Nightwood*'s masculine-feminine overlay is not overtly marked.[17] That Nora's body and dress are unmarked is in keeping with sexological theories current at the time in which one partner of a lesbian couple was viewed as an "invert" and the other was never "satisfactorily defined" (Ruehl 1991, 35). Robin is described as boyish—wearing trousers, playing with toy soldiers and wind-up cars—and these "masculine" attributes and games predominate in her characterization. But Robin is also a mother. Not only that, but at one point she dresses accompanied by "chimes of cosmetic bottles and cream jars; the faint perfume of hair heated under the electric curlers" (58). In another passage she moves from "boy" to parodic "husband": "'Sometimes,' Nora said, '[Robin] would sit at home all day looking out of the window or playing with her toys, trains, and animals and cars to wind up, and dolls and marbles and soldiers. . . . Sometimes, if she got tight by evening, I would find her standing in the middle of the room in boy's clothes, rocking from foot to foot, holding the doll she had given us—"our child"—high above her head, as if she would cast it down, a look of fury on her face'" (147). This textual gender play in which boyish Robin is also a biological mother frames the conventional masculine-feminine positions involved in some power exchanges: as in a traditional white middle-class marriage of the period, Robin has adventures and Nora stays home, Robin silently withholds her feelings and Nora endlessly expresses hers. At the same time, Nora remains the patient constant in Robin's inconsistent life. The ambiguous gender context, in which Robin is both Woman-who-reproduces and boy-who-plays-with-soldiers, unsettles the seeming conventionality of Robin and Nora's masculine-feminine exchanges. Rather than adopting gendered stereotypes, holding them constant, and pleading for understanding as *The Well of Loneliness* does, *Nightwood* inserts them in a more complicated palimpsest of lesbian erotics where they form only one overlay— the one least emphasized.

III

> You, who should have had a thousand children
> and Robin who should have been all of them.
>
> —Matthew to Nora in *Nightwood* (101)

The mother-child trope figures most crucially in *Nightwood*'s palimpsest. Like positions of gender, mother-child stereotypes abound in discussions of lesbian relations. Both Freudian and non-Freudian psychoanalysis posit mother-daughter etiologies for lesbian desire. Helene Deutsch counters Freud's emphasis on the "masculinity complex" by delineating "repressed longing for the mother" as the origin for desire between women; Charlotte Wolff suggests that lesbians want "to re-establish a lost paradise—the union with [the] mother," to cite only two of many such analyses (Deutsch 1944, 346; Wolff 1973, 60). More recently, Bonnie Zimmerman points to lesbian-feminist revisions of this stereotype of lesbian desire and cites especially Lorde, Cherrie Moraga, Michelle Cliff, Paula Gunn Allen, and Alice Bloch (Zimmerman 1990, 58). Esther Newton describes "mother/daughter eroticism" as "a central component of lesbian sexuality" (1984, 571). Bertha Harris writes in *Lover,* "There is no intimacy between woman and woman which is not preceded by a long narrative of the mother" (1976, 173). Others theorizing lesbian erotics are not as convinced; de Lauretis argues that lesbian eroticism is not "pre-oedipal, in the sense of the 'mother-child dyad' dear to much of so-called psychoanalytic feminism" (1991a, 257). From an entirely different theoretical perspective and in the context of ethics, Sarah Hoagland criticizes the efficacy of the mother-child relation as a model of caretaking because it is too insular and too often does not take into account the inequitable social realities of the world (1991).[18] *Nightwood* enters this debate both by figuring mother-child positions as part of its lesbian erotics and by "disfiguring" the hegemonic positions these erotics delineate, as I will argue.

Nora's narrative reproduces some cultural conventions of the mother's position vis-à-vis the child's, a binary that also implies gender: Nora is the home, Robin the wanderer; Nora protects, Robin is protected; Nora fears, Robin is feared for. In these exchanges, Robin has the most visible power because she initiates action and Nora responds to it. At the same time, however, Nora provides Robin with safety. No matter how often Robin wanders, she returns to Nora—returns to a faithful lover who will keep her safe. So, despite Robin's more obvious command, Nora's power balances Robin's because Nora is the guarantor of stability. Desire is a function of absence in these exchanges, and initially it is mutual. Nora thinks constantly of Robin, and occasionally Robin misses Nora: in one of Robin's early wanderings when she sees a sculptured head that both she and Nora love, "a quiet joy radiated from her own eyes; for this head was remembrance of Nora and her love, making the anticipation of the people she was to meet set and melancholy" (59–60). Temporary absences create desire in both lovers, but exchanges of power in the "mother-child" positions keep the couple slightly off-center so that stasis (and boredom) is endlessly deferred. Nora as "mother/wife" worries about Robin's safety but provides a center of stability; Robin as "child/husband" has a home to which to return, but only when she chooses to do so. As Nora tells Matthew, "If I asked her, crying, not to go out, she would go just the same, richer in her heart because I had touched it, as she was going down the stairs" (151). For both, tension results from never knowing absolutely that each will maintain her position for the other. The form of the narration helps suggest that Robin has the greater power. The omniscient narrator first describes Robin's increasingly frequent nights out; then Nora recollects their years together. Both voices, together with the fact that representation of Robin's consciousness is largely absent from the narration, make it apparent to the reader that Nora is the obvious bearer of pain, the voice of anguish, the subject divided from her like subject who defers to Robin's ostensibly greater freedom by always being there in times of need. Despite the narrative construction of Robin as the lover who controls, however, it is finally Nora who makes the decision to end the relationship.

Ostensibly, Nora comes to this decision because Robin not only begins a sexual relationship with Jenny Petherbridge, but denies that she loves Nora as well. But in her retrospective narrative, Nora recognizes how she is implicated in Robin's flight. Before Nora and Robin part, the mother-child dynamic, shaped primarily by its protector/protected guise, shifts to a configuration that has an added moralistic dimension—rescuer/rescued. This maintains the mother-child discourse, but also lays over it a good girl/bad girl relationship, again a staple of lesbian narratives. The point comes when Nora is so eager to protect Robin that she can no longer wait at home but must follow Robin and rescue her from her "dissolute" companions. This pressure sends Robin from anonymous encounters to the relationship with Jenny in which she tells Jenny that she and Nora are "'just good friends'" (141). The betrayal of their intimacy brings Nora to "str[ike Robin] awake" by telling her their relationship is over (145). Robin in turn "wakes up" to her own corruption, and flees with Jenny. Nora then goes to Matthew, where she realizes what she has been to Robin, "a fixed dismay" (157). The maternal protection that becomes impetus for rescue finally functions as control—as power to determine Robin's movements and to define her morally. No longer a safe home to which Robin always returns, Nora is instead an overpowering threat from which Robin must escape. When Nora realizes her culpability in destroying the delicate balance of difference between "mother" and "child," she stops talking to Matthew and leaves to find Robin. In the brief last chapter, both lovers find themselves at Nora's private chapel in America. But the enigmatic final scene in which Nora collapses at the chapel door and Robin eventually lies weeping next to Nora's dog suggests that the women cannot live together in the world of the day.

IV

She is myself.

—Nora in Nightwood (127)

Like the trope of mother-child that operates so pervasively in *Nightwood*, fictional portrayals of love between two lovers who are perceived as "the same" evidence negative constructions of the gay and lesbian erotic in dominant culture. Both early sexology and some post-Freudian psychoanalysis pathologize the same-sex erotic dynamic as extreme self-enclosure under the rubric of narcissism.[19] But Freud's classic essay "On Narcissism" (1914b) remains the touchstone for psychoanalytic accounts of narcissism as self-enclosure. I now turn to that essay in a reading that emphasizes the difference between primary and secondary narcissism, a difference often enlisted in pejorative accounts of homosex as "sameness."[20] *Nightwood* references self-enclosure as a negative, but it also rewrites "sameness" as a crucial component of erotics between women. By offering two fictions of "sameness," the novel returns Freud's distinction between two kinds of narcissism (a distinction often collapsed by nontechnical references to narcissism as a pejorative) and, more important for women's erotics, rewrites "sameness" as "resemblance."

Freud's "On Narcissism" begins by delineating primary from secondary narcissism, suggesting that primary narcissism is the "libidinal complement to the egoism of the instinct of self-preservation, a measure of which may justifiably be attributed to every living creature" (74). Secondary narcissism indicates a withdrawal of the libidinal instincts from objects to the ego: "The libido that has been withdrawn from the external world has been directed to the ego and thus gives rise to an attitude which may be called narcissism, a secondary narcissism superimposed on the primary one" (75). In the second part of the essay, he turns from his examination of schizophrenics in whom he observed the withdrawal of libido from external objects back into the ego, to three other examples through which to understand narcissism more clearly. The third of these (in addition to the study of organic disease and of hypochondria) is the erotic life of the sexes. In this section he distinguishes anaclitic from narcissistic object choice—a distinction that *Nightwood* revises, as I argue in the next section.

Freud's distinction between object choice and both primary and secondary narcissism is important for my purposes, since "narcissism" and its companion forms "narcissistic" and "narcissist" function in contemporary psychoanalytic discourses as a pathology (e.g., "narcissistic personality disorder") and outside them as a pejorative descriptor. "On Narcissism" moves from its account of primary narcissism as "normal" and secondary narcissism as a pathology, to narcissistic object choice as a type of erotic life first observed "especially clearly" in "perverts and homosexuals." But the discussion of the role of narcissism in erotic life and erotic object choice focuses not on homosexuality but on the differences between anaclitic and narcissistic object choice in "the male and female sexes" and specifies from the beginning that both "paths" are open to everyone, that "we are postulating a primary narcissism in everyone, which may in some cases manifest itself in a dominating fashion in his [*sic*] object choice." In so moving, Freud follows his frequent practice of theorizing from clinical observations of his own or others (he notes that Otto Rank describes the "extensive presence" of narcissism so that it might "claim a place in the regular course of human development" [73] to a nonclinical population. Both his assertion that anaclitic and narcissistic object choices are related to primary narcissism (that is, to the original protosexual attachment to one's caretaker *and* one's self in acts of autoerotic self-preservation) and his subsequent discussion of the erotic life of men and women suggest that sexual involvement with someone else maintains a connection to primary narcissism, while the self-enclosure of secondary narcissism makes other-directed object choice more difficult. He notes, however, that clinically even secondary narcissism frequently brings about "only a *partial* detachment of the libido from objects" (86). My point in reviewing this part of Freud's argument is to underline the distinction in "On Narcissism" between secondary narcissism and other-directed narcissistic object choice because, as I have suggested, the two are commonly conflated to connote a version of Freud's secondary narcissism—which is then used as a dismissive label for same-sex erotics.[21]

Nightwood includes specific reference to the kind of self-enclosure Freud attributes to secondary narcissism, but the novel also offers a version of "sameness" as a ground for Nora's passion. Here is Matthew's description of Robin, a description that coincides with Freud's account of secondary narcissism and with nonanalytic dismissal of self-absorption: "'[Robin] can't "put herself in another's place," she herself is the only "position"'" (146). It is important to note that this classic portrayal captures what Matthew sees as the self-absorption of Robin as a single figure; it does not refer to the erotic between two women. On the contrary, when Nora speaks of loving one who is like herself, she describes not the singular narcissism Matthew attributes to Robin, but relational connection between two mutually vulnerable lovers. That Robin is self-absorbed finally does not matter; Nora loves her anyway, and in the end that loving drives her to America to find Robin once again.

Nora discovers the strength of her connection in her retrospective narrative, where she often frames their identification as desire. Here is a representative passage: "'There's nothing to go by, Matthew,'" she tells Matthew about her love for Robin. "'You do not know which way to go. A man is another person—a woman is yourself, caught as you turn in panic; on her mouth you kiss your own. If she is taken you cry that you have been robbed of yourself. God laughs at me, but his laughter is my love'" (143). Nora locates herself outside of heterosexual desire and conventional religiocultural boundaries—outside, but defiantly outside. Nora loves Robin despite the absence of erotic rules and affirms her love in the face of a laughing God. Her connection to Robin is explicitly embodied, explicitly sexual; their bodies are both different and alike: "'on her lips you kiss your own.'" Difference precedes sameness in the syntax of this sentence, just as the differences stressed in the omniscient narration precede the "self-sameness" Nora discovers in her retrospective narrative of desire. Nora finds that in loving and losing Robin she has lost herself as well, whereas earlier she had thought of Robin merely as "Other." So her previous "other" set-ups of Robin, in, for example, Robin's position as child to Nora's mother, or as bad girl suffering from Nora's need to rescue, keep Nora's discovery of herself in Robin from being narcissistic enclosure. What she finds is not self-annihilating *sameness* but crucial *resemblance*, a relation of identity layered with figures of alterity.

Throughout the text, the women occupy differing positions of gender and nurturing with mutual but nonsimultaneous vulnerabilties: Nora needs to be needed, for example, and Robin needs to be safe. The tensions of difference drive the erotics between them, preventing boredom; passages in Nora's narrative that assert identity read less like narcissism than like doubled subjectivity. This doubleness is suggested by word play in the early omniscient narration: "[Nora] would go out into the night that she might be 'beside herself,' skirting the cafe in which she could catch a glimpse of Robin" (59). In the retrospective narrative, Nora comes increasingly to voice their doubled subjectivity: "'I thought I loved her for her sake, and I found it was for my own'" (151); "'Matthew,' she said, 'have you ever loved someone and it became yourself?'" (152).[22]

Nora's declaration "'she is myself'" (127), repeated throughout her narrative, is grounded in the figures of difference that have preceded it and traces of which adhere to the rhetoric of identity. I stress this layering of differences in *Nightwood*'s erotics between women because lesbian relationships are conventionally described as self-enclosing, and in danger of fusion even in contemporary lesbian communities. Therapists warn against loss of boundaries (see, e.g., Nichols 1987, esp. 107–108); writers of sex manuals stress the importance of importing difference into sexual life (see, e.g., Loulan 1990, 206–208). In *Nightwood,* the erotics emphasize sameness only in the context of the overlays of difference. The novel captures the unconscious exchanges of power between lovers who are joined by their resemblance as same-sex lovers, yet play out variously figured differences. In these exchanges Nora and Robin become what French lesbian writer/theorist Michèle Causse calls "semblables-differentes" (Gonnard 1987, 64). Difference in the context of resemblance in *Nightwood* works much as Causse suggests: "Difference frightens, seduces, astonishes, stupefies, and in the end it is absolutely instructive" (Gonnard 1987, 65). Indeed, Nora's declaration of her mutuality with Robin comes from the "instruction" of her retold narrative of differences, in which she re-experiences the intensity of her loss, restages her desire, and recognizes her own culpability. The doubled subjectivity Nora proclaims as she recalls her lover works not as paralyzing self-enclosure that precludes love, but rather as crucial connection.

V. Same/Difference: Narcissism and *Nightwood*

Reading Freud through Nora's narrative of desire (a kind of intertextual palimpsest) makes obvious the missing maternal voice in his work and revises some theoretical connections between narcissism and homosexuality.[23] Throughout his writings, Freud privileges a phallic specular economy and inscribes "the law of the father," as feminist commentators have regularly pointed out (Irigaray 1985a; de Lauretis 1988; Roof 1991, esp. 174–215). Although Freud ponders homosexuality more often and from a more progressive position than he is sometimes given credit for, when focused on two women his gaze sees them as in some way masculine. He does not imagine desire between women as women because he believes that "the object choice of the homosexual woman is determined by *masculine* desire" (Irigaray 1985a, 99). Early in his work (1899), he wrote to one of his intellectual "fathers," Wilhelm Fliess, for whom he said his feelings included a homosexual component: "What would you say if masturbation were to reduce itself to homosexuality, and the latter, that is, male homosexuality (*in both sexes*) were the primitive form of sexual longing. . . . If, moreover, libido and anxiety both were male?" (my emphasis)(Freud 1985, 2, 380). Even in his later formulation of psychoanalysis, the lesbian—the woman who desires another woman sexually and emotionally—does not appear in his account. Like all women, the lesbian in Freud inhabits what Luce Irigaray identifies as "the economy of the Same," in which the universality of the male/masculine subsumes the possibility both of sexual difference and of woman's self-representation. The lesbian in Freud is thus subject to what de Lauretis, commenting on Irigaray's critique of Freud, names "sexual indifference."[24]

All of which is not to say that Freud completely neglects homosexuality in women. The female "invert" is there in *Three Essays on the Theory of Sexuality* (1905). More than the male invert, she exhibits the mental characteristics of the opposite sex. The "female homosexual" is also present, in Freud's narrative of female sexuality in "Femininity" (1933).[25] She has a "masculinity complex" and cannot give up her desire for a penis. In his one case study of female homosexuality, "The Psychogenesis of a Case of Homosexuality in a Woman" (1920), he ascribes the woman's love for women like her mother to a function of her anger at her father, so that the girl's mother-desire is not primary but secondary. Similarly, in "Femininity" (1933), Freud suggests that female homosexuality occurs after a woman has taken her father as a love object and somehow been disappointed. Thus "the lesbian" in Freud either occupies a masculine position or is defined in terms of her father-relation.

Female homosexuality is barely mentioned in Freud's work on narcissism.[26] But the erotics of *Nightwood,* structured as they are by difference and resemblance, illuminate the gaps in certain of his formulations, especially the declaration that object choice may be either narcissistic (like the self) or anaclitic (like the mother). The textual dynamics of *Nightwood* help fill the lesbian lacunae opened by Freud's articulation of gender and object choice in his narratives of narcissism. At the same time the novel gives voice to the unvoiced in Freud, spoken "maternal" desire.[27] In using Barnes's narrative to intervene in Freud's texts, I am prompted not only by their similar historical moments and the culturally problematic nature of psychoanalytic discourse for women in general and lesbians in particular, but also by the form of *Nightwood*'s narrative. Nora's retrospective account of her love for Robin both revises the identificatory model that is delineated in Freud's narratives of male homosexuality and narcissism, and writes the maternal position that is largely absent in his work.

In *Leonardo da Vinci and a Memory of His Childhood* (1910) and a 1910 footnote to *Three Essays on the Theory of Sexuality* (1905), Freud recounts how male homosexuality results in part from the child's identification with the mother. In *Leonardo* he explains that a boy may repress his love for his mother in order to preserve it, then identify with her and determine instead to love only others like himself (Freud 1910, 98–101). As the note to *Three Essays on Sexuality* indicates, this identificatory mechanism predicts desire of men for "a young man who resembles themselves and whom *they* may love as their mother loved *them*" (Freud 1905, 145 n. 1; 1910). By analogy, it might be argued that the same dynamic of identification and love for one who resembles the self pertains also to desire between women. Obviously, however, it could not work in a parallel way given that both child and mother are female. But the process of identification would allow something otherwise largely absent in Freud—a position from which the adult woman desires one who resembles a younger version of herself.[28] Because resemblance pertains to mother and daughter in a way it does not to mother and son, male homosexual desire in which love for others like oneself is secondary to the original love for the mother becomes, hypothetically in the lesbian erotic, both primary and secondary. One identifies with the mother to love those like oneself and, in so doing, continues the love for the mother, which is now extended rather than repressed. Freud, of course, would not have theorized in this way since his figuration of female-female desire requires "changing into a man."

When lesbian desire is figured in *Nightwood,* Freud's etiological emphasis is replaced by a narrative of difference-in-resemblance conveyed in familial terms.

Nightwood posits that the dynamic of identification with and love for one who resembles the self holds in part also between desiring women, with the crucial difference that the culturally constructed trope "Mother" substitutes for Freud's familial figure. In the mother-child overlay of *Nightwood* there is a child's position (Robin's), a maternal position (Nora's), and the intervention of a third term, a Mother position, constructed textually from cultural conventions of what constitutes mothering and to which both Robin and Nora are subjected.[29] By "maternal position" I mean that in her relationship with Robin, Nora acts as the nurturer, the protector, the rescuer, and the controller. "Mother position" refers to the idealized expectations associated with mothering as a socially constructed and racially and historically specific institution that determine Nora's role.[30] Nora's maternal enactments may thus be viewed as a playing out of a culturally scripted part called "Mother."

From her introduction in the section appropriately titled "Night Watch" (Nora the Mother watches protectively over Robin and keeps a safe home for her while she wanders the night streets of Paris) to her final recognition of herself as her lover's tormentor, Nora identifies with this Mother construct. Even before that chapter, the narrator says that Nora "robbed herself for everyone; incapable of giving herself warning, she was continually turning about to find herself diminished" (51). This Motherly self-abnegation at first has no specific focus; she is "endlessly embroiled in a preoccupation without a problem" (53). But "then she met Robin" and increasingly becomes her Mother as well as her lover (53). Their house has a fountain with "a tall granite woman bending forward with lifted head; one hand was held over the pelvic round as if to warn a child who goes incautiously" (55). Matthew frequently refers to Nora in such terms as "the mother of mischief . . . trying to get the world home" (61) or "[y]ou, who should have had a thousand children and Robin, who should have been all of them" (101). By arguing that Robin "put you cleverly away by making you the Madonna" (146), he names the specific cultural Mother whom Nora comes to see as the figure of her downfall. In retrospect, Nora recalls retracing Robin's steps in the back streets of Naples. She looks into a room in which a young girl sits in front of an icon: "Looking from her to the Madonna behind the candles, I knew that the image, to her, was what I had been to Robin, not a saint at all, but a fixed dismay" (157). In this scene Nora recognizes the consequences of having acted as Mother; in her zeal to protect, she becomes to Robin both accusatory ideal and invasive savior. Nora's unconscious identification with the Mother and her love for Robin, someone "like herself," revises Freud's account of narcissism in *Leonardo* by suggesting not etiology but ideology as a source for Nora's performance as Mother: The origins of her lesbian desire are never an issue in the text. Instead, her performance is increasingly marked by a culturally specific maternal pressure—providing a safe home, protection from harm, and inculcation of the dominant culture's moral values. That identification interferes with her position as lover. While Freud's *Leonardo* predicts that love for another woman will preserve love for the mother, Nora recognizes how her attempts to "mother" drive Robin from her. Robin and Nora's story escapes from the "pre-oedipal sandbox" of lesbian desire (de Lauretis 1991b, 15) because it is neither about blissful union nor finally dyadic; the Mother, a position which Nora fills in her protecting and rescuing, interrupts that possibility. *Nightwood* thus rewrites the hypothetical analogy of familial identification in Freud, voices the "maternal" desire that is largely absent from his work, but at the same time critiques culturally specific social constructs of "mothering" and the Mother.[31]

Robin's story does not engage Freud's work on narcissism as directly as does Nora's, both because Robin is not the teller of her own tale and because the initial source of her love for Nora is not represented. Her narrative suggests how the need to be mothered, represented in the novel by her looking to Nora for protection, becomes the need to escape first from an excess of protection, then from an excess of rescuing. In hoping Nora will be her protector, Robin enacts a turn on her role as the only actual mother in the novel. She never identifies with the maternal position despite the fact that she herself is a mother while Nora is not. This ironic reversal underscores another tension at play in the erotics between them: difference between public status and private desire. In the mother-child overlay, Robin the mother is always Nora's child.

Just as *Nightwood*'s critique of the Mother intervenes in Freud's account of narcissism and identification, so too the erotics of Nora's relation with Robin revise Freud's thinking on object choice. In one of the most frequently quoted sentences from "On Narcissism," Freud writes: "We say that the human being has originally two sexual objects: himself and the woman who nurses him, and in doing so we are postulating a primary narcissism in everyone, which may in some cases manifest itself in a dominating fashion in his object-choice" (Freud 1914b, 88). He labels these two directions *anaclitic,* based on the mother who is the original caretaker, and *narcissistic,* in which the model is one's own self. Though he assumes that both paths are open to each individual, he maintains the theoretical distinction between the two and argues that men more often follow an anaclitic direction, women a narcissistic one. The mother-child erotics in *Nightwood* argue instead that the two choices are really one, that they coincide rather than remain distinct: I desire one who is like me and who also fills the Mother position constructed as an ideal by dominant discourses about mother love. For Robin, who at first returns home to be protected, who is often childlike and boyish, Nora begins as idealized Mother as well as lover. The narrative then criticizes that construction, as I suggest above.

Because the mother is ghostly or "spectral" in Freud, his essay does not account for Nora's story.[32] Her narrative must be written in Freud's "space-off," a term de Lauretis uses in another context to describe those spaces which are not represented in a discourse, but which are inferable from its frame (de Lauretis 1987, 26). Writing Nora's maternal voice again makes visible a blindness in Freud and argues for the importance of lesbian texts for lesbian theory.

As an intervention and critique of Freud, Nora's narrative in *Nightwood* deconstructs an influential dominant narrative of sexuality. I imagine the intervention, the novel, and the erotics it displays as palimpsestic: layering Nora's narrative over Freud's writes a lesbian story in the gaps of a canonical text; that lesbian story emerges in *Nightwood* when Nora layers her retrospective account over the version presented in the omniscient narration; finally the erotics of Nora's account depend on exchanges of power among paired figures layered so that traces of one "show through" on another. The narrative as palimpsest thus not only intervenes in Freud but, more importantly, theorizes its own lesbian erotics, in which the implicitly sexual plays out in a wider emotional and intellectual context. It stresses the importance of lesbian relationship—what Diane Hamer calls "a negotiation between two desiring partners" (1990, 148). In the novel these negotiations depend on the tensions of differences in power played out against the doubled subjectivity of resemblance that Nora discovers in remembering Robin. The narrative structures these negotiations as movements from discursive positions that are themselves disfigurings of culturally constructed differences of gender and nurturing. In so doing, Nora's story, read as an erotics of complicated dynamics of exchange, as one text among many theorizing desire between women, contributes powerfully to a deeper understanding of how we conduct the intimacies—and confront the dangers—of our lives.

2. WRITING TOWARD *NIGHTWOOD:* SEDUCTION IN THE "LITTLE GIRL" STORIES

Nightwood is Barnes's most famous text and most intricately detailed account of erotics between women. But earlier, shorter fictions also trace in a less fully realized way the dynamics of Nora's narrative. By way of demonstration, I want to turn to three short stories written ten years before the publication of *Nightwood* that begin to work out the novel's preoccupations even though they are not yet marked by the narrative complexities of loss and retrospection so crucial to *Nightwood*. I will argue that these three stories, linked by the "little girl" who narrates them, delineate an early version of the erotics of nurturing. These stories, so called because of the original titles of two—"A Little Girl Tells a Story to a Lady" and "The Little Girl Continues"—culminate in a third that is a direct precursor to *Nightwood*, "Dusie." All three play on gender identifications and familial relations in the production of an erotics. In the earlier two stories, a submerged sexuality charges the erotics, although they do not surface as overtly sexual. In "Dusie," both emotional and sexual dynamics inform the narrative. My reading of all three looks to the shadows rather than to surfaces in focusing on textual figures of resemblance that will become the palimpsest of *Nightwood*.

Beneath the surface of their conventional prose, the three "little girl" stories anticipate the figures of nurturance central to Nora's narrative. The stories are held together not only by their common narrator, but by the common interrogation of gender and sexuality that shadows the text. In all three stories, a young woman tells a story to a lady. The narratives themselves are stories of one kind

of seduction or another, seductions that have one younger and one older participant. The stories about seduction imprint on the narrative situation a forbidden
atmosphere—the seduction of female by female, by older of younger, with the
erotics of the mother-daughter trope shadowing the shadows. The narrator
herself has the absolute autonomy usually reserved for men. She travels all over
Europe, alone or with her sister; she decides how long she will stay, how she will
live, when she wants to leave one place and move on to another. The narratee,
the mysterious "Madame," we know less about. But the narrator wants her to
listen. "Nicht wahr," she says; "n'est pas," "is it not so?" always seeking information, looking for assent. Even in the midst of the stories themselves, the narrator
intrudes with direct address or little asides to her listener so that we never forget
she is a "little girl" telling her stories to "a lady": "'Then this last autumn, before
the last winter set in (you were not here then, Madame)'" or "'Sometimes it is
beautiful in Berlin, Madame, *nicht wahr?*'" (1925b, 25). Of course, the narrator is
not a little girl at all, but a precocious young woman who implicates herself and
her sexuality even as she seems with innocent nonchalance to be recounting some
other woman's story to the presumably attentive "Madame." Her three stories,
increasingly overt in their sexual content, are themselves a fictional seduction of
the older "madame" by the young narrator, Katya.

In "Cassation" a mysterious older woman tries to convince Katya to come and
live with her and take care of her child. Literally, that is, sexually, it is not a
seduction story, yet there hangs over it a sexual atmosphere not unlike that of
Nightwood. Originally "A Little Girl Tells a Story to a Lady" and first published
in 1925, the story was revised and retitled "Cassation" for *Spillway*. The new title,
come upon long after Barnes's Paris days and her denial of her own involvement
with women, stresses what is now the standard reading of all the *Spillway* stories:
the fascination with the void, with negativity, with the abyss at the heart of the
world. Such a reading also connects "Cassation" to *Nightwood,* but it misses the
radical nature of the text's questioning of conventional gender difference and
sexuality. As usual in Barnes's fiction, plot is a minimal pretext. Katya several
times sees a mysterious and dramatic woman in a cafe; one day they are drawn
together, and the woman invites the girl home. After they have lived together for
a year, the woman, Gaya, asks Katya to stay forever to care for her mentally
impaired child. Katya refuses, leaves, returns to say good-by, and finds Gaya in
bed with the child, both making the same wordless sound of vacancy.

The plot operates in a world of unconventionally marked gender and sexual
likeness. The only man in the story is Gaya's husband, a sort of feminized ghost.
He is little, dainty, dreamy, uncertain, appears infrequently, and does not participate in the action. Gaya does attribute to him what several generations later
would be called "the power of the weak," the mark of woman. Conversely, the
women, both Katya and Gaya, are independent and autonomous. In their year
together they take walks, admire military cannons, and have intellectual conversations about philosophy and the state of civilization. During these brief scenes
in the first half of the story, the women in their assertive autonomy generally

occupy positions conventionally marked as masculine rather than as feminine. But within this reversed gender structure, there are still differences in power. The older woman has the active/male role, the younger the passive/female role. Katya does what Gaya asks.

Halfway through the story, however, there is a shift in power. In the first half of the story, Gaya has been the stronger force, leading the girl home, ensconcing her in a bedroom for a year, treating her in part as a child, in part as an intellectual equal. When, in the story's second half, Gaya must finally become mother to her vacant child because of the child's growing need for care, the power shifts to the participant narrator. Katya exercises a masculine power of refusal in ignoring Gaya's pleas to stay, and Gaya, in turn, is reduced to childlike helplessness.

This, then, is the gendered structure of the story: the women marked by traditional masculine traits, the man by traditional feminine ones; the women present, the man absent. The reversal that drives the narrative comes when the older woman must assume the "trap" that Irigaray describes in "Et l'une ne bouge pas sans l'autre," the most institutionalized female role possible—the role of the mother (Irigaray 1981, 61). When she does so, the power dynamic shifts, and with it the positions filled by the two women. The "little girl" now controls the action. The mother cannot prevent her going and collapses into vacancy. This gendered narrative is written in language charged with sexual meaning complementing/complicating the structure. Throughout the story the two women, though never lovers, act out child/mother relationships like those referenced in the passages of *Nightwood*. Reading particular scenes and particular turns of phrase in the light of *Nightwood*'s erotics illuminates the sexual subtext of the narrative.

Early in the story, the women go home together:

> "Then one evening we came into the garden at the same moment. It was late and the fiddles were already playing. We sat together without speaking, just listening to the music, and admiring the playing of the only woman member of the orchestra. She was very intent on the movements of her fingers, and seemed to be leaning over her chin to watch. Then suddenly the lady got up, leaving a small rain of coin, and I followed her until we came to a big house and she let herself in with a key. She turned to the left and went into a dark room and switched on the lights and sat down and said: 'This is where we sleep; this is how it is.'" (14)

This scene resembles that of Robin and Nora's first meeting in *Nightwood* when they are brought wordlessly together at a circus with a lioness bowing in recognition. In "Cassation" the women's first meeting begins with Katya walking elsewhere, looking at the statues of emperors (who look like widows, in keeping with the story's gender reversals) when she suddenly thinks of the cafe and the tall woman she has seen there. She returns; Gaya is there and speaks to her for the first time in a "'voice that touched the heart'" about her home with its Venetian paintings "'where young girls lie dreaming of the Virgin'" (13). The narrator sums up for Madame: "'I said I would meet her again some day in the garden, and we could go 'home' together, and she seemed pleased, but did not show surprise'" (14). Then follows the passage quoted above. As in the *Nightwood* scene, the two women come together silently; one leaves suddenly and the other follows. In between, they focus not on a lioness but on the intensity of the only woman member of the orchestra. Here it is not the recognition of the animal appropriate to Robin's beast-self, but sexual difference, that only woman musician, that sends them home to the bedroom. Once there, the narrator takes time to describe the massive dimensions and great disorder of the room, but saves her most lavish description for a great war painting, which runs together "'in encounter'" with the bed. On it "'generals, with foreign helmets and dripping swords, raging through rolling smoke and the bleeding ranks of the dying, seemed to be charging the bed, so large, so rumpled, so devastated'" (14). So much for men in the bedroom.

In this narrative preparation, the two women have been drawn together by the repetitions of chance and the power of a woman's music; conventional expectations lead the reader to expect a sexual encounter. Here they are in front of the bed, the narrative action has been stopped to point to male violence, and then? In any popular lesbian pulp fiction, they might fall onto the bed, overwhelmed by Destiny or True Love. In "Cassation," they are prevented from so doing; a child lies in the center of the pillows, "'making a thin noise, like the buzzing of a fly'" (14). The charged atmosphere shifts from incipient sexuality to the needs of the child. But Gaya does nothing except drink a little wine, insist that Katya stay, throw herself on the bed, her hair spread around her, and fall asleep. Later that night she puts Katya to bed as she might a child, or a young lover, by loosening and braiding her hair. Katya stays a year.

After that year together, when the condition of Gaya's child worsens, Gaya, in the central monologue of the story, tries to convince Katya to stay and care for the child. She promises to be like her mother, her servant; she denies their previous intellectual sharing:

> "Now you will stay here safely, and you will see. You will like it, you will learn to like it the very best of all. I will bring you breakfast, and luncheon, and supper. I will bring it to you both, myself. I will hold you on my lap, I will feed you like the birds. I will rock you to sleep. You must not argue with me—above all we must not have arguments, no talk about man and his destiny." (18)

The sexual undercurrents of their coming together have earlier been bound up with Gaya's playing at the mother's role. Faced with actually mothering her own helpless child, the woman of power has become the suppliant who wishes to make her friend into her child's caretaker. As she continues her plea, she literally confuses her own child with Katya; friend and child become the same, as if Katya could fill in the vacancy of Gaya's daughter. Her actual daughter cannot provide the companionship that such theorists of the maternal as Chodorow and Irigaray stress is basic to the mother-daughter relation; instead, the child's mental absence calls only for the mother's caretaking role. Not only is Gaya confronted with the institution of motherhood, but experientially, she must mother a child who can never be her companion.[33] To avoid such mothering, Gaya tries to convince Katya to become her child's caretaker; in her speech, she merges Katya as caretaker with Katya as daughter substitute. Were she successful, she, like Nora in *Nightwood,* could have her intimate as her "child" and be both her companion and her caretaker. But Katya, her independence threatened by Gaya's attempts to make her a dependent "daughter" rather than a playful intimate, refuses, just as Robin eventually refuses Nora's need to rescue. Katya's need for differentiation, as Chodorow might say, is as great as Gaya's confusion between her desire not to mother at all and her need for a daughter-companion. Their parting, like their meeting, is shadowed by longing:

> "Then Madame, I got up. It was very cold in the room. I went to the window and pulled the curtains, it was a bright and starry night, and I stood leaning my head against the frame, saying nothing. When I turned around, she was regarding me, her hands held apart, and I knew that I had to go away and leave her. So I came up to her and said, 'Good-bye my Lady.' And I went and put on my street clothes, and when I came back she was leaning against the battle picture, her hands hanging. I said to her, without approaching her, 'Good-bye my love' and went away." (19)

Katya now has the power that initially was Gaya's. In the final scene, Gaya is no longer differentiated from her vacant daughter. She sits beside her child, imitating her mad sound, the seductive woman-turned-mother-turned-child fallen into the void.

Read in the context of *Nightwood,* this story confirms its configuration both of difference in likeness and of mother-child dynamics between women intimates. Of course the story is "about" cassation, as Gaya's long monologue and the ending indicate. But it is also about a little girl telling a story to a lady, one woman speaking to another about attraction, the power of women, the devastation of motherhood, and the conflation of child and intimate. It assumes a female world, then gives up the shifts in power, conventionally marked masculine and feminine, as a comment on the consequences of the ultimate female role—mothering.

The second story in the sequence, "The Grande Malade," continues the subtexts of gender and of sexuality/nurturance. Its original title, "The Little Girl Continues," connects it to "The Little Girl Tells a Story to a Lady," just as its revised *Spillway* title, "The Grande Malade," is linked to "Cassation" in its implication of annulment by disease. Unlike the earlier story, however, its unconventional structuring of gender implicates the male as well as the female characters. Again the story involves pairs of the same sex. Significantly, although the plot purports to be about a heterosexual couple, Moydia and Monsieur X, we never see them alone as a couple or hear anything of their relationship. Instead, the narrative construction subverts the ostensible focus of the plot by concentrating on the couples, Moydia and her sister, Katya, and Monsieur X and his patron, the Baron. Katya, here again active and autonomous, is both narrator and participant. The story is of a cap, a cape, and a pair of boots, all marking transgression of gender and blurring of lines of difference. Katya has given up flowered hats in favor of a cap. Only the women listen to her, whereas men adore her sister Moydia. Moydia is feminine difference in this pair marked by female likeness. If "Cassation" is shadowed by the sexuality of the mother-daughter trope, "The Grande Malade" suggests instead the problematic attraction of father-daughter couples. Moydia chooses as her lover Monsieur X, who himself is paired with the Baron, a man of "aged immaturity" who taps around after Moydia with his cane. With the Baron she is a gamine, teasing him in her childlikeness, sitting in his lap, playing either the "'kitten or the great lady as occasion demanded'" (24). He plays the passive but receptive older "father" to her spoiled child.

The story opens with Katya's description of Moydia's physical beauty. Its first half establishes them as a pair, always together, walking in the Tuilleries, hanging lace curtains over their beds to smoke and talk of lovers. They differ in their appearance; Moydia is clearly feminine, while Katya has her trousers and her cap like her father's. The sisters are like, an inseparable "we," but different not only in their appearance but in their relation to father figures. Katya wants to be her absent father; Moydia wants to take him as lover, substituting for him the available presence of the old Baron.

The males in the story, however, spend more time with each other than with the sisters. Monsieur X seems particularly unsuited as a lover for Moydia: "'He was the protege of a Baron. The Baron liked him very much and called him his "*Poupon prodigieux*," and they played farces together for the amusement of the Fauberg. That was the way it was with Monsieur X, at least in his season when he was, shall we say, the *belle-d'un-jour* and was occupied in writing fables on mice and men, but he always ended the stories with paragraphs *tres acre* against women'" (24). Moydia leaves town to visit her actual father, the one who lives so strongly in the imagination of Katya. During her absence, Monsieur X dies with the Baron at his side. The narrative's only repeated passage, its doubling appropriate in a story where likeness defeats conventions of sexual difference, recounts Monsieur X's death and refers obliquely to the unconventional strains of the story. Katya tells Madame of Monsieur X's death: "'When the Baron saw that Monsieur X was truly going to die, he made him drink. They drank together all night and into the morning. The Baron wanted it that way. "For that," he said, "he might die as he was born, without knowing"'" (27). A page later Katya repeats the scene and the quote for Moydia when she returns from her visit. What is it that Monsieur X doesn't know? Among other things, surely, that his ties to the Baron were greater than those to Moydia.

Katya asked the Baron for something of Monsieur X to give as a remembrance to Moydia. He gives her Monsieur X's cape. Given the fame of Djuna Barnes's own cape, familiar to all who knew her in Paris at the time of the story's publication in *This Quarter* (1925), it is difficult not to see the story's cape as something of a private joke. But more than that, it marks a further transgression of gender identification, passing from a man of uncertain sexuality to a woman who in wearing it always, as the story tells us, comes to resemble her dead lover. By wearing his cape, she becomes not only a masculinized woman who replaces the feminized man, but also the "protege" of the old Baron/father with whom she earlier has had such a sexually coy relationship. Meanwhile, the boots that Monsieur X had earlier promised to Katya are quite forgotten. So while Moydia puts on a man's cape, Katya must forgo her man's boots; for both, clothes mark their move away from boundaries of gender identity toward an ambiguous center, "neither one and half the other," as Matthew O'Connor says. The matrix of gender and sexuality in "The Grande Malade" is not that of "Cassation," yet both stories are shadowed by outlawed transgression of difference boundaries. In their undercurrent of familial eroticism and their fascination with likeness and difference within that likeness, they anticipate the overt emergence of these ideas in *Nightwood*.

"Dusie," like *Nightwood*, brings the undercurrents to the surface. Published in a collection called *American Esoterica* and not included in *Spillway*, perhaps because of its unambiguous lesbian subject matter, "Dusie" directly anticipates many of *Nightwood*'s preoccupations. Like other queer texts, the story's very existence challenges theories of sexual difference. Within its theoretical structure of sameness, difference appears at the textual level in the variety of women presented, but particularly in the condemnation of one who commits an act of violence. Like *Nightwood*'s Jenny, she disappears before the narrative closes. The women who remain, like Nora and Robin, participate in the familiar mother-daughter-lover configuration.

The story is set entirely in a world of likeness. In Madame K's lesbian salon there are no men, only women with different roles. Questions of conventional gender give way to an explicit focus on sexuality. Dusie is the prototype of *Nightwood*'s Robin. She dresses in trousers, plays with dolls and toy soldiers, has many women lovers who call her pet or beast "according to their feelings" (1927, 78). In a description that looks forward to Matthew's *Nightwood* speech on the third sex as "uninhabited angels," the narrator says, "You felt that you must talk to Dusie, tell her everything, because all her beauty was there, but uninhabited, like a church, *n'est-ce-pas,* Madame?" (78). Like Robin she has brief outbursts of temper coupled with an unheeding absence. She has a "strong bodily odor" not yet elaborated as the earth-flesh, fungi perfume of *Nightwood*. Her movements are "like vines over a ruin," just as Robin recalls the "way back" of prehistory (78). Others talk in front of her about her death. But she doesn't notice, and "that made it sorrowful and ridiculous, as if they were anticipating a doom that had fallen already a hundred years" (79). Other descriptions look forward just as directly both to the character and to the language of *Nightwood*.

Clarissa anticipates Jenny just as Dusie does Robin. Both Clarissa and Jenny are thieves of others' lovers. Both mark difference in their female worlds; they counterpoint the other pairs of women lovers by their acts of violence and their narrative disappearances. Both are completely dependent on everyone they know. Jenny, the squatter, lives by appropriating others' words and loves. Clarissa seems "as if she lived only because so many people had seen and spoken to her and of her. If she had been forgotten for a month, entirely by everyone, I'm sure she would have died" (77). She knows how to teach evil, just as Jenny does, and the story's brief action, Clarissa's mutilation of Dusie's foot, shares the power of physical violence with *Nightwood's* carriage scene in which Jenny attacks Robin, making bloody scratches on her face. In both scenes the violence has a sexual context: after the carriage ride, Robin goes with Jenny as lover to America. Clarissa says to Dusie, "You must think, too, about the most terrible virtue, which is to be undefiled because one has no way for it; there are women like that, grown women, there should be an end" (81). These are the last words "the little girl" overhears before she falls asleep. When she awakes, Dusie is asking her to leave the bedroom. When she returns, Clarissa is gone and Dusie's foot is crushed. In this context, it is difficult not to hear the sexual implications of "defiled."

Set against this violence, the mother-daughter-lover dynamic in Dusie's relation with Madame X is warmer, but no less problematic. Though the story does not address the dynamic as directly as *Nightwood* does, it shares the novel's ambivalence about mothering one's lover. Dusie's dolls and tin soldiers, her vulnerability and her self-absorbed absence signal her childlikeness. She clings to her lover, Madame K, as "the only reality." Madame K is mistress of the house, a large, very full blonde Frenchwoman who, the narrator reminds us, is childless. When she is with Dusie, she looks "like a precaution all at once" (77). The narrator says she does not fear for either of them because of the way they "were with each other always" (81). In the final moments of the story, when Madame K returns from a visit to her own mother[34] and finds Dusie with her foot crushed, she takes the foot in her lap and says to the narrator: "You see how it is, she can think no evil for others, she can only hurt herself. You must go away now" (82). Her maternal protectiveness, like Nora's of Robin, is unable to prevent Dusie's defilement. Despite this failure, the story, like "Cassation" before it and *Nightwood* after, makes clear how bound up with sexuality women's attempts to nurture are in Barnes's work.

Nightwood, with Robin as Nora's "child" and lover, works out more elaborately what we see in Dusie as a character just as the novel contains the story of Dusie, Clarissa, and Madame K writ large. What is missing in *Nightwood* is the "little girl" as narrator. Indeed, the little girl's role in "Dusie" is considerably reduced from what it was in her first story, "Cassation," where she is half of the pair central to the story, and from "The Grande Malade," where she puts the story of Moydia in relief by her difference from her. In "Dusie" she is more strictly a narrator and less a participant, though she does consent to stay with Dusie when Madame K goes off and thus can report something of the goings on between Dusie and Clarissa. But clearly her role is fading. In "Dusie" she no longer has a name; in *Nightwood* she disappears altogether. The novel's narrative voice sounds like that of the unseen birds in Robin's hotel room—present but not assigned to a character.

"Dusie" has a related figure for its narrative and that of the other "little girl" stories. In Dusie's room are two canaries, "the one who sang and the one who listened" (76). As the "little girl," the one who is only a year younger than Dusie, sings her stories to "Madame," she becomes increasingly explicit in the sexual nature of her tales. We never learn how Madame responds, but we listen as Barnes works her way toward the erotics between women that is most fully presented in *Nightwood*. From "Cassation" with its shadow story about mothering, through "The Grande Malade" and its sexual uncertainty, to "Dusie" and *Nightwood*, where women's erotic connections and meditations on inversion preoccupy the central characters, Barnes puzzles over likeness and difference, self and other, sexuality and gender. Only with the more sophisticated palimpsestic narration of *Nightwood* do the complicated attractions and inevitable losses of erotic nurturing between women emerge fully formed.

Part Two

JEANETTE WINTERSON
THE EROTICS OF RISK

I. *Nightwood* and the Narrative of *Written on the Body*

Contemporary British novelist Jeanette Winterson belongs to the genealogical "symbolic community" of Barnes not because Winterson acknowledges Barnes as a direct influence in any of the ways Bertha Harris does, but because the instructive erotics between women in *Written on the Body* (1992) return some of *Nightwood*'s textual and affective preoccupations.[1] Despite the historically specific details of their narrative references, *Written on the Body*, like Nora's narrative in *Nightwood*, meditates on an erotic connection made more intense by the extremity of loss in the context of the specifically sexual. Both narrations are retrospective and construct fictions of a lost love; both end ambiguously in similar settings with the lovers problematically reunited. At the level of plot, both narrators fall in love with women married to Jews who attempt to deny their ethnicity.[2] Both deploy sketchy plots as a pretext for commentaries on passion, love, desire, and loss; even Winterson's language in the commentaries sometimes echoes Barnes's. Like *Nightwood*, *Written on the Body* figures its erotics in terms of likeness and difference, and calls on paradigms of gender and nurturing. But more immediate and more pervasive than those Barnesian preoccupations is its theorizing of the risks that charge affective exchanges between women. As a fiction of theory, *Written on the Body* works out ideas begun in Winterson's earlier novel *The Passion* and details a dynamics of risk-taking that both depends on and defends against the same-sex resemblances layered in *Nightwood*.

I have argued that the erotics of Nora's narrative may be read in part as a palimpsest in which power circulates between and among paired positions of difference in tension with the resemblance that marks same-sex lovers. *Written on the Body* references a more explicit palimpsest that both recalls *Nightwood* and suggests its own narrative method and erotic preoccupation.

> Written on the body is a secret code only visible in certain lights; the accumu-
> lations of a lifetime gather there. In places the palimpsest is so heavily worked that
> the letters feel like braille. I like to keep my body rolled up away from prying eyes.
> Never unfold too much, tell the whole story. I didn't know that Louise would
> have reading hands. She has translated me into her own book. (89)

In elaborating the novel's title, this passage, part of a longer meditation on
making love, centers on the secret codes of one lover's body and the ability of
the other to read them. It is also a passage about risk-taking between lovers. The
language calls attention to the specifics of decoding (the body of) a lover for
whom giving permission to read risks making herself vulnerable in unaccus-
tomed ways. "Accumulations of a lifetime," especially the circumstances of the
narrator's past loves, leave traces that help determine why, as the narrative progresses, "Louise" is able to read a secret code previous lovers could not. The
private body that is "rolled up away from prying eyes" and open only to Louise—the lover who reads through touch—and the incorporation of one lover
into another through translation all signify in the erotics of the novel because
they imply the narrator's reluctance to risk being easily read. At the same time
that it marks the hesitation to risk vulnerability, the imperative never to "tell the
whole story" infuses the novel's narrative method in which time, locations, and
order of events are nonsequential and partially relayed. Of course, the passage's
opening sentence also reads: *Written on the Body* "is a secret code only visible in
certain lights," a tease manifested in the novel's most frequently noted feature,
the ambiguous sexing of the narrator, "I." Just as "I"'s sex-unspecified body is a
palimpsestic recording of the past, so the emotional and sexual codes of various
narrative moments are layered in this titular passage which, in the end, becomes
emblematic of the erotics of risk and resemblance in the novel as a whole.

Given that both *Nightwood* and *Written on the Body* play with the palimpsest
trope, it is not surprising that Winterson's novel, like Barnes's, is lightly plotted
but has a complexly layered narrative. The chronological order of events in *Written on the Body* is simple enough: after a series of brief affairs with women, many
of whom are married, and with (apparently) single men, "I," whose sex is not
specifically given, settles down with Jacqueline, with whom "I" has comfort, but
not passion. "I" soon abandons Jacqueline, having fallen in love with Louise, who
in turn leaves her husband, Elgin, and moves in with the narrator. They have been
together about five months when Elgin tells the narrator that Louise has terminal
cancer. "I" then leaves so that Louise may return to Elgin, a cancer specialist who
convinces the narrator that he may be able to save Louise's life. After living
miserably in the country obsessing about Louise, the narrator returns to look for
her in London. Unable to find her there, the narrator goes back to the country,
where Louise finally appears, perhaps in a fantasy, in the last pages of the book.

The erotics of the novel, both hermeneutic and diegetic, depend on the narrative complications of this chronology. Again like *Nightwood*, the narrative is
retrospective, but unlike the palimpsest in which Nora's version is layered over

that of the omniscient narrator, *Written on the Body* has only the first-person narrator's singular story. As a consequence, the intensity of the erotics is heightened because there are no intervening points of view to alleviate the obsession with the lost lover. The retrospective telling works not so much as an act of rediscovering desire but as a series of meditations on passion, comfort, risk, loss, and body desire.

By "hermeneutic erotics," I mean those features of narrative form that capture the reader by setting out the diegetic erotics of the story itself. "Why is the measure of love loss?" begins the book; seemingly the end of the story to follow is known from the start so that plot-as-suspense isn't the point. Instead, "love" and "loss" become subjects of the narrator's meditations and agents of the reader's captation. As textual affects, they exist in no single moment or location but continue throughout the story. The narration produces this sense of ever-present affect by moving back and forth between recent and distant recollections intercut with meditations on emotion told in a kind of suspended temporality; often these meditations use present-tense verbs even though they are seemingly "I"'s thoughts at the time being recalled. The effect is one of a past-tense present-tense that places the meditations rather than the plot or characters at the center of the book.

The location of the narrator is similarly diffused. The narration begins with "I" alone somewhere in a single bed thinking back to a lover's moment with Louise, but the location and moment of this opening frame are never precisely specified. This lack of specificity becomes part of the hermeneutics when the reader substitutes the desire to know a plot outcome with a desire to locate both temporally and spatially the sequence of narrated events. In so positioning the reader, the narration forces attention away from simple event outcomes and on to a more complicated performance of how past decisions haunt future choices. Loss of the lover is a given from the first sentence forward; how loss measures love and how the narrator might be implicated in that loss keep the reader reading.

While the reader participates actively in the text in this quest for temporal, spatial, and causal location, the novel's most frequently noted feature, the unmarked sex of the narrator, creates tension for the reader in a less immediate but more crucial way. In general, conventions of reading fiction require knowing whether an "I" is a man or a woman.[3] Because *Written on the Body* focuses on romance, it especially compels a choice of sex for "I," so that the reader may enter the novel at the simplest level of "love story." The reader depends on conscious and unconscious psychic preferences and on the more overt context of the novel's composition, including its historical moment and the biography of the author, to make such a choice. Winterson's self-identification as a lesbian together with her fame as the author of *Oranges Are Not the Only Fruit* (1985), an explicitly lesbian narrative about the coming out of its protagonist "Jeanette," drives the decision to imagine "I" as Louise's woman lover. The many references to mirrors, twins, and other occasions of doubling in *Written on the Body* playfully encourage such a reading without fully determining it.

Oranges is Winterson's only explicitly lesbian text, but it is also her best-known, since a version of it has been televised both in Britain and in the U.S. At the same time, however, liminal sexuality rather than lesbian identity is a feature of the books written after *Oranges* and before *Written on the Body*. *The Passion* (1987) and *Sexing the Cherry* (1989) have male and female narrators and references to queer sex of various sorts.[4] So, in *Written on the Body*, while most reviewers assume "I" to be a woman, sexual ambiguity still haunts the text, and Winterson's past novels leave room for various psychic investments to determine "I"'s sex.[5] (Indeed, Winterson recounts stories of male publishers' sales representatives praising her ability to capture the male psyche in *Written on the Body* [Bush 1993, 55].) I, however, read her as a woman.

What's interesting for me isn't this coy hermeneutic plot game or even the reader's operative choice, but the function the possible narrator ambiguity serves in reading an erotics of risk otherwise at work between women: the unspecified sex of the narrator acts as a defense against the language of incorporation and loss of boundaries that both entices and threatens two lovers whose bodies are similar. Such a defense works only in the context of the emotional and sexual processes in the novel's foreground. Where *Nightwood* puts in place exchanges of power as a mark of difference between women lovers, *Written on the Body* uses an ostensibly sexually unmarked narrator to guard against the threat of loss in a plot underwritten by a dynamics of body likeness. Linking chance of loss with recognition of the self in the other, the novel articulates a dynamic of emotional risk-taking at the same time that it reworks the erotics of resemblance so crucial in *Nightwood*. In theorizing the threat of boundary loss, *Written on the Body* extends arguments about chance and fear first advanced in *The Passion*. Just as Barnes's fiction intervenes in psychoanalytic discourses on narcissism and nurturance, Winterson's two novels speak with and against cultural discourses on risk by writing another narrative of erotics between women.

II. Some Contemporary Discourses of Risk

Contemporary discussions in a variety of cultural settings frame risk as danger. Its charge is negative. As François Ewald observes, "risk has an allusive, insidious potential existence that renders it simultaneously present and absent, doubtful and suspicious" (1993, 221). Such suspicion manifests itself in various contemporary discourses by assuming risk as something to be avoided, something that often cannot be controlled and so must be taken into account, "assessed" in daily life as in corporate ventures. Economic and sociological theories of rational choice posit individuals as risk-averse. Late modern corporations develop risk assessment as a scientific technology disciplining contemporary lives through such institutions as the insurance and investment industries. Medical discourse sums up life circumstances and family histories by labeling groups "at risk" for such diseases as breast cancer and osteoporosis. Experimental medical procedures often require imposing risks on human subjects just to determine the potential dangers of new procedures designed to cure. AIDS discourse describes risky sexual and drug-using practices in its prevention campaigns. Obviously these campaigns aim to eroticize safer sex rather than high-risk practices.

But risk has not always been constituted as danger. In its history as a Western cultural phenomenon, "risk" has shifted from rhetorical neutrality to its present status as a negative signifier. It has moved, that is, from suggesting "chance" to implying "danger." Cultural anthropologist Mary Douglas traces this shift from the terminological emergence of "risk" in the seventeenth century. In that historical moment it had its origins in gambling and meant "the probability of an event occurring, combined with the magnitude of the losses or gains that would be entailed" (1992, 23).[6] In the eighteenth century, the cultural focus on probability continued and was used in the developing of insurance, especially marine insurance. Chance of profit was measured against chance of a ship's loss. A century later, the neutrality of the term began to shift to the negative, as risk aversion became paramount in economic decision-making. In the late twentieth century, Douglas argues, use of the term moves even further away from "chance" and now is bound semantically almost entirely to "danger": "whereas originally high risk meant a game in which a throw of the die had a strong probability of bringing great pain or great loss, now *risk* refers only to negative outcomes" (3). At the same time, she differentiates risk from taboo, specifying that being at risk involves being vulnerable to events caused by others, while being under taboo means instead being viewed as the cause of harm to others (7).

Both risk and taboo would seem relevant discourses for contemporary s/m sexual practices, a context in which risk might be assigned a positive rather than negative valence by s/m practitioners. The extended feminist and lesbian debates about s/m between and among women make clear that the so-called "sex wars" of the early eighties have survived into the nineties and that s/m remains highly taboo for many women, whatever the sex and gender of their lovers.[7] Surprisingly, risk as an erotic has received little attention by women writing about s/m between women. Instead, the most repeated touchstones are "negotiation," "consent," "safety," and "trust." Risk remains the shadow of trust—a given—little remarked as a dynamic in accounts of scenes eroticizing (among other things) pain, humiliation, shame, dominance, and submission in the context of crossing physical, psychic, and emotional boundaries. Pat Califia writes in the introduction to *Macho Sluts,* "[L]et me say explicitly, at the risk of sounding foolish, that this [book] is a valentine in its original form, a cunt held open by a woman's trusting fingers" (1988, 10). Because the s/m stories in *Macho Sluts* and other collections depend on an erotics of risking pride, subjectivity, consciousness, even death, it is something of an irony that the only mention of risk is the risk of "sounding foolish." Still, the sentence implies trust as a romance; without risk, such trust would be contentless.

In fact, Califia's introduction does not discuss the specifics of trust, negotiation, or other s/m dynamics. Rather, the chapter takes up *writing* about lesbian s/m and defends it against charges of pornography. In so doing, the introduction suggests a connection between taboo and risk that collapses Douglas's differentiation. Dykes are "at risk" of being verbally or physically attacked because they often visually embody homosex as a taboo: "The same cues that alert other lesbians to our availability and sexual prowess seem odd, annoying and unattractive to straight people. And they don't have any tact about letting us know it" (14). But at the same time, as signs of a cultural taboo, visible sexual outlaws put the "social contract" at risk.[8] Califia appropriates the language of anti-gay fundamentalists to make her point with humor: "Minority forms of sex have to be repressed or the social contract will hang in tatters. People will look to their friends and lovers for warmth, affection, love and support instead of to their biological families. Women and children will have no protection from male violence. . . . Nobody will go to church. . . . I suspect what is really being protected by censorship, anti-abortion and homophobic campaigns is the self-image of the so-called majority" (15). Because she writes from the position of taboo subject, Califia opens a space for Douglas's observation to be made into a political point about how risk and taboo work together rather than separately.

Califia's introduction does take up risk in a sexual context, but not to theorize it.[9] Instead, she notes that her publisher (Alyson) does not permit its writers to eroticize high-risk sex, and so she has had to rewrite some of her stories, however reluctantly. But making high-risk sex erotic is not the same as eroticizing risk itself; on that topic, the introduction has little to say. In a later essay, she comes back to the subject of risky practices and AIDS by acknowledging her own "slippages" in the passion of the moment. The essay itself is commendable in its honesty about the difficulty of always practicing safer sex, but one passage seems highly problematic, even in its lyricism. Of unsafe slippages she says, "The desire itself is always honorable. Always. Even if it carries unwelcome microbes among with it. . . . Never be sorry that you have touched another human being intimately, drawn a part of them into your body. It is worth the price" (1993, 223). The rhetorical slippage between fantasy and act doesn't have to make risk explicit to imply its erotic—and deadly—potential.

Amber Hollibaugh provides a seeming counter to Califia's position in a recent interview, also focused on women and HIV/AIDS. In talking about the need for women to be able to say what they desire, but also to say yes or no to various sexual practices, she makes explicit what Califia leaves unsaid, but inferable: "'Safer sex' is about intelligence and passion and responsibility and desire. And I've always been interested in that long before HIV became a cutting edge. HIV just makes it clearer. If you don't think beforehand, you may have to think after. I don't want to have to think after. I really don't think it's necessary for us to risk our lives for shame'" (Goldstein 1994, 43). "La Belle Dame Sans Merci" notwithstanding, this particular tradition of risk and romance reads as a cautionary tale in the age of HIV/AIDS.

III. Theorizing Risk in Winterson

As fictions of theory, the Winterson novels intervene in and extend these various risk discourses. Rather than confirm the contemporary idea of risk as negative, *The Passion* and *Written on the Body* eroticize it. Instead of following contemporary discourses in posing risk only as danger, the novels argue that both the original sense of chance and the current cultural signification of danger constitute risk: when one subject chances emotional and sexual pursuit of another "like" subject, danger ensues. They also suggest, as Califia does, that the "danger" of same-sex lovers makes them at once "at risk" and "under taboo." Further, both Winterson novels might be said to "theorize" emotional risk-taking in the context of the explicitly, but seldom explicitly represented, sexual. Thus, precisely because, unlike Califia's work, neither novel details explicit sexual practices—risky or otherwise—their theorizings are able to highlight the risk-taking *affective* exchanges that ground textual erotics. In so doing, they speak concretely to the varieties of ways in which risk itself underwrites the versions of emotional exchange produced in these fictions.

Whether "risk" has a positive or negative valence in its various and historically shifting discursive contexts, it connotes the threat of loss. Winterson's novels both extend risk discourses and recall the Barnes tradition by specifying how the threat of loss is crucial to sexual and emotional dynamics. Winterson's novels, for example, condense Douglas's argument that "risk" shifts in meaning over time from chance as a neutral idea to danger as an inevitable outcome; in the novels, the pleasure of gain depends on the danger of loss. "It's the thought of what we might lose that excites us," Villanelle says in *The Passion*. Threat of loss is the fulcrum of desire, or, as the opening sentence of *Written on the Body* has it, "the measure of love."

Like her theorizing more generally, Douglas's arguments about risk are determinedly social, rooted in the idea of community and not of the individual. In writing about "the self as risk-taker" in the context of AIDS, for example, she makes clear that "no subtle or subjective concept of the self is to be used here. Psychology, emotions or aesthetics play no part. It is an outside view of the self" (1992, 102). Clearly risk engages not only the psychological (as Douglas acknowledges elsewhere in *Risk and Blame* [41] even though her own investments lie in the politicalization of danger in public policy) but also the psychoanalytic, as Califia's narrative mix of fantasy and practice suggests.[10] Winterson's novels implicate loss in their erotics not only by detailing the specifics of risk-taking, but also by revising psychoanalytic discourses of anxiety. *The Passion* and *Written on the Body* argue that in an eroticizing of anxiety, the danger of loss functions as a barrier between two like lovers, creating a pleasurable tension and a defense against fusion. To invoke anxiety in the context of loss is to recall the specific discourses of Freud in *Inhibitions, Symptoms and Anxiety;* to distinguish barriers in the service of emotional and sexual dynamics is to turn in addition to contemporary theorists of homosex. In what follows, I argue that by staging scenes of sex and gender masquerade, *The Passion* theorizes risk as loss and lure, an idea that *Written on the Body* elaborates and extends in scenes posing passion against comfort. As fictions of theory, both novels intervene in the theoretical fictions of psychoanalysis by specifying how chance of loss produces both pleasure and danger in an erotics between women.

IV. Cross-dressing as Risk in *The Passion*

The Passion suggests that risk-taking functions in sexual and emotional dynamics between women by eroticizing the fear of loss that comes with taking chances. As a novel written in the 1980s but set in the early 1800s, it plays off of the historically shifting meanings of "risk" and its origins in gambling discourse. The novel's brief affair between women depends especially on scenes of cross-dressing that chance various losses when one woman teases another by unsettling culturally specific gender expectations.[11] Just as meditations on love and loss constitute the heart of *Written on the Body*, so miniature meditations closer to aphorism mark *The Passion*. The erotics of risk function thematically and rhetorically by bringing together over several pages repeated variations on two aphoristic phrases. One reads: "You play, you win, you play, you lose. You play." The other reads: "Somewhere between fear and sex passion is." When taken alone, the phrases recall easily enough familiar conventions of heterosexual romantic passion; however, from the event contexts in which they appear, these aphorisms delineate the specific risks and fears occasioned by an erotics between women. To risk is, by *OED* definition as well as by implication in contemporary risk discourses, to chance loss; *The Passion* also insists that "what you risk reveals what you value" (43). In the novel, risk, loss, chance, and value form by accretion a loose semantic chain; as it moves through and helps construct the narrative of events, this chain comes also to include fear, passion, and sex in an erotics linking Villanelle to her lady.

The Passion, set in Europe during the Napoleonic wars, has two alternating narrators, one male, one apparently female. Henri's passions are for Napoleon and for Villanelle; the first brings disillusionment, the second disappointment. Villanelle's passion is for the Queen of Spades, a married woman with whom she has a brief, intense affair. The first appearance of risk comes not in Villanelle's voice but in Henri's. He sees a game of noughts-and-crosses left by children: "You play, you win, you play, you lose. You play. It's the playing that's irresistible. Dicing from one year to the next with the things you love, what you risk reveals what you value. . . . Does it matter whom you lose to, if you lose?" (43). Henri's emphasis is on the competition of the game, in keeping with his longer meditations about war. The opposite player doesn't matter; the winning does.[12]

The next variation is Villanelle's. Dressed as a young man, she works as a card dealer in a casino in Venice. One night she moves her cards of chance to an outdoor masquerade festival, where she meets a beautiful, mysterious woman. What began in Henri's thinking as competitive play becomes in Villanelle's scenes the scent first of risk, then of passion: musing on gambling in general, she thinks, "Queen of spades you win, Ace of clubs you lose. Play again. What will you risk? Your watch? Your house? Your mistress? I like to smell the urgency on them. Even the calmest, the richest, have that smell. It's somewhere between fear and sex. Passion I suppose" (55). Here she introduces passion into her variation on Henri's win-lose-play motif and attaches it abstractly to risk of losing possessions (hence "mistress," a term appropriate to the male gamblers she usually serves). In so doing, she connects chance, risk, loss, and passion.

A few pages further, her abstract passion becomes specifically sexual when Villanelle comments on kissing from odd angles: "The lips and the lips alone are the pleasure. Passion is sweeter split strand by strand. Divided and re-divided like mercury then gathered up only at the last moment." Directly following, in a single-line paragraph comes love: "You see, I am no stranger to love" (59). In the next line the mysterious lady, whom the text names the Queen of Spades after her having chosen that winning card in a match with Villanelle, appears. The narrative sequence expands the earlier sense of "risk" simply as a chance taken in gambling by linking it with fear and sex, then increasing its erotic charge by references to love, and finally by associating it with a specific erotic subject—the Queen of Spades. By inviting accumulation of meanings through semantic chaining and narrative sequence, *The Passion* moves "risk" from an abstraction in gambling to a specific sexually-charged context; the novel reveals risk as a positive erotic in the shadows of contemporary discourse and highlights its disruptive potential.

After winning at cards, the Queen suddenly strokes Villanelle's cheek and disappears into the masquerade. Villanelle determines to find her lost lady and repeats, "Somewhere between fear and sex passion is" (62). She suffers the throes of conventional romantic love, but the language emphasizes her fear, a link in the chain previously named but not elaborated until now: "With this feeling inside, with this wild love that threatens, what safe places might there be? . . . If I were a little different I might turn passion into something holy and then I would sleep again. And then my extasy would be my extasy but I would not be afraid" (63). In the chain of linked signifiers, "fear" enters Villanelle's narrative in the context of a lost woman whom she pursues, and the erotics of risk takes on a cast increasingly specific to passion between women.

Fear is the name the novel gives to one affect of risk-taking. But because the narrative semantics gradually specify risk as an erotic, fear comes, again by textual accumulation, to be associated also with "extasy"-as-pleasure in Villanelle's encounters with her lady. With the sudden disappearance of the Queen from the textual stage, the novel emphasizes a feature of Villanelle's job at the casino—her cross-dressing—and the pleasure and fear it produces. In her work she dresses as a boy because "it was part of the game, trying to decide which sex was hidden behind tight breeches and extravagant face-paste" (54):

> She thought I was a young man. I was not. Should I go to see her as myself and joke about the mistake and leave gracefully? My heart shrivelled at this thought.

To lose her again so soon. And what was myself? Was this breeches and boots self any less real than my garters? What was it about me that interested her? You play you win. You play you lose. You play. (65–66)

With these thoughts in mind, she accepts a dinner invitation from the Queen, fearing that her sex will be discovered and her lady again lost. Two of the fears that partially frame risk as passion are specifically named here: fear of discovery and fear of loss. But rather than deter her, they propel her forward in an eroticizing of the risks she is taking, risks that are consequences of the cross-dressing game.[13]

Cross-dressing grounds the complicated erotics of risk in the novel because it produces at least three trajectories of desire. The first is Villanelle's, who is dressed as a boy because it is part of the game of the casino. The setting of the game, in which dice and card-playing have moved from the casino to an outdoor carnival, strengthens the connection of risk-taking to its original sense of proba- bilities in gambling. In that setting, Villanelle's guise gives her a chance not only to play at liminality, but to question the congruence of sex, gender, and the unitary self ("Was this breeches and boots self any less real than my garters?" [66]). Inside the casino, masqueraders, whose anatomical sex is not known and may or may not be congruent with their gender performances, deal cards to players whose pleasure consists in part in the indeterminacy of not knowing which card is next. There, Villanelle's cross-dressing is merely an accessory to the important (because monetary) risk-taking of the card players. Her sartorial plea- sure in the casino rises from dressing so that she "knows" her anatomical truth and knows too that the gamblers are invited in their flirtations to guess without consequence.

But her controllable gender masquerade is countered by one strange body feature: she was born with the webbed feet usually anatomically proper only for male babies who are destined to be boatmen on Venice's canals. Although she refers to herself as a woman and takes pleasure in gender play, Villanelle is already a border creature. Her webbed feet must remain forever hidden because they pose too great a threat to epistemic order.[14] In fact, their presence reduces the significance of costumed gender play by providing an even riskier possible reve- lation that she must hide by passing-as-gender-masquerade. However purposeful and seductive her disguise, it cannot match her more essential body secret. The contrast in these different border crossings makes gender play just that—play. Discovery of her webbed feet would more permanently unsettle the borders of gender: I dress as a man in the casino, and according to the rules I might be either a man or a woman. I take pleasure from knowing what you don't know. But I also know what you can't even guess. Like a mythical stand-in for a hermaphrodite, I am both and neither.

When she leaves the casino to meet her lady, Villanelle's shift of space increases her risk: what inside the carnival atmosphere of the casino tantalizes, outside chances the more tangible fear of "body truth" discovery. Villanelle worries: "She thought I was a young man. I was not." Despite this fear (and no doubt also

because of it, since the novel eroticizes risk), Villanelle pursues the lady beyond
the safe casino gaming space. In one meeting, the fear of discovery leads directly,
as well as covertly, to passion. The lady challenges Villanelle's costume, but not
necessarily her gender:

> "You're not a soldier."
> "It's fancy dress."
> I began to feel like Sarpi, that Venetian priest and diplomat, who said he never
> told a lie but didn't tell the truth to everyone. Many times that evening as we ate
> and drank and placed dice I prepared to explain. But my tongue thickened and
> my heart rose up in self-defense.
> "Feet," she said.
> "What?"
> "Let me stroke your feet."
> Sweet Madonna, not my feet.
> "I never take off my boots away from home. It's a nervous habit."
> "Then take off your shirt instead."
> Not my shirt, if I raised my shirt she'd find my breasts. (70)

To stop this inquiry, Villanelle kisses her. In the scene, fear of body discovery
ends in the passion of body talk; deferring the risky moment of undressing and
the uncertainty of whether sex or loss will follow maintains the erotic tension of
the moment.

What is unwritten in Villanelle's narration but apparent from the Queen's
sexual interest are the erotics of sex/gender ambiguity. The Queen's interests
constitute the second trajectory of the cross-dressing scenes—the desire of the
viewer, rather than of the dresser. Villanelle's ambiguity flaunts conventional
binaries, and momentarily permits the Queen, as viewer, to play out her desire
in a space where sex, gender, and sexuality may or may not be congruent. Since
in the casino space the Queen doesn't know Villanelle's sex, she may assume she
is male and play out her own heterosexual desire as a cover for a homosexual
possibility.[15] Or she may focus her desire on the possibility of decoding
Villanelle's ambiguity, an erotics which invites entry into the body-as-text in
order to "read," unravel, and thus control the mystery of the ambiguity.
Villanelle's fear of discovery comes from the first ("She thought I was a young
man. I was not" [65]). As it turns out, the erotics of decoding is more operative.

Villanelle's first-person narration forecloses direct presentation of the Queen's
decoding-as-erotic. But the close of the scene, which began with kisses to deflect
the Queen's sartorial inquiries, makes clear her discovery of Villanelle's sex:

> As I was leaving she said, "My husband returns tomorrow."
> Oh.
> As I was leaving she said, "I don't know when I will see you again."
> Does she do this often? Does she walk the streets, when her husband goes away,
> looking for someone like me? . . . Does she invite them to supper and hold them
> with her eyes and explain, a little sadly, that she can't make love? Perhaps this is

her passion. Passion out of passion's obstacles. And me? Every game threatens a wild card. The unpredictable, the out of control. Even with a steady hand and a crystal ball we couldn't rule the world the way we wanted it. There are storms at sea and there are other storms inland. Only the convent windows look serenely out on both.

I went back to her house and banged on the door. She opened it a little. She looked surprised. "I'm a woman," I said, lifting up my shirt and risking the catarrh.

She smiled. "I know."

I didn't go home. I stayed. (71)

The Queen has successfully decoded Villanelle's sexual masquerade, though how and when remain unstated. Instead, this passage suggests other sources of the Queen's passion and power. If for Villanelle passion leans in part on risk of discovery and fear of loss, Villanelle imagines for the Queen a passion dependent on the necessity of creating barriers, and for the two of them, on what she calls earlier the "sweet and precise torture" (67) of separating their pleasures. By the end of the scene, it is clear that for both women the Queen's marriage (initially) furthers their desire by making their attraction harder to act on. The Queen's home becomes another version of the casino. In it, they play dice and more intimate games of control. I want you more if I create an obstacle for you to surmount. I regulate our erotics by controlling the height of the barrier. Villanelle is the Queen's perfect lover, since she wants precisely "the unpredictable, the out of control." She pleases the Queen by overcoming the challenge of the obstacle and by giving herself over to her lady's control at the same time that she indulges her own passion for risk and unpredictability.

The Queen's marriage, which gives her economic and legal power, conditions their risk just as the cross-dressing scenario enables the risk of sexual unmasking. Their secret passion shares its intensity with other such romantic liaisons across literatures and sexualities, but is heightened by the specific risks taken by like lovers: they operate under the social taboo against homosex as well as against extramarital sex. This unease, of course, conditions most lesbian romances; what is specific to *The Passion* is its articulation of risk as the center of an erotics between women.

Villanelle contrasts her passion with the Queen's by saying that the Queen seeks "passion out of passion's obstacles," while she is drawn by the "wild card, the unpredictable, the out of control" (71). Both the possibility of being sexually unmasked and rejected and the danger of a doubly illicit affair inform the attraction of being out of control. As in the dynamics of cross-dressing, where different gazes produce different erotics, the contrast between two sources of erotic tension suggests how each participant operates out of her own phantasmic scene.

The Queen's interest in "passion's obstacles" recalls and revises de Rougemont's well-known account of passion in *Love in the Western World*. In his extended reading of the Tristan and Iseult story, de Rougemont argues that passion requires obstacles and that Tristan constructs them when they are no longer externally imposed. Tristan's ultimate insistence on chastity is a symbolic suicide, "hence Tristan's inclination for a *deliberate obstruction* turns out to be a desire for death" (de Rougemont 1956, 45). But as Adrienne Rich writes in countering the Tristan and Iseult story, women know the difference between love and death (1978, XVII). "Passion out of passion's obstacles" in *The Passion* leads not to death but to deferment of pleasure ultimately taken. It marks one lover's delight in having control over the circumstances of her extramarital affairs, while permitting the other lover's desire for being "out of control" to come into play in their dynamic.[16]

The hermeneutic agency of the reader constitutes the third trajectory in the Villanelle–Queen of Spades scenes. By responding to and filling textual gaps, readerly desire also helps construct the first two trajectories; but such desire also extends beyond those trajectories because the reader's extradiagetic knowledge imagines an erotics that is not possible for Villanelle or the Queen to "create" individually. Primarily readerly desire is, as Peter Brooks and other narrative theorists argue, a desire to know what happens. Reading conventions for romance, regardless of the sexualities in play, push toward consummation. The reader of *The Passion* imagines possible outcomes for Villanelle and the Queen from their first meeting forward. And the conventions teach that brief unconsummated encounters followed by disappearances usually result in reappearances. So this first meeting disposes the reader to imagine various scenarios predicated on attraction between women in the context of cross-dressing. Some of Villanelle's concerns become the reader's (always structured, it goes without saying, according to individual readers' investments in and resistances to such attractions and such contexts). But fear of sexual discovery might well give way to anticipation of such a discovery, while fear of permanent loss may generate either readerly anxiety if it triggers memories of such loss in the reader, or readerly protectiveness/concern for the character as a "child" of the reader's creation. At the same time, the reader may visualize a scene in which the erotics of gender ambiguity are about to be enacted for the reader's "viewing" enjoyment.

The literary apparatus positions the reader outside the scene as a voyeur attentive to its erotic possibilities. Take, for example, the casino scene where Villanelle and the Queen of Spades first meet:

> It's getting late, who comes here with a mask over her face? Will she try the cards?
> She does. She holds a coin in her palm so that I have to pick it out. Her skin is warm. I spread the cards. She chooses. The ten of diamonds. The three of clubs. Then the Queen of spades.
> "A lucky card. The symbol of Venice. You win."
> She smiled at me and pulling away her mask revealed a pair of grey-green eyes with flecks of gold. Her cheekbones were high and rounded. Her hair, darker and redder than mine. (59)

The touch, the smile, the unmasking of one woman who may not know that the dealer is also a woman, and certainly does not know that she has the webbed feet of a boatman, set up the reader's desire for consummation, whether sexual or epistemological. That moment comes when Villanelle bares her breasts, and the reader's desire is redirected from the desire to know what is going to happen in the discovery scene to whether that initial passion will be sustained.

V. Fiction as Theory, Theoretical Fictions: Anxieties of Loss in *The Passion* and Freud's *Inhibitions*

All three trajectories of desire in the narrative of cross-dressing turn on the threat of loss. While Douglas traces the etymological shifts in risk from "chance of loss or gain" to "danger," psychoanalysis may be said to ground threats of danger in (remembered) loss and to theorize both not as risk but as anxiety. In foregrounding risk, *The Passion* makes use of both its historical setting and its contemporary moment to suggest how risk acquires a positive valence in women's sexual and emotional dynamics: the novel eroticizes both chance and danger in the scenes of cross-dressing. At the same time, the novel intervenes in Freud's formulations of anxiety by specifying how cultural expectations of gender function in narrativizing an erotics between women that depends on danger and on versions of loss.

There are at least two kinds of loss threatened in the novel: loss of the lover and loss of self-control. Freud connects them in his writings on "danger-situations" as determinants of anxiety. His early formulations about anxiety suggest that it is produced by unexpressed sexual tension ("On the Grounds for Detaching a Particular Syndrome from Neurasthenia" [1895]). Laplanche and Pontalis also list first "the accumulation of sexual tension" in their citing of the aetiologies of anxiety neurosis (39). Freud's later texts on anxiety never quite let go of the libido's connection to anxiety; in *Inhibitions, Symptoms and Anxiety* he writes that "anxiety arises directly, by a kind of fermentation, from a libidinal cathexis whose processes have been disturbed" (123). But most of the argument in *Inhibitions,* his most extended treatment of anxiety, focuses more specifically on "danger-situations" as giving rise to anxiety as affect. Danger situations are fundamental sites of object loss which have as their prototype birth trauma and a sense of helplessness; in later life, danger-situations may trigger either involuntary or voluntary responses. Voluntary anxiety is the ego's response to the threat of remembering such situations of loss and helplessness, and works as an ego defense. Freud summarizes: "Anxiety is the original reaction to helplessness in the trauma and is reproduced later on in the danger-situation as a signal for help. The ego, which experienced the trauma passively, now repeats it actively in a weakened version, in the hope of being able itself to direct its course" (1926, 166–67).

In *The Passion,* the threat of loss of the lover (in the situations of cross-dressing and the transgressive affair) and loss of control (in Villanelle's desire to seek the unpredictable, the out-of-control) drive the erotic and make specific Freud's arguments about anxiety. In part the threat of the lover's loss contributes generally to "passion out of passion's obstacles," since it works as an obstruction to their romance. But by specifying threat of loss as the particular obstacle at work between the women, by eroticizing it, and by articulating it as risk, the novel extends classic psychoanalytic fictions to theorize its own erotics.

In the context of the novel's women lovers, threat of the lover's loss occasions anxiety because it triggers threat of self-loss as well. In fact, self-loss might be said to be doubly threatened: once through the potential loss of self-boundaries and possibility of fusion (loss of the self *in* the other like-self), and again through the lover's departure (loss of the self *with* the other like-self). The ego, in its drive for self-protection, guards against the helplessness of boundary loss by voluntarily producing anxiety, an anxiety that protects the ego from fusion through reproduction of the trauma. That protection also helps sustain subjectivity by differentiating subject from object, reconfirming boundaries, and reasserting the presence of the object.

Such an argument is crucial to Samuel Weber in his intricate reading of Freud's shifting theories of anxiety. Weber notes that the reproduction of the trauma in the production of the danger signal "is nothing less than the manner in which the ego constitutes itself by setting itself apart from the indifferentiation of the primary processes" (1982, 54).[17] *The Passion* further specifies for women lovers that deliberate anxiety is not only a defense against helplessness as boundary loss, but also a necessary means of differentiating subject from object, self from the like-self, in the construction and maintenance of subjectivity. At the same time, *The Passion* gives deliberate anxiety an erotic charge and names it fear.[18] Villanelle connects fear with ecstasy, and the narration repeatedly asserts that passion lies between fear and sex. These textual moments make clear that the production of anxiety in response to the threat of loss, whether of self or of lover, constitutes a risk worth taking.

What the novel calls fear and what psychoanalysis calls anxiety extends not only to danger situations that threaten the loss of the lover and/or the self, but also to loss of control. Villanelle specifies playing the "wild card," by which she means taking a woman lover (94), as a mark of unpredictability and also as a way of being out of control (71). In so doing she not only plays with the language of gambling as risk, but specifies what captures her emotional and sexual interest. As a danger-situation recalling helplessness, Villanelle's desire to be out of control suggests vulnerability as a feature of women's erotics. But, the novel argues, loss of control must be both chosen and temporary to constitute its risk as erotic. In so arguing, *The Passion* opens for specific dynamics between women another space in Freud's thinking about anxiety. What in Freud is reproduction of anxiety as protection against the helplessness endemic to danger-situations becomes in Winterson's novel the giving up of control as an enactment not of helplessness but of vulnerability as an erotic. Villanelle "wagers" her heart and willingly relinquishes control in entering into the game and the affair with the Queen; in exchange she gets "a passion I had not felt before," a brief time in which they live "naked and not ashamed" and are happy (95).

Villanelle's risk of control depends partially on cultural gender expectations. Just as in *Nightwood,* where hegemonic constructions of the Mother play a part in the erotics between Nora and Robin, so too in *The Passion* (as well as in contemporary social scripts between some women lovers) normative culture's construction of white women as emotionally and sexually vulnerable cannot help but ground the novel's emotional and sexual dynamics.[19] Whether women as lovers respond to the construction of woman-as-vulnerable by enacting it in a kind of willful mimicry, acting against it in a show of butch bravado, or eroticizing it in playing out of character (that is, against gender expectations, which may be culturally or subculturally constructed), agentic vulnerability reconstitutes a danger situation as one source of pleasure.

I refer to "mimicry" in Irigaray's sense of deliberately assuming the feminine role. But unlike the context of her theorizing in which woman mimics the feminine as a path toward "'destroying' the discursive mechanism" of a "masculine economy," the narrative of *The Passion* has already established Villanelle as transgressing the borders of such an economy by cross-dressing and by possessing those "masculine" webbed feet (Irigaray 1985b, 76). Risk of feminine vulnerability in willfully and temporarily giving up control, performative masculine cross-dressing, and hidden bodily secret play off each other in the text so that mimicry unsutures and destabilizes sex, gender, and humanness. The ambiguity of such gambles for both players also operates in the erotic between them.

At the same time, mimicry itself is a risk since it replays the cultural construction of (white) Woman as vulnerable. As June Reich argues, "mimicry problematizes the real by representing both the presence and absence of a construction. It's hard to keep it up though, as meaning is an excess, an effect the performer cannot control" (1992, 123). That is, choosing to lose control temporarily is an eroticizing of the feminine whose effects themselves are not always in control of the performer. Thus such a choice must be framed, as it is in the novel, by constructing it as willful. Given the power of ideology in the formation of the unconscious, however, such acts can never completely erase the traces of dominant cultural expectations adhering to a sexed body. When the Queen acknowledges Villanelle's bared breasts, what Villanelle experiences as a risk of vulnerability through a giving up of control, the Queen may view literally—not as a risk, but as a cultural, ideological, and bodily given with which she may play. Such a scenario might well constitute both pleasure and danger.

I have said that *The Passion* "theorizes" risk, especially as it is conditioned by loss and passion. The trade-off between passion and comfort so central to *Written on the Body* also appears briefly in *The Passion.* The novel contrasts the two near the end of the Villanelle–Queen of Spades narrative when Villanelle ponders the possible longevity of their affair in the face of the Queen's marriage. After she reveals her womanness and begins her liaison with the Queen, she voices a new fear: "Can a woman love a woman for more than a night?" What begins in *The*

Passion with the interweaving of two repeated but separate phrases moves as the narrative progresses from the abstraction of competition—risk, fear, winning, losing—through the connection of those abstractions to sex and passion, to the specific dynamics of Villanelle's passion for the Queen. After Villanelle reveals herself, the risk shifts once again—this time to the risk of sustenance: can a flirtation become something longer-lived when it depends on the complications of same-sex erotics? Their passion is "brief and fierce" (72), its fierceness attributable in part to its risk of discovery by her husband. Villanelle looks in on her one night and is about to knock when she sees her lady's husband bend and kiss her. She muses that "they did not live in the fiery furnace she and I inhabited, but . . . had a calm and a way that put a knife to my heart" (75). This brief glimpse of married comfort and its contrast with lesbian passion will become in *Written on the Body* a fully operative dynamic.

Only when Villanelle tells the story of her passion for the Queen of Spades to Henri eight years later is its outcome known. Unlike Nora's in *Nightwood*, Villanelle's retelling is not itself an act of desiring; its tone is reflective rather than obsessive. But if the retrospective narrative does not produce desire, it does repeat the earlier linkage of passion with risk. Where Nora's narrative reopens her search for Robin, Villanelle's leads to closure with the Queen. Villanelle tells Henri that working at the casino taught her "what it is that people value and therefore what it is they will risk" (89). She realized that what she had valued was her heart, that she lost it to the Queen of Spades, but that there was "no sense in loving someone you [could] never wake up to except by chance" (95). So after nine consecutive nights together while the husband was away, Villanelle gave up the Queen because a life together was not possible. But she literally left her heart with her lady; she enlists Henri to rescue it for her, and he does. Though the two women have one last conversation years later, they never again are together as lovers.

The sight of marital comfort ends the lesbian erotics of *The Passion*. In a reversal of some lesbian narratives in the 1940s and 1950s, in which the married woman abandons her lover to return to her husband, Villanelle chooses to leave the Queen so as not to lose the intensity of their passion, "that valuable fabulous thing that cannot be replaced" (96).[20] Since erotics between women in *The Passion* depends on risk and gaming, it is apt that Villanelle's closing portrayal of her circumstance tropes on gambling: "What you risk reveals what you value," and the narrative argues that pleasure between women is that irreplaceable "valuable thing."

VI. The Erotics of Risk and Resemblance in *Written on the Body*

Written on the Body might be said to rewrite, extend, and complicate the erotics of *The Passion*. In *Written on the Body* the meditations have more to say about the pleasures and dangers of comfort; the power dynamics between a married woman and her unmarried lover continue to determine the erotics. The novel turns upon a plot in which the passion of brief affairs first leads to the comfort of a lesbian "marriage" and is displaced by True Love with a married woman, a relation in which both passion and comfort seem possible. As a consequence of the lovers' different marital histories, versions of emotional risk remain a crucial component of the erotics between the narrator and Louise. Rather than test the epistemology of cross-dressing, the erotics of risk in *Written on the Body* depend on the unequal marital class status of the lovers and the inherent chance of loss it threatens. What in *The Passion* is the risk and transgressive thrill of body discovery becomes in *Written on the Body* the risk of commitment and intimacy in the face of potential loss. But, as the plot I summarize in my chapter's opening pages indicates, *Written on the Body* takes also what might be called the risk of genre, so that it undercuts the conventions of its romance plot by foregrounding its own use of romantic clichés. Such a strategy permits both the meditations on an erotics of intimacy and a metacommentary on the risk of attempting to write such meditations at all. When, for example, the narrator recalls the dynamics of her past affairs as a trade-off between passion and comfort, the text plays on a traditional romance tension familiar from such formulations as de Rougemont's. But the narrator's position as queer lover living outside the boundaries of marital sanction tinges her commentaries on such conventions with both bitterness and irony. She's bitter because she does not have the economic protection of marriage and because her lovers leave her for the safety of their husbands. Ironically, however, her most pointed meditations on the ordinariness of contentment without passion refer not to heterosexual marriage but to her own passionless lesbian relationship. As a revisionist romance, *Written on the Body* deconstructs its own clichés and generic conventions at the same time that its narrative writes an erotics once more grounded in the threat of losing a lover.

The discursive risk taken by Winterson in using an unnamed narrator of unspecified sex to talk about love and loss exceeds even her play with romantic convention and cliché. In my chapter's final section, I argue that such chancing responds to a relation of identity and alterity similar to the one between Nora and Robin in *Nightwood* and Villanelle and her lady in *The Passion*. In writing an erotics of resemblance, *Written on the Body* ultimately extends Douglas's sense of risk by suggesting how resemblance chances the loss of self in the lover and defends against it by leaving the sex of the narrator undeclared. In so doing, it continues *The Passion*'s intervention into Freud's formulations of anxiety. At the same time, as a narrative theorizing affect between like lovers, the novel also recasts the more recent psychoanalytic fictions of Melanie Klein on projective identification and Beverly Burch on lesbian complementarity.

VII. Passion, Comfort, and the Risk of Intimacy

In *Written on the Body,* an erotics of risk is first framed by the narrator's meditations on the trade-off between passion and comfort, the chance one takes in risking the comfort of the familiar for the lure of the new. Of course, such tension exists in the relationships of many couples who struggle to stay together over time. But between white middle-class women in Britain whose cultural specificity constitutes the social surround for the novel, this tension plays out with particular force, because of both their specific cultural and subcultural ideological productions as (white) women and their distance from the conventions provided by heterosexual marriage.[21] Under the pressure of learning to perform as Woman, that is, to act in accordance with what contemporary middle-class Anglo-British culture proscribes in order to be considered a woman at all, white middle-class women most frequently grow up with a primary concern for the relational.[22] They are trained by ideology to maintain their relationships through emotional labor.

This ideological demand might even be said to loom twice as large when two women are involved. So one version of lesbian lore portrays women lovers moving quickly to live together in a kind of date-and-mate syndrome (as in the recent American joke, "What do lesbians do on their second date? Rent a moving van"), just as white popular culture imagines the heterosexual single woman constantly plotting for marriage, and the wife giving up everything from her job to her self-esteem to keep her marriage together. This ideologically constructed desire for comfort (read: living together monogamously in a mutually committed "forever" relationship) is many times at odds with the passion, both sexual and emotional, attached to a new love.[23]

At the same time, contemporary erotics between women often still exists, as *Nightwood* asserts, without rules to go by so that the comforts "guaranteed" by centuries of heterosexual cultural productions about marriage and family are missing when women lovers risk short-term passion for long-term comfort.[24] *Written on the Body* meditates on this tension and argues, like the good romance that it is, that Right Love will permit, even encourage, both passion and comfort for the lovers. The novel's specific erotics involve risk-taking not only in the passion/comfort trade-off, but in the narrator's past preference for affairs with married and hence only temporarily available women. Her preference ensures the presence of passion and absence of comfort with lovers previous to Louise. With Louise, other risks—of intimacy, commitment, and loss of control—come crucially into play.

Early in the novel, the narrator recalls a scene with a lover (later revealed as Louise) in which they swim nude in front of a disapproving married couple. This small moment sets up the ongoing tension in the novel between the comfort of marriage and the thrill of a new affair. The two women take delight in crossing boundaries of sexual and familial propriety and in risking condemnation from conventional heterosexual onlookers whose gaze helps to establish marriage as the Other to erotic pleasure in the novel. Just as in Villanelle's affair with the Queen of Spades, the narrator's pre-Louise romances in *Written on the Body* are largely with married women who delight in the risk and pleasure of the affair, but ultimately return to their husbands. Unlike Villanelle, however, who gives up her lady rather than be fitted in around a spouse, "I" recounts losing her lovers to the conventional comforts of boring marriages. When she tires of the temporary passionate highs and final sexual losses built into her affairs, she forms a "marriage" of her own with Jacqueline, but both the narrative set-up of marriage as boring comfort and her meditations on comfort make it inevitable that the arrangement will be short-lived.

In an early commentary, she summarizes how she got into affairs with married women: "The door was open. True, [the wife] didn't open it herself. Her butler opened it for her. His name was Boredom. She said, 'Boredom, fetch me a plaything.' He said, 'Very good ma'am,' and putting on his white gloves so that the fingerprints would not show he tapped at my heart and I thought he said his name was love" (15–16). These affairs thrive on being "drugged out on danger" (72), the risk of discovery, but they always end with the wife returning to the marriage bed, where "[h]er husband lies over her like a tarpaulin. He wades into her as though she were a bog" (73). Such things, she says, "lead the heart-sore to the Jacquelines of this world" (74). Thus her affair with Louise is predicated on the risks she knows attend any affair with a married woman, and the risk of losing Jacqueline, who she has temporarily convinced herself provides a safe harbor from the storms of desire and loss.

During her time with Jacqueline, she describes herself as "an apostle of ordinariness. I lectured my friends on the virtues of the humdrum, praised the gentle bands of my existence and felt that for the first time I had come to know what everyone told me I would know: that passion is for holidays, not homecoming" (27). But she soon discovers that she misses that holiday of passion; Jacqueline gives her comfort that is ultimately unsatisfying: "Jacqueline was an overcoat. She muffled my senses. With her I forgot about feeling and wallowed in contentment. Contentment is a feeling you say? Are you sure it's not an absence of feeling? . . . Contentment is the positive side of resignation. It has its appeal but it's no good wearing an overcoat . . . when what the body really wants is to be naked" (76).

And so the "Jacquelines of this world" lead back to affairs. But the affair with Louise turns out to provide both passion and comfort, as a reworking of the "overcoat" metaphor suggests: "I" remembers waiting for Louise and being sorry when she arrived, only because Louise's presence ended the pleasure of anticipating her arrival. "It was the pleasure of walking in the snow in a warm coat, that choosing to be alone. Who wants to walk in the snow naked?" (181). Jacqueline as "overcoat" muffles the narrator's feelings; the anticipation of Louise warms her waiting like a coat. Instead of stifling "I"'s senses, Louise stimulates them. "I" might have wanted to walk naked, but not without knowing that Louise was (semi)available to her. One lover provides comfortable boredom, the other, comfortable anticipation.

Risk marks the difference between the two relationships. For some time the affair with Louise is clandestine and shares the conventional romance of all such secrets. But when they decide to leave their "spouses," risk depends on the dangers of commitment and intimacy. Previously almost all "I"'s affairs have lasted only six months or so. While they employ risk of discovery as a sexual charge, their repetition also suggests that in her affairs the narrator protects herself (or has been protected from/kept from) the dynamics of intimacy. When

Louise says she'll leave her husband to live with the narrator, "I" recognizes that passion and comfort are both possible: "With Louise I want to do something different. I want the holiday and the homecoming together. She is the edge and the excitement for me but I have to believe it beyond six months. My circadian clock . . . has a larger arc that seems set at twenty-four weeks. I can override it, I've managed that, but I can't stop it going off" (79). The text invokes two extended metaphors to capture the narrator's sense of risk. She imagines her circadian clock exposed to light. "Sun like a disc-saw through the body. Shall I submit myself sundial-wise beneath Louise's direct gaze? It's a risk; human beings go mad without a little shade, but how to break the habit of a lifetime else?" (80). Here the body risks being burned, in a trope that is really an extension of Villanelle's question in *The Passion:* can a woman love a woman for more than a night? It is a question in part of intensity of focus; with Louise she'll have none of the protection provided by her experiential knowledge that short-lived affairs are tempestuous but serial. But it's also a question of longevity and commitment, risks raising the stakes of loss.

Just after the narrator has questioned risking loss, in language recalling Nora's in *Nightwood,* she opts for the comfort of protection:

> I put my arms around her, not sure whether I was a lover or a child. I wanted her to hide me beneath her skirts against all menace. Sharp points of desire were still there but there was too a sleepy safe rest like being in a boat I had as a child. She rocked me against her, sea-calm, sea under a clear sky, a glass-bottomed boat and nothing to fear. (80)

In this passage, the language of nurturing gives way to the second figure of risk: love as a difficult journey made in this boat. "Love it was that drove them forth. . . . The journeys they made were beyond common sense; who leaves the hearth for the open sea? especially without a compass, especially in winter, especially alone. What you risk reveals what you value. In the presence of love, hearth and quest become one" (81). The passage echoes *Nightwood*'s child/mother figuration, repeats Villanelle's observation about risking what you value, and unites comfort and passion as "hearth and quest."

But it does not yet specify what valuable thing one risks in making hearth and quest one. That specificity follows shortly:

> I was holding Louise's hand, conscious of it but sensing too that a further intimacy might begin, the recognition of another person that is deeper than consciousness, lodged in the body more than held in the mind. . . . I'd never known it myself although I'd seen it in a couple who'd been together for a very long time. Time had not diminished their love. They seemed to have become one another without losing their very individual selves. (82)

For the promise of intimacy that can sustain itself over time, "the recognition of another person that is deeper than consciousness," she risks losing her boundedness, her singularity. But with Louise she takes just that risk in a belief that they, like the old couple she remembers, can have it all.

The novel casts these classic romance questions—how long will it last? can I go so emotionally naked? can I chance disaster?—as risks that not only inform the erotic but in large measure determine it. At the level of plot, these risks mark steps taken in the context of the narrator's previous history of affairs with married women. Even remembering this history, the narrator is willing not only to risk Louise's return to her husband Elgin, but also to take what for her is the most frightening risk of all—a step over the abyss of intimacy. Near the end of the novel, after the disappearance of Louise, the narrator realizes why intimacy is so risky. Her desperate, fruitless search for Louise leads her to strike out physically at Elgin. She thinks back on her actions:

> It horrifies me to think about that madness, I've always had a wild streak, it starts with a throbbing in the temple and then a slide into craziness I can recognize but can't control. Can control. Had controlled for years until I met Louise. She opened up the dark places as well as the light. That's the risk you take. (174)

The actual scene with Elgin is comedic, but the more serious retrospective meditation gets at the consequences of intimacy. Intimacy risks (among other things) being especially vulnerable to rejection, and endangering the boundaries of subjectivity. Risking intimacy opens up "dark places" in the self; in this scene the loss of the lover who is known "deeper than consciousness" produces loss of control in a moment of violence. Taking such a chance, losing control, also intensifies the loss of the lover/intimate who has occasioned the risk and been worthy of it. From those "dark places" opened through intimacy with Louise come the grief and anger at her loss.

VIII. The Risk of Genre and Cliché

These pages write every pair of lovers' dream: having it all—if only for a brief time. But lest the language of love and risk in this passage and others be pulled under by the weight of its lyricism, the text throughout takes another kind of risk that paradoxically sustains the level of inflated language by calling attention to the almost inevitable connection between love and cliché.[25]

It is obvious from the opening pages that the narrator meditates on the discourse of love as intensely as on its practice. "'I love you' is always a quotation," she says on the first page (9) and, in a reference to another Other outside dominant mores, aligns herself with Caliban, who cursed those who taught him language. "Love demands expression." She goes on, but "it's the clichés that cause the trouble" (9, 10). This opening passage also establishes the floating character of event time in the novel. She is alone but thinking back to a time when she and "you" (Louise is not yet named) were "in love." But the meditation on love and cliché is cast in the present tense so that it permeates the recollected past events as well as the present meditative moment and thus reads with relevance for both. Love for her is "so terrifying" that she needs to sit in "the saggy armchair of clichés" where "millions of bottoms" have sat before: "They did it . . . now I will do it won't I, arms outstretched, not to hold you, just to keep my balance, sleepwalking to that armchair. How happy we will be. How happy everyone will be. And they all lived happily ever after" (10). The time of the opening two pages in the sequence of plot events is not precisely fixed, so that the sarcasm about living happily ever after applies both to her decision to leave the safety of the saggy armchair of clichés and risk the terror of loving Louise, and to her eventual separation from Louise. At the same time the opening passage invokes the fairy-tale romance formula that repeats with a difference in the novel's final sentence: "I don't know if this is a happy ending but here we are let loose in open fields" (190). Since Louise's return in the final scene may be read as either fantasy or actuality, the "happy ending" formula is at once invoked and made problematic.

Other clichés about love have a similar life in the text; thematically they set the narrator's briefer, clichéd affairs against her more committed life of passion and comfort with Louise. But these clichés, by calling attention to the hackneyed language of love, also contextualize the risky lyric language that describes Louise. Foregrounding how clichés function suggests a level of textual self-reference that paradoxically permits the lyrical flights of language about love to resonate. Describing her previous brief affairs, she thinks, "I suppose I couldn't admit that I was trapped in a cliché every bit as redundant as my parents' roses round the door. I was looking for the perfect coupling; the never-sleep non-stop mighty orgasm. Ecstasy without end. I was deep in the slop-bucket of romance" (21). Clichés cause trouble because they function as an ideology of expectation; phrases earn their status as cliché through cultural repetition that in turn produces a truth-effect: "I" expects to become part of a "perfect coupling" because she has heard so often that love brings "ecstasy without end." Clichés also write the dichotomy between passion and comfort that marks the narrator's experience before Louise. To do so, they condense dominant cultural myths of romance into a verbal shorthand that the novel thematizes, and then uses as a measure against which the story of Louise can be set and above which it can rise.

Yet even the novel's ultimate story of "true love" doesn't pretend to escape from romance conventions and cliché. Instead, it echoes various literary discourses of love, appropriately in keeping with the narrator's job as a translator. The opening page speaks of love in biblical tones: "It will not stay still, stay silent, be good, be modest, be seen and not heard, no. It will break out in tongues of praise, the high note that smashes the glass and spills the liquid." Then the metaphor abruptly changes: "It is no conservationist love. It is a big game hunter and you are the game. A curse on this game. How can you stick at a game when the rules keep changing?" (9, 10). The comic shifts in repertoire from biblical echo to big-game hunting signal the language games the various discourses will engage throughout the novel. In her first meal with Louise, the narrator parodies poetic conceits: "When she lifted the soup spoon to her lips how I longed to be that innocent piece of stainless steel. I would gladly have traded the blood in my body for half a pint of vegetable stock. Let me be diced carrot, vermicelli, just so that you will take me in your mouth" (36). Such passages differ from the direct discussions of cliché that critique her other relationships, whether the passion of a six-month affair with a married woman or the homey but loveless comfort of Jacqueline, and thus separate them from her love for Louise. But the conceits recall traditional discourses of love, so that even her newly found depth of feeling is never couched naively. The text risks lyricism at the same time that it guards against sentimentality.

Though it is filled with knowingly lyrical meditations on the language of love that accompany the playing out of the romantic, *Written on the Body* cannot really be called a romance. Or can it? Its narrative, with its indeterminate relation between chronological and narrated time and its foregrounding of language and form, at first seems distant from the simple plot lines and straightforward narration of popular romance. The retrospective narrative has roughly three sections, none of them chronologically linear. The first section presents "I"'s courting and winning of Louise from her husband. It ends with "I"'s decision to leave so that Elgin may take care of Louise in her illness. The second section is a short series of meditations on the (now lost) body. The third recounts "I"'s mourning, followed by a seemingly unsuccessful search for Louise. The novel closes with their reunion, which may or may not be a fantasy. But the complicated narration actually tells a "romantic fiction with a twist," to invoke the subtitle of a collection of contemporary romances that Jeanette Winterson edited in 1986. Like the emphasizing of clichés, references to genre occur in the text: "I" is accused of wanting to live in a novel (160); a friend calls her relationship with Louise "the perfect romance" (187). As a romance, however, it is, indeed, "twisted."

If from the medieval quest through the Renaissance fashioning of gentlemen, the romance genre was masculine in its origins (though not so marked until recent readings by feminist critics), from the late nineteenth century to the present it has become increasingly feminized. Today, "a romance" (gender unmarked) suggests the popular mass-market productions of Harlequin or a Mills and Boon formulaic love story. So connected to women both in readership and, largely, in authorship has the romance become that a "masculine romance," in which the dominant concerns are the "values and codes of masculinity" (Batsleer et al. 1985, 80) as depicted in westerns, war stories, and thrillers, must be named by gender as well as genre. And as commentators point out, since contemporary masculine romance often shuns much attention to heterosexual love as story in its fascination with male bonding, it is at pains to emphasize descriptively the heterosexuality of its heroes precisely to prevent any measure of "homosexual panic" in its (male) readers. (Batsleer et al. 1985, 76). I stress this "gendering" of the genre because *Written on the Body* may be read in part as a parodic critique of contemporary romance conventions, which depend heavily on a heterosexual plot and strict gender codes for hero and heroine. It performs its parody most obviously through the device of the sex-unspecified narrator and the possibility of fantasy in the closing scene. At the same time, a reading casting its erotics as lesbian also suggests its resonance with one plot convention of lesbian romance: the courtship of a married woman by an experienced dyke. This convention, too, gets reworked, if not parodied, in the novel.

The heterosexual romance genre written by women, as Tania Modleski, Janice Radway, and others have pointed out, depends on a plot focused on "a man and a woman meeting, the obstacles to their love, and their final happy ending" (Radway 1984, 199). Moreover, it cannot just relate a courtship, it must capture "what it feels like to be the object of one" (64). In the Harlequin subgenre described by Modleski, for example, a young woman becomes involved with a more experienced handsome man who, despite his interest in her, treats her poorly before he reveals his love, and the two live happily ever after (36). The heterosexual dynamics ground every movement of the plot; the gender codes of the characters, though they may shift with the historical moment, are rigidly conservative: the woman must be Feminine, the man Masculine, as the dominant culture of the historical moment uses these terms.

The language of love in *Written on the Body* risks the sentimental to focus on feeling, and the plot in the first part of the novel is the tale of a lover who meets an object of desire, overcomes obstacles so they might be together, and finds requited love. Indeed, the entire novel might also be said to have this plot, with Louise's illness simply another obstacle that is overcome by her return in the final pages. Obviously its love story is a romance; its loss-and-return format is also a convention of the genre (Batsleer et al. 1985, 88). But just as obviously, the unspecified sex of the narrator emphasizes by contrast the degree to which the specificity and stability of sexual identity make the heterosexual romance genre possible. In turn the plot conventions of the romance require individual readers to sex the narrator according to their own desires. Yet even reading Louise's lover as male forces a rethinking of heterosexual romance conventions. If "I" were male, the romance convention that the woman's experience of love be the plot focus disappears. Similarly, "I"'s language is obviously a discourse of feeling so foreign to the mysterious and distant heroes of contemporary romance that reading the narrator as male at the very least critiques the sometimes brutal masculinity of the romance hero. And "I"'s affairs with both women and men previous to Louise clearly transgress the rigid codes of heterosexuality.

Reading "I" as a woman, as I do, focuses attention on the novel as a version of lesbian romance. The novel recalls a specific subgenre of lesbian romance, not to critique it, as it may be said to do in its connection to heterosexual romance, but to revise it more positively. What exists in mid-twentieth-century lesbian popular fictions as a subgenre with a frequently unhappy ending becomes in Winterson's version a joyous celebration, at least briefly. In a rereading of lesbian popular fiction of the 1950s, Angela Weir and Elizabeth Wilson note that romance between a married woman and her unattached single friend was a familiar convention. Often in these plots marriage wins out not because the protagonist is going through a phase but because the pull of emotional and economic security is so strong (Weir and Wilson 1992, 96). Their reading of these novels argues that they are often more radical than such fictions are given credit for. Sometimes the women do go off together, and lesbian romance in these novels often challenges "the inauthenticity and alienation of mainstream American life in the 1950's" (97). In *Written on the Body,* Louise leaves the comfort of her marriage to live with the narrator, so at the level of plot convention, at least, this novel rewrites the kind of lesbian popular romance in which the girl loses the girl back to the husband.

Finally, however, *Written on the Body*'s interventions in romance genre traditions, whether straight or lesbian, depend on the reading performance of the ending. Early on, the narrator is sarcastic about happy endings. "And they all lived happily ever after" is one of those clichés that cause trouble (10). Near the end she says that "happy endings are compromises" (187). She realizes that she should not have made compromises in her trust of Louise; instead she should have allowed Louise to make her own decision about how she wished her illness treated. So when in the final scene "I" arrives back in her country house, sits in the "saggy armchair," with its unstated reference back to the "saggy armchair of cliché," and wonders, "Is this [being without Louise] the proper ending?" it is difficult not to read it as a set-up for Louise's miraculous reappearance on the final page. That reappearance is further problematized by a brief conversation "I" has just before Louise appears:

> "I couldn't even get near finding her. It's as if Louise never existed, like a character in a book. Did I invent her?"
> "No, but you tried to," said Gail. "She wasn't yours for the making." (189)

Strikingly, both this exchange and the reappearance of Louise recall *Nightwood.* "I," like Nora, searches the city for her lover, then returns to her country house where Louise appears. Just as "I" worries about her invention of Louise, Nora, when she recounts her search to Matthew, recognizes that her sense of Robin-as-child was a destructive fiction. Both narrations produce ambiguous endings, though *Nightwood*'s conclusion does not recall romance conventions as *Written on the Body*'s does. Both novels, however, point to a danger in any romantic relationship—the danger of fictionalizing one's lover—suggest their narrators' culpability in losing their lovers, and emphasize invention in narratives already filled with self-referential comments on storymaking.[26]

When, in *Written on the Body,* "I" immediately remembers Louise's saying "it's the clichés that cause the trouble," the reader keeps that phrase in mind when Louise makes her reappearance. It's worth quoting the ending, since it opens itself to be read as either the narrator's fantasy or Louise's actual return, or, more likely, the ambiguity of both possibilities. "I" is speaking:

"'What can I do?' Louise once said, 'It's the clichés that cause the trouble.' . . . I'd like to be able to tell her the truth."

From the kitchen door Louise's face. Paler, thinner, but her hair still mane-wide and the colour of blood. I put out my hand and felt her fingers, she took my fingers and put them to her mouth. The scar under the lip burned me. Am I stark mad? She's warm.

This is where the story starts, in this threadbare room. The walls are exploding. The windows have turned into telescopes. Moon and stars are magnified in this room. The sun hangs over the mantelpiece. I stretch out my hand and reach the corners of the world. The world is bundled up in this room. Beyond the door, where the river is, where the roads are, we shall be. We can take the world with us when we go and sling the sun under your arm. Hurry now, it's getting late. I don't know if this is a happy ending but here we are let loose in open fields. (190)

Read straight, the language deploys the "green world" metaphor that Bonnie Zimmerman says is typical of contemporary lesbian romance. Zimmerman details how such fictions depend on Western romantic (heterosexual) metaphors and plots; she names nature, isolation, and transcendence as "pervasive motifs" in recent lesbian romance (1990, 79). Certainly parts of *Written on the Body* share these features. The lovers spend their most romantic holiday in isolation away from the city, feeding each other plums and swimming naked in a river. The lyrical language suggests that in their brief time together they are able to transcend the difficulties of leaving their previous lovers to begin a fulfilling life together. Such language also directs one reading of the ending as the generically necessary happy one. Read in the context of a narrative that frequently invokes discourse about cliché, invention, and the fictionalizing power of retrospective narration, however, the ending points instead to Louise's return as fantasy, "an imaginary scene in which the subject is the protagonist and in which, in distorted manner, a wish is fulfilled. Phantasy is the setting for the desire (wish) which came into being with its prohibition (absence of object)" (Mitchell 1984, 242). Read in the context of *The Passion,* with its frequent refrain, "Trust me, I'm telling you stories," "I"'s statement that she wants to tell Louise "the truth" seems especially suspect.

The ending makes a definitive closure impossible, even as it invites readers driven by romance conventions to conclude that Louise has returned. The language of love with its clichés that are undercut by foregrounding the nature of cliché creates an atmosphere of romance that recalls the popular romance genre only to be in tension with it. That is, the novel writes the language of love that readers associate with popular romance; the love story (or as one negative reviewer called it in reference to Erich Segal's popular but critically savaged novel, "the *Love Story*" [Vaux 1992, 20]) follows the romance plot outline, but much more obviously parodies its excesses by not gendering its narrator and by calling into question the genre's most important characteristic: the happy ending. In its play with cliché and genre, *Written on the Body* risks attack from reviewers and irritation of readers who miss its citational references. Such rhetorical and formal chances ground the narrative of risk crucial to the erotics between women in the novel.

IX. Risk, Fear of Loss, and the Dynamics of Power

Because risk chances loss, fear of losses of various kinds runs beneath the meditations on love that a revision of the romance genre risks and that the foregrounding of cliché makes problematic. The thematics of the novel privilege love as the only force stronger than desire, and assert that passionate desire and comfort can coexist in the kind of True Love the narrator thinks she has with Louise. But these narrative assertions are never tested, since the lovers live together only five months before the narrator learns from Elgin that Louise has leukemia. The threat of her death brings to the surface the tensions around fear of loss that have all along accompanied the lyrical language on love and the comic commentary on cliché that allows the discourse of love to function without becoming cloying. The novel's erotics work in part as a comment on the powerful anxiety about loss, which in turn largely underwrites the thrill of risk so crucial to the novel's commentary on love and desire. If in *The Passion* passion lies between fear and sex, in *Written on the Body* it is fear of loss that marks the power exchanges between the narrator and her lover. Reading the narrative of past events as a condition for "I"'s fears focuses attention on the dynamic between women when one is married and one is not. Reading the narrative of tropes in "I"'s meditations suggests that a fear of self-loss runs as an undercurrent to the discourse of love between like lovers.

That several of "I"'s previous involvements have been with married women who leave her not only makes her attraction to Louise a risk, it allows Louise a power that the text leaves largely oblique. The narrator is at pains to assert that the power dynamic between them is an equal, if complicated, one. Unlike *Nightwood*'s ultimate crisis, in which the dynamics become unbalanced as Nora drives Robin from her, here the relationship is shown to be mutually constitutive ("'You started this, Louise,'" says the narrator. "'I acknowledged it. We both started it,'" Louise replies [53]). They are equally "sunk in each other" (91). What's more, again in contrast to *Nightwood*, these dynamics are occasionally the subject of the narrator's meditations. She describes Louise's sexuality as demanding a kind of mutuality in "a game between equals who might not always choose to be equals" (67). She says she chose to be possessed by Louise and that she "wanted her to be the leader of our expedition" (91).

This rhetoric of choice revises the lesbian erotics of Nora and Robin's early relationship by seeming to make the balance of power between "I" and Louise overt. In *Nightwood* the trade-off between power invested unequally in masculine/feminine and mother/child dichotomies remains textually covert. In *Written on the Body*, the text clearly describes the lovers as invested in a mutuality that sometimes involves the conscious choice to play out power differences. Historical shifts in lesbian sexual politics account for the contrast. In the fifty years between the two novels, the language of mutuality has become not only permissible, but something close to required in fictional representation of erotics between women. Mutuality counters the stereotypes of sexology in which the female invert seduces the heterosexual woman, and reverses the convention of heterosexual romance in which true love often defeats inequality of social position.

But the stated investment in mutuality in *Written on the Body* does not prevent the functioning of a covert struggle for control. Louise takes the lead in their coming together. Though the narrator believes they first met by accident, she learns much later that Louise had followed her home. When they spend their first afternoon together, it is Louise whose kiss of greeting lingers a moment longer than it should. When they continue to spend time together, Louise is the one who asks, "Are we going to have an affair?" thereby making overt the sexual tension which the narrator experiences but leaves unvoiced. In taking up positions of power signed by language of nurturing, Louise comforts ("I was in Louise's arms and she was bending over me, fingers on my forehead, soothing me" [69]); "I" describes Louise as the person who "will warm me, feed me and care for me" (51); she names herself as "lover and child" (81). Thinking of their sexual dynamic, it occurs to the narrator that Louise might be a volcano and she a Pompeii.

This language and these plot events construct Louise as having a power that attracts the narrator; indeed, of their lovemaking "I" says, "I had no dreams to possess you but I wanted you to possess me" (52). Thus the erotic is structured both by Louise's assertiveness and by the narrator's consenting desire to be possessed. This dynamic is a private one, however; overtly, the narrator is the "roué" who tells her lover tales of her many, often humorous conquests. In the scenes leading up to their affair, she recalls herself as driven to see Louise, in spite of her living with Jackie. In the first stages of their friendship, she thinks of their eventual coming together as being only a matter of time ("Is it nobler to struggle for a week before flying out the door or should I go and get my toothbrush now" [39–40]). In part what balances their desire is this trade-off between the one who appears to pursue and the one who takes/is given the lead.

But what makes commitment to Louise a particular risk for the narrator is Louise's position as Married Woman in the narrator's private history, which is scarred by past losses of just such women. Early in the narration, "I" recalls her thoughts when Louise makes the crucial decision to leave Elgin. The passage echoes the novel's opening line, "Why is the measure of love loss," and through that repetition both fixes its thematic importance and names the specific nature of the fear at the heart of the erotic:

> You said, "Why do I frighten you?"
> Frighten me? Yes you do frighten me. You act as though we will be together for ever. You act as though there is infinite pleasure and time without end. How can I know that? My experience has been that time always ends. . . . If I rush at this relationship it's because I fear for it. . . .

You said, "I'm going to leave."

I thought, Yes of course you are, you're going back to [your marriage].

You said, "I told him before we came away. . . . "

This is the wrong script. This is the moment where I'm supposed to be self-righteous and angry. . . .

You said, "I love you and my love for you makes any other life a lie." (18–19)

"The wrong script" is the one written in several earlier references and stories of the narrator's being left by wives who return to their husbands. Whatever fear there is of losing Louise is multiplied by her position as a married woman and the narrator's earlier history of loss. This question of who will suffer the loss, who will be the one to leave, often operates as a control mechanism in lesbian relationships, since both dominant culture and lesbian subcultures teach women that being alone is somehow not normal. At the same time, risk of loss in part constitutes the transgressive desire at work between women. In this novel, as in *Nightwood,* the risk of being left for another, either husband or lover, helps constitute their mutual vulnerability and desire.

The balance is lost, however, when the risk of being left becomes the risk of loss through death. Here, too, however, the marriage imperative plays a part. Elgin's pronouncement that Louise is dying and that only he can save her speaks to the power of the speaker and the discourse of medicine. Conventional social structures authorize both, even though the text works to deconstruct the power of the husband. The narrator's decision to leave Louise against her own stated wishes reinforces the legitimacy and power of the legal husband over the love of the "illegal" lover, and counters the earlier rhetoric about the inability of marriage to prevent loss of the heart. The discourse of medicine with its seeming power of life over death captures the narrator, who leaves Louise so that Elgin may save her life.

The last third of the novel is given over to her recognition that this decision was a mistake, made out of the desire to be right. The text suggests that the narrator is subject to the ideological regulatory power of medical discourse and the social power of the doctor-husband who wields it despite her claim that she makes a decision independently to leave Louise in Elgin's care. "I"'s retrospective narrative comments additionally on another possible source of her loss: her attempt to reinvent her lover in her own image, to decide for her what she might need contrary to Louise's request that they stay together. This decision too is an issue of control, and the narrator wins the point by following what she takes to be her own way, but loses the match when her decision separates her from her lover. At the same time, the fear of loss and the fear of who will be the loser come into play as well. The narrator may also be said to leave in order not to be left when Louise dies.

X. The Erotics of Resemblance

If fear of loss of the lover plays out as an unacknowledged struggle for control, fear of loss of the self in the lover emerges in this novel, as in *The Passion,* as crucial to the erotics between them. The language of difference and sameness, incorporation and engulfment, twinning and mirroring promotes a reading of lesbian affective connection. These are traditional literary tropes for such textual liaisons, and their repetition here is reminiscent not only of *The Passion* and *Nightwood* but of novels quite removed from the *Nightwood* tradition such as *Desert of the Heart.*[27]

The language of incorporation is most pronounced in the meditations on the body. This bodily emphasis reinforces an erotics of resemblance with its seduction and danger: seductive because loving the other-like-the-self may strengthen self-love ("On Narcissism," by contrast, argues that the more one loves another, the more one takes away from the self), and dangerous because the language of *Written on the Body,* much more explicitly than that of *The Passion,* suggests that such love risks the trauma of self-engulfment and incorporation into the like-self. Both Winterson novels, however, eroticize the "danger-situation" (to recall Freud's term) of boundary loss. The seduction of self-love and the eroticized danger of resemblance as they play out especially in the body meditations not only continue *The Passion*'s revisions of Freud, but also resonate with recent psychoanalytic thinking on lesbian relation. Below I take up particularly the work of Beverly Burch, which recasts Melanie Klein's classic writing on projective identification in light of the perceived likeness between women as lovers.

In *Written on the Body*'s central section, the narrator finds "a love poem to Louise" in the impersonal language of an anatomy book she reads obsessively to understand Louise's illness (111). The prose poems she creates from the medical text critique covertly the power of Elgin's medical discourse that has helped take Louise from her. Their lyrical tropes script a narrrative in which "I" imagines herself first inside then outside Louise's body, trying to protect it, know it, claim it, honor it in an act of love. But the language of love includes the language of self-recognition; as a result, fear of loss of the lover sometimes also becomes fear of loss of the self.

Such a fear emerges in passages contextualized by what might be called the rhetoric of identity. Like *Nightwood*'s, this rhetoric establishes resemblance by tropes of mirroring, twinning, and entwinement that sometimes pose the danger of engulfment, even as they serve also as a lure. The first of these comes in a repetition of the scene discussed above in which Louise surprises the narrator by deciding to leave her husband:

> You said, "I'm going to leave him because my love for you makes any other life a lie."
> I've hidden those words in the lining of my coat. I take them out like a jewel thief when no-one's watching. They haven't faded. Nothing about you has faded. You are still the colour of my blood. You are my blood. When I look in the mirror it's not my own face I see. Your body is twice. Once you once me. Can I be sure which is which? (98–99)

The passage returns Nora's more frantic assertion of loss and identity in *Night-wood*: "a woman is yourself. . . . If she is taken you cry that you have been robbed of yourself" (143). Winterson's mirror trope also strengthens the erotics of resemblance in recalling by contrast Woolf's famous figure of sexual difference: "Women have served all these centuries as looking glasses possessing the magic and delicious power of reflecting the figure of man at twice its natural size" (1929 [1957], 35). The importance of Winterson's passage is marked by both its occurrence in a repeated scene and its shift in verb tense to convey ongoing, rather than momentary, emotions. The body is the complicated site of the tropes.[28] "You are my blood" signs the narrator's experience of Louise's life sustaining her own, of Louise's body in her own, but it also suggests Louise as created by the narrator's recollection of her, a Louise given life by the narrator's fiction of memory. Nora, too, fictionalizes in remembering Robin, and *Nightwood* makes use of the blood trope to suggest incorporation: "In Nora's heart lay the fossil of Robin, intaglio of her identity, and about it for its maintenance ran Nora's blood" (56). In both novels the lovers are either one body or two bodies in one; in *Written on the Body*, "I" cannot be sure which is which.

These same preoccupations mark the meditations on the body that follow soon after this passage. Sometimes the desire is to be inside Louise's body to protect her ("Will you let me crawl inside you, stand guard over you" [115]) or to be an archaeologist of her body, exploring "that impressive mausoleum." She sees "myself in your skin, myself lodged in your bones" (120). Other lines reverse the trope so that projection of her body becomes incorporation of Louise's. She remembers Louise as "milk-white and fresh to drink" (125). She imagines embalming her in her memory (119) or being marked by her lover's bite, noting also that "the L that tattoos me on the inside is not visible to the naked eye" (118).[29] The language of mirroring raises the stakes by suggesting not only that the lovers incorporate each other but that they are like each other. "I" describes Louise's face as "mirror-smooth and mirror-clear. Your face under the moon, silvered with cool reflection, your face in its mystery, revealing me" (132). Later, she says, "She was my twin and I lost her" (163). At other times the language is closer to identification: "if you are broken then so am I" (125); "if Louise is well then I am well" (154). Or, in a phrase that might have come from *Nightwood*, she responds to advice to forget Louise by replying, "I may as well forget myself" (148).[30]

Given this rhetoric in which lovers become part of each other and resemble each other, it is not surprising that other tropes speak to fear of loss of the self in the lover: recall that the narrator describes her meditations on Louise's body as "drowning myself in her." In one section she imagines "I dropped into the mass of you and I cannot find the way out" (120). In the closing meditation the language suggests both drowning and immolation as "I" imagines "floodings of you running down the edges of the sky on to the brown earth on to the gray stone. On to me. Sometimes I run into the sunset arms wide like a scarecrow, thinking I can jump off the side of the world into the fiery furnace and be burned up in you" (138). Similarly, nearer the end of the novel she says, "She flooded me and she has not drained away. I am still wading through her, she beats upon my doors and threatens my innermost safety" (163).

This rhetoric of identity interwoven with fear of self-loss writes out a dynamic between women lovers familiar in feminist psychology. The fluidity of boundaries postulated by many feminist theorists as a feature of women's development is sometimes doubled in erotics between women, and can result in a merging of subjectivities so that individual boundaries are not only crossed but lost. In her book *On Intimate Terms: The Psychology of Difference in Lesbian Relationships* (1993), on the dynamics of lesbian relation, psychoanalyst Beverly Burch gives a more positive cast to this threat of boundary loss that psychotherapy sometimes refers to as "the merging problem." Burch asserts that boundary fluidity promotes what she calls "complementarity," so that rather than see loss of the subject in the other, she argues that complementarity works between women lovers to enhance attraction, bonding, and transformation (80). The tropes of engulfment that run concurrently with the rhetoric of identity in the novel's body meditations touch on this kind of boundary loss.

Burch's theory of complementarity recasts the analytic concept of projective identification most frequently connected with the work of Melanie Klein. Klein theorizes projective identification as the "prototype of an aggressive object relation" (1946 [1986], 183). While for Freud projection is usually a defense mechanism, an attempt to expel interior "cause[s] of unpleasure," as he describes in "Instincts and Their Vicissitudes," Klein's version privileges identification (Freud 1915a, 136).[31] When the ego splits off bad parts of itself and projects them onto another (in Klein, originally the mother, but subsequently others as well) in an attempt to control and injure, it also identifies with this bad mother so that other-hatred becomes partial self-hatred as well. Klein goes on to discuss the projection of good parts of the self as necessary for good object relations, but perhaps because of her emphasis on projective identification's function as a prototype of aggressive object relation, the term retains a negative cast in most contemporary psychoanalytic theory.[32] Kristeva, for example, who explicitly theorizes what she sees as a gap in Klein's descriptions of depressive and schizo-paranoid positions, focuses on projective identification in Klein as "sustained by the 'hostile' as well as guilt-ridden desire to take the place of the persecuting mother out of envy" (1986, 249).[33]

Burch's recent work, however, rethinks Klein's terms in the context of lesbian relations. Though most of *On Intimate Terms* details a theory of relation between what she terms "primary" and "bisexual" lesbians, her thinking on projective identification begins to suggest how projection works positively rather than negatively in women's erotic relations. Burch departs from Klein not only in her stress on projective identification as positive rather than pathological, but also in her focus on interpsychic rather than intrapsychic processes. Her theory of complementarity in lesbian relationships is structured around the mutuality of projective and introjective identifications. In processes that are sometimes conscious, sometimes unconscious, each lover takes up and acts out projections of the other so that differences and possibilities can be lived out through cross-identifications. Both ideals and fears can be projected and enhanced or lessened through these processes. Obviously, the discourse of such mutuality itself inscribes an ideal, but Burch's text stresses the potential for self-enhancement in the context of relationship because it is arguing against a tradition which details the pathological aspects of excessive projective identifications.

Written on the Body's meditations on likeness narrativize an unexamined assumption in Burch's theory—why projective identificatory processes should be particularly crucial between women lovers. The novel argues that an erotics of resemblance grounds projective identification, both with its Kleinian emphasis on fear and loss and its Burchian insistence on the power of projection as a mechanism of sexual and emotional bonding. By "erotics of resemblance" I mean sexed body likeness and, by extension, psychic expectations that two like bodies will also have been similarly marked by socialization.

What constitutes "likeness" depends in part on the culturally specific positionings and identifications of each lover, which well may be indiscernible to the other. In the novel, where both women are white and where class difference resides most obviously in differing marital statuses, body likeness, as evidenced in the tropes of mirroring and twinning, gives rise to psychoanalytic identifications such as Klein and Burch describe. Even when resemblance privileges sexual likeness and keeps dominant racial likeness invisible because the advantages it brings are not conscious, the similarity of subjectivity is of course illusionary since, as Sedgwick pointedly notes, "people are different from each other" (1990, 22). Nevertheless, the illusion of resemblance, based on the lovers' "similar" bodies, not only grounds but heightens projection in the most general sense: because we are both women, what I feel must (at least) be close to what you feel.

In the more specifically analytic process of projective identification, this feeling of emotional connection is, in Juliet Mitchell's reading of Klein, a consequence of the ego's projecting its feelings into the object "which it then identifies with, becoming like the object which it has already imaginatively filled with itself" (1986, 20). The "likeness" Mitchell refers to is intensified in an erotics of bodily resemblance. But because this likeness is finally illusionary, it inevitably also produces error. In the novel, the narrator leaves Louise because she decides on Louise's behalf what she might want; "I" projects her own feelings partially as a defense against being abandoned and partially as an attribution of her own fear of death to her lover.

At the same time, Mitchell's emphasis on the "imaginative filling" resonates with the fiction-making process itself. The novel's first-person retrospective narration makes Louise a fiction constructed by the narrator under the pressure of loss. When the novel opens "Why is the measure of love loss?" the reader is poised ambiguously between mourning and melancholia, so to speak. Whether Louise's loss is temporary or permanent is never made certain; until word of her leukemia appears halfway through, the possibility of her death (rather than her return to her husband) does not threaten. The narrator's fictional construction of Louise would seem to take place under the aegis of depression brought on by recalling the threat of loss of love rather than actual loss of the lover. Narrative suture is sustained not by delay of event outcome, which is noted in the opening line, but by engaging the reader in the erotics of "I"'s relation to Louise, a relation that narratively works as a kind of projective identification on the narrator's part.

Reading the narrator as a woman is easy in these meditations on the body. The unidentified sex of the narrator is most subject to determination in this section because of its tropes of identity, incorporation, and projection. At the same time, this sexual indeterminacy acts as a defense for the reader constructing an erotics between women from the narratives of events and tropes in the novel. Though such a reader most likely will, by psychic investments and habits of reading, fill the sexual aporias by reading "I" as a woman, the ghost of the alternative reading never quite disappears even in the body meditations. Thus, in the scene of reading (and perhaps also in the scene of writing), the specter of a male lover defends against the anxiety of identificatory engulfment just as in the diegetic scene eroticized anxiety defends against the fear of boundary loss. In the body meditations, the ghost is playful:

> It was a game, fitting bone on bone. I thought difference was rated to be the largest part of sexual attraction but there are so many things about us that are the same.
> Bone of my bone. Flesh of my flesh. To remember you it's my own body I touch. Thus she was, here and here. (129–30)

The passage reinforces a reading of the two lovers as alike, even as one. But as the passage teases, it's still a game, since Louise may be "here and here" through identity ("to remember you it's my own body I touch") or through "I"'s memory of Louise's tactile presence on a differently sexed body. The ghost of difference defends against the tropes of drowning and immolation that threaten the narrator and the narrative space being filled in the performance of reading. But given the fictional convention of an unambiguously sexed narrator, the ghostly defense remains a subterranean one.

Part Three

REBECCA BROWN

THE EROTICS OF EXCESS AND THE
DIFFICULTIES OF DIFFERENCE

In 1986, one year before Jeanette Winterson published *The Passion,* she edited a short fiction collection called *Passion Fruit: Romantic Fiction with a Twist.* The book's romances are definitely not the sort of stories found in Harlequins or Mills and Boon. *Passion Fruit*'s cover art signals the volume's twists of romance conventions: in the place of the usual heterosexual couple, the cover parodies Roy Lichtenstein's famous pop art piece "Crying Girl," by featuring a single transgenderal figure; s/he is a boyish weeper with beard and mustache. The stories themselves, while mostly about heterosexual romance, script assertive women, receptive men, and offbeat settings. Contributors include such well-known contemporary writers as Sara Maitland, Fay Weldon, Marge Piercy, Bobbie Ann Mason, and Angela Carter. Only one author has two stories in the collection: the opening piece, "Forgiveness," and the closing one, "Junk Mail," are by Rebecca Brown, an American whose novels and shorter fiction collections, well-known and widely reviewed in Winterson's Britain, are just now beginning to receive mainstream critical attention in the U.S.[1] "Forgiveness" begins: "When I said I'd give my right arm for you, I didn't think you'd ask me for it, but you did." The story relates how "I" literally gives up an arm to a lover who takes it out to have it bronzed, keeps it temporarily on the mantelpiece, then departs altogether, bronzed arm in hand, only to return unarmed in the end. The comic literalness of a lover's sacrificing her limb, and her accompanying ironic observation ("It is an old saying after all"), is kin to the comic commentaries on clichés that Winterson will embed in *Written on the Body.* Ultimately, both representations defend against the poignancy of loss that marks the center of each fiction.

Brown's "Forgiveness" and "Junk Mail," again like the later *Written on the Body,* have sex-unspecified narrators who refer to their equally unspecified lovers as "you." But when Brown published the stories as part of her novel-in-stories, *The*

Terrible Girls (1990), she set them in a longer lyrical narrative of obsession, loss, power, and emotional difference between women lovers. *The Terrible Girls* recalls *Nightwood* in its erotics, and Brown has already been compared to Barnes by Joan Nestle on the novel's back cover: "Like a modern Djuna Barnes, Brown creates a language of telling that is fiercely beautiful and honest. This book is a love story unlike any you have read before. Its subversive and passionate transformations carry the lesbian literary voice into the 21st century." Erotics between women in *The Terrible Girls,* again reconstructed by a narrator in retrospect, pointedly critique the asymmetries of power that originally structure "I"'s relation to her lover, "you." Although the novel's resolution classifies it as a romance, its various erotics identify it as something other, depending as they do both on the lovers' differences and on the self-critical ironic voice that recalls them.

Because fiction in the Barnes tradition engages both "sameness" and difference, it prompts (re)reading psychoanalytic fictions of narcissism. I earlier posed *Nightwood* as an intervention in Freud's essay "On Narcissism," in part by suggesting the difference between Robin's enclosing self-absorption and Nora's relation to Robin in an erotics not of "sameness" but of resemblance. *The Terrible Girls* also recognizes the structuring importance of resemblance in eroticism; Brown's novel-in-stories, however, contributes specifically to a theorizing of women's affective and sexual dynamics by focusing more immediately than *Nightwood* does on the difficulties of difference.

As a novel in the *Nightwood* tradition, *The Terrible Girls* also figures affects in the context of a lover lost; both its tropes and its events might be plotted in a sequence of episodes designating loss, separation, and incipient recovery. In representing loss, Brown's novel recalls and revises a second well-known essay of Freud's, "Mourning and Melancholia" (1917), in which Freud continues his thinking on narcissism and writes as well about another structuring relation of affect: identification. In reading *The Terrible Girls* as a partial revision of the classic psychoanalytic fictions named narcissism and identification, I will detour through "Mourning and Melancholia" and consider especially its collocating formulation, "narcissistic identification." I argue that *The Terrible Girls* continues from *Nightwood* in its rewriting of "sameness" as resemblance, and, in addition and more significantly for women's erotics, theorizes the alignment of identification with desire. My discussion also frames *The Terrible Girls* as a theoretical fiction that comments not only on the psychoanalytic understandings of "identification" and "desire," but on these scripts as they engage the performing reader as well. It is finally individual performances by culturally and historically located readers that enact the novel's erotics.

I. Dynamics of Power: The Frame-up

As a novel-in-stories, *The Terrible Girls* is a loosely constructed narrative of betrayal and redemption. Its seemingly separate tales weave together a parable in which "I," damaged by her obsessive love for "you," is restored to wholeness by the intervention and guidance of "she." In its barest outline, the narrative has a classic humanist plot in which a noncontradictory subject loses, then regains a heart lost in love: The first story, "The Dark House," features two women in a tantalizing game of desire deferred, during which an infatuated "I" serves "you"'s every whim. Suddenly "you" decides that they should run from their current lives. They arrive at a dark house occupied by an unidentified third person who seems to be waiting for "you." After a three-story interruption that begins with a meditation on the erotics of attraction, then recounts the excesses wrought by power imbalances, the threads of the opening narrative resume in the fifth story, a tale of "I" and Lady Bountiful, née "you." Now both members of a failed underground resistance, "you" has left "I" (and the movement) to marry Lord Bountiful; "you" visits "I" occasionally under the guise of charity to the less fortunate. "I" fantasizes scenes of revenge, but is freed from her obsession with "you" only in the final story when she is guided by her new lover, "she," first to "you"'s house for a last confrontation, and then to the ruined city where "I" has hidden her heart. (Earlier, it has been taken from her by the "terrible girls," but they are so busy fighting each other that they lose track of it.) Together "I" and "she" unbury the lost heart and restore "I" to wholeness.[2]

The novel might be said to have two narratives—a frame-tale narrative of events (related primarily in the opening and closing stories, and in the tale of Lady Bountiful) constituting the plot, and an interpolated narrative of affect (stories 2, 3, and 4—"Isle of Skye," "Junk Mail," and "Forgiveness") complicating the lesbian dynamics suggested by the frame-tale events. The erotics between the two women begin in the opening story, "The Dark House," but play out primarily in the three-story interpolation immediately following. The frame provides the closed event narrative into which the narrative of affect is inserted. In my reading, the stories of Lady Bountiful and the terrible girls narrated in the frame-tale are less compelling, perhaps because more polemical, than the emotional narrative of "I" and "you."[3] As a consequence, I give more space in my subsequent discussion to the triad that interrupts the framing plot. But the frame-tale remains crucial for its rendering of skewed power dynamics, both at the micro level of the subject, where "you" controls "I," and at the macro level of economic class, where "you" rises from impoverished revolutionary to Lady of the land.

In the frame-tale, Lady Bountiful figures not only as an embodiment of "you" who takes "I"'s heart, but also as the representative of social power. By the time of the closing story, the land ruled by the greedy and repressive Lord Bountiful and his Lady has been ravished by drought and beset by roaming "terrible girls." The "terrible girls" allegory may be read as critiquing the destructive disregard of one generation for the preceding one to whom it is indebted for privilege (e.g., chic queer girls who condemn 70s feminists with their "puritan tales about the bad old days," "their cheaply xeroxed flyers and their tacky tracts," and "their sensible old maid shoes, their mannish overalls and ratty sweat-shirts" [128]), or more generally as the breakdown of revolutionary community through individual self-interest. In the final story, Lady Bountiful reappears in the now-polluted land as the unnamed "you," whom "I" and "she" visit on their way to find "I"'s heart. "I" encounters "you," older but still beautiful, asleep in an ordinary house, perhaps the same "dark house" as in the opening story. Just as "I" decides not to hack "you"'s heart from her in revenge, "you" awakes and apologizes for the terrible (personal and social) pain she has caused. "I" departs, knowing she can now move forward with her life, and continues with "she" to the city where they recover "I"'s lost heart.

The frame-tale is primarily a retrospective narrative. Iniquities of institutional and personal power drive the dynamic, but because "I" retells them from a position of recovery, her narrative distance allows a critique in a near-comic tone. Unlike in *Nightwood* or *Written on the Body,* loss does not occasion a renewed search for the lover; instead it prompts a desire to (re)construct a subjectivity from a body-in-pieces.

The seeming success of the frame-tale's humanist search for wholeness is destabilized by the stories that interrupt it, and undone by the narrator's final misrecognition of unified subjectivity. The disruptive stories present a narrative of affect dependent on tropes rather than on event; that is, they count on linguistic detail and especially on extended body references to convey the subtleties of emotional exchanges in a sexual context. The tropological narrative of affect is governed by excess, incompleteness, and nonidentity between lovers; their traces haunt the frame-tale's final vision of the restored body: "There was something against my body, there was an opening, a blaze, there was the heart" (136).

II. "The Dark House": "Someday, if I wait . . . "

The opening story, "The Dark House," establishes both the dynamics between "I" and "you" that play out in the frame-tale events, and the conditions of loss elaborated in the affective narrative that interrupts the enframing plot. The opening paragraph introduces power differences:

Never, you said, not me. Don't waste your time waiting.

But after a while you said, Well possibly.

Then after a longer while you said, Well maybe. But whatever you might do, if you did anything, you'd certainly make no promises and one would be wrong to assume or expect. Then you cocked your head a little and said that if anything were perhaps to happen it would take a long, long time. But if one were around anyway and felt like it, one might wait.

This was your way of saying Someday. Of telling me to wait.

"You" has the power because she (her sex is made clear in the next paragraph) is desired and controls by deferring "I"'s desire. The story aligns "you"'s control with her social status. For most of the story, "you" hosts a conference (which, ironically, features speeches of a clinical psychology sort) where the seemingly endless deferral takes place; "I" is the conference's "coffee-cart girl." More important, the roles of conference hostess and coffee-cart girl stand in for their positioning in heterosexual culture. "You" addresses the conference on the dangers of "coffee-cart girls" at the same time that she functions as hostess, so that she both produces a minoritizing discourse from a position of prestige and reproduces a traditional feminized role that keeps her professional status from threatening an institutional gender hierarchy. That "I," who comes from an unmapped land beyond the river, keeps trying to persuade "you" to escape to that unknown terrain with her, and that "you" resists because she hasn't studied the maps and worries that she might not like the new territory, marks "I" as a lesbian and separates her from "you."

Such tropological marking is confirmed in "I"'s account of the address "you" makes at the conference about "coffee-cart girls"—the way they dress, their gestures, and the questions of origin: "What makes one turn into a coffee-cart girl? Heredity or Environment? Dominant-submissive or submissive-dominant? Childhood clothing and games? How long one is breast fed? Or simply something very, very wicked? Then you launched into How to Deal with Them. Are they to be pitied or reviled?" (11). The retrospective narration provides both an account of "I"'s attraction to the hostess/clinician ("You had made me the coffee-cart girl") and hindsight knowledge (which foreshadows for the reader her inevitable betrayal.) "I" is doubly abject in that her working-class status and sexual preference determine her position as an outsider in the (dominant) culture of the conference. But at the same time, her assertion of her role as the subservient "coffee-cart girl" and her willingness to wait for "you"'s attention acknowledge the complexity of her desire. She foregrounds the social differences that figure her attraction to "you," though whether she eroticizes the pain of abjection or fantasizes the conquest of the (seemingly) more socially powerful isn't clear. She also attests to the well-known pleasure of deferral.

The frame-tale's alignment of class, sexual preference, and desirer-who-waits establishes an "I"-"you" power dynamic that drives their waiting game. Despite her protests ("I'm not like that, you said"), "you" turns out to be a "coffee-cart girl" also, but is willfully blind to what her audience can see: "Why is she lying, they whispered, Why is she saying such dumb archaic stuff? . . . The person who you were lying for was you" (11). What complicates these differences in power is the retrospective narration and the comic tone; they recount "I"'s attraction at the same time that they make clear her ultimate knowledge of "you"'s manipulation and self-blindness.

In the story's opening paragraph, "I" represents "you"'s voice of deferral ironically. The prose style becomes a commentary on the content. The move from "never," to "well maybe," to "a long, long time" signals "I"'s retrospective awareness of "you"'s use of promise to entice. The reader might take refuge in this narratorial knowledge if it weren't for the last line of the opening: "This was your way of saying Someday. Of telling me to wait" (1). Here "I" makes a fiction of what she's been told—she interprets rejection as hope. In so doing she reaffirms the power of deferral and participates in a familiar Barnesian erotic by rescripting what she hears. By the end of "The Dark House," she, like

Nightwood's Nora, comes to see her own fiction-making, but unlike Nora, she speaks directly to it: "I'd gotten so used to hearing what you said the way I wanted to that I couldn't tell what you really said. I wanted, when you had said to me, I'm not, I'll never, for you to have been lying. I wanted someday for you to stop lying and be with me" (9). Such commentary affirms the reader's trust in the narrator's self-knowledge; it also prepares for the eventual closure of the event narrative in the last story when "I" declines to destroy "you" in revenge, and is instead restored to wholeness when her body and heart literally and figuratively are returned to her.

But before the novel moves to unify the subject in a vision of seeming wholeness, it sets up a narrative of the body-in-pieces as a marker for, and consequence of, loss.[4] "The Dark House" ends with "I" and "you" leaving the conference (at the moment that "you" chooses, of course), crossing the river (with "I" holding "you," who can't swim, of course) to a dark house where "I" expects they'll be together. But when they arrive, someone, sex unspecified, is waiting for "you." "You" asks "I" to leave, and the last sentence of the story echoes the opening: "I wave to the hand but it does not wave back. But it leaves a small, thin opening where someone could wave through. I close my eyes and imagine your hand waving out to me. You leave that opening for me, a sign for me, a way of saying, Someday, if I wait" (24). By this point, the narrator has shifted from retrospective to the lyric present tense, a shift that leaves open the question of whether "I"'s awareness of her fiction-making, her scripting of what she requires, has been only momentary. There's still that "small, thin opening," that promise, that maybe "you" is only temporarily lost. The deferral continues.

The narrative of affect that interrupts the frame-tale begins in the next story, "The Isle of Skye," continues through "Junk Mail," and ends with "Forgiveness." In each story an "I" meditates on separation and loss involving a "you." Though "I" and "you" may not be the same figures in all three interpolated stories, and though they may also not be identical to "I" and "you" in the frame-tale, the two have similar power dynamics throughout *The Terrible Girls.* Or, more accurately, as the affective narrative moves from "Isle of Skye" to "Forgiveness," the relation between "I" and "you" comes increasingly to look like that between the coffee-cart girl and the conference hostess, between two women occupying lesser and greater power positions in their relationship. What begins as a meditation on difference and the difficulty of speech ends with the narrator's claiming agency through her attempts to recover a part of herself given up for love.

All three of the stories have sex-unspecified narrators, but their placement after the tale of the hostess and the coffee-cart girl and preceding the fable of "I" and Lady Bountiful makes them read as explicitly lesbian.[5] Indeed, the references to lovemaking ("I find I'm not a foreigner when my tongue finds the warmth between your thighs"; "one of our tongues is on one of our breasts" [29, 30]) would strongly suggest two women even without the frame-tale. All three stories follow from the close of "The Dark House," in which the women separate. The separation of "Isle of Skye" is seemingly more mutual, but the next story, "Junk

Mail," is all about extremity of loss. In it, loss of the lover occasions "excess without reason" and leads to the hacking off of the arm in "Forgiveness." If one of the determiners of loss in *Nightwood* is Nora's excess of control, in *The Terrible Girls* the chief determinant of loss is the absence of self-control or "I"'s willingness to part with too much of herself.

"Isle of Skye" represents likeness and difference in geographic and linguistic figures. The story has a minimal plot: "I" takes time from her travels to visit "you," her sometime lover, whom she has seen occasionally in the past. They don't communicate well verbally, but they speak articulately in their lovemaking. "I" secretly wants to be asked to stay on, but "you" reads her public gestures as a wish to continue traveling. After four days, "I" leaves and returns to her own country; she writes, not sure that "you" will recognize either the postmark or the script. The narrative of affect plays the difficulty of spoken communication against the more reliable nonverbal language of desiring bodies. Since "I" is a traveler, tropes of geography and its coding in cartography, and of communication and its coding in verbal systems, constitute the fields of reference.

The two lovers come from different worlds but share like bodies and like dreams. When they wake, it is from the same nightmare. Though neither can remember the dream's specifics, their interior meditations suggest that "I" fears leaving and ending up alone in a country where no one can understand her, while "you" fears that even if she asks "I" to stay, "I" will leave her at some future point. When they wake from their mutual nightmare, "I," the traveler, reaches for her passport, and "you," the homebody, turns on the familiar bedside lamp. In some ways the most poignant story in the novel, and the only one in which "you"'s voice (marked in the text by italics) alternates with "I"'s, "Isle of Skye" recalls Nora and Robin's exchange of home and away, but comments more directly on the lack of communication that keeps "I" wandering even when she wishes to stay. Their erotics of attraction, while testifying to the need for talk as well as for touch, also gets at the same tension that sustains Nora and Robin in *Nightwood* and will be romanticized in *Written on the Body*: passion vs. comfort. Throughout the story, likeness grounds the differences that keep the lovers interacting, but only for brief, intense visits. While they are together, the interplay of similarity and difference produces ambivalence. After they have separated, ambivalence gives way to longing, and in the next story, to obsession.

I discuss in Part One the tension between sameness and difference that becomes more accurately in *Nightwood* a palimpsest of differences inscribed on like lovers. "Isle of Skye" does not provide even the few details of the lovers' psychosexual dynamics that Barnes's novel does, but it does use difference/sameness more generally as a founding discourse in which the likeness of bodies counters differences in language and origin. In so doing it recalls the traditional romance's appeal not just to the nonverbal expressions of sexual passion, but to cultural and subcultural technologies that produce same-sex lovers as outside the law and so dependent on their own knowledges as they travel "new countries" where "there are no maps."

III. The Return of Difference

Before turning fully to "Isle of Skye," I want briefly to put into play some theoretical discourses of sameness and difference that Brown's story counters or extends. I have already begun to discuss one gatekeeping technology of "sameness": psychoanalytic narratives of narcissism, often popularized (and sometimes careless) versions of "Freud" in which *Nightwood* intervenes. I will revisit narcissism shortly, in one of its specific guises—narcissistic identification. In the late-twentieth-century United States, however, homophobic cultural discourses do not require psychoanalysis to pathologize same-sex object choice.[6] Despite the recent emphasis of queer theory on sexual acts, object choice and ensuing definitions of fixed "sexual orientation" remain the foundation of bigotry. Not (or not only) what you do but with whom you do it enrages conservative extremists, prompting recurrent efforts to deny civil rights to gay men and lesbians. The recent attempt to prevent passage of legislation protecting homosexual acts and persons in Washington State also speaks to object choice when it explicitly forbids "same-gender marriage."[7] Even institutional juridical discourse that seeks to distinguish "person" from "act" is not consistently applied. The Uniform Code of Military Justice, for example, criminalizes the act of sodomy; the military, however, can retain personnel who commit homosexual acts if it finds that those acts were "an aberration" and the persons performing them were not "actually" homosexuals but heterosexuals who momentarily strayed (Hayes 1990, 29 n. 7). Such attempts to police homosex demonstrate Lee Edelman's point that perceived "sameness" of homosexual lovers is made to signify difference in order to preserve the "norm" of heterosex (1994, 3–23).

Homophobic rhetoric's attempts to deny civil rights protection on the basis of actual or presumed same-sex "orientation" or "preference" rest on conditions of perceived "sameness"; however, some feminist theorizings of difference are also problematic in their implications for (homo)sexualities. "Difference" in its various guises has been the primary touchstone for virtually every mode and intersection of poststructuralist and feminist theory for more than two decades; obviously it informs more empirically oriented discussions of social issues as well. One feminist discourse in the social sciences, to give only one of an ever-proliferating number of examples, is sometimes referred to as the equality vs. difference debate, by which is meant that arguments for women's rights may be framed by arguing either "that sexual difference ought to be an irrelevant consideration in schools, employment, the courts and the legislature" or that "appeals on behalf of women ought to be made in terms of the needs, interests, and characteristics common to women as a group" (Scott, 138). In this succinct summary Joan Scott adopts, for purposes of critique, long-standing feminist practice in using the term "sexual difference" to mean the difference between men and women. Necessary criticisms by women of color, on the one hand, and attention to poststructuralist discourses of difference and *différance,* on the other (as Scott points out), have led to feminist specifying of "difference" as differences among women as well as the differing race, class, ethnic, and sexual preference positions of any singular subject.[8] Such emphases produce an understandable and necessary privileging of difference as part of structural dominance, but one that may have the unintended effect of reinforcing in a less than conscious way the denigration of "sameness" as it operates between women as lovers. In an unrelated but equally influential argument of Luce Irigaray's, for example, Sameness intervenes in theories of sexual difference by standing pejoratively for the phallocentric regime that colonizes women in an economy in which the feminine cannot stand on its own in signification, but can be posited only as other to the masculine (1985a, 32–34; 1985b, 221).

In queer theory, as in feminist theory, "sameness" and difference inevitably turn up as analytics. Eve Sedgwick observes in *Epistemology of the Closet* that same-sex lovers are often read as being *literally* the same: "though the two etymological roots of the coinage 'homo-sexuality' may originally have been meant to refer to relations (of an unspecified kind) between persons of the *same sex,* I believe the word is now almost universally heard as referring to relations of *sexuality* between persons who are, because of their sex, more flatly and globally categorized as *the same*" (1990, 158, n. 31; emphases in the original). Sedgwick, in a point that is crucial for her investment in cross-sex identification, discounts the idea that same-sex relations "are much more likely to be based on similarity than are cross-sex relationships" (159). Perhaps they are not, but fictions in the Barnes mode and many other representations of erotics between women portray the attractions and dangers of "sameness." I think, for example, of the flip popular edict that lesbian erotics turn on the "three M's": mirrors, mothering, and masculinity—that is to say, on myths of sex resemblance as well as of gender difference.[9]

Sedgwick's reference to homosexuality's being "almost universally heard" to imply lovers who are "the same" may be intended to mean "heard" by non-gay- or -lesbian-identified hearers; in any case, discourse produced by and for self-identified lesbians, dykes, gay women, queer girls, and other participants in erotics between women often inscribes difference as a structuring relation, per-haps to counter that "universally heard" sameness, but to resist boundary loss, and to import erotic tension as well. Recent emphases on visible difference in butch-femme enactments or discussions of s/m sexuality in such magazines as *On Our Backs* and *Bad Attitude* also have a specific political and historical context. As examples of U.S. 1990s representations of power differences in women's erotics, images and language in these magazines may be read in part as reacting against a discourse of lesbian-feminism that emphasized equality between lovers. What began in the 1970s as a political rhetoric of "equality" in sexual exchanges came to be seen a decade later as a myth of "sameness" that implied no erotic charge, no hot sex.

As a fiction of the 1980s, "Isle of Skye" counters that myth by scripting a dynamic in which the complexities of emotional and sexual exchange demand difference to charge desire and depend on likeness to facilitate touch. But Brown's fiction also complicates theory by refusing to valorize difference in the abstract, and by portraying bodily "sameness" as insufficient to overcome the specific differences that emerge in the exchanges.

IV. "Isle of Skye": "Loving difference causes pain"

The first lines of the story set up the narrative of afffect by referring to similarity and difference in geographic and linguistic terms:

> Hello is easy. It's the same most places. And if not, a smile or nod will do. But then again, in some countries, a smile means sadness; and greeting is expressed with an open mouth shaped like the letter "O."
> . . . .
> In my country, you say, people live in homes.
> That's like my country too.
> So far so good. (25)

Throughout the story, the passage's language of geographic comparison stands in for what might be more general differences between lovers, especially those of belief as they influence erotics, and thus produce varying customs from two "countries": monogamy/nonmonogamy, same-sex experience/bisexual or heterosexual experience, or "out" lover/closeted one. In its tropes of travel to another country, the story recalls "The Dark House," in which "I" tries to persuade her lover to escape with her to a similarly suggestive, unnamed, unknown terrain, but "you" protests that she doesn't have papers, hasn't had shots, and hasn't studied the maps (2).

The geographical difference also manifests itself linguistically so that the lovers must use a phrasebook for their attempts to communicate; largely those tries fail, so that their differences become interpretive as well: "We try to talk and think we do, but we are each afraid. We know when we say blue that we mean blue. But maybe when you say blue, you mean sky. And maybe I mean water" (26). That language and geographic differences stand in for emotional and ideological ones is clear in that "I" refers to U.S. place names and "you" to nearby British landmarks. They resemble each other in that both speak English, but they differ since they still can't catch what the other thinks she's said. Difficulty in communication between lovers is a truism that matters "differently" between same-sex lovers, because it is one of many versions of difference that structures desire.

The failure to understand just what the other means centers on whether "I" will stay or leave again, and reveals "you" as the better reader of "I"'s verbal texts. Or, if not "better," at least more able to exercise control on the basis of her understandings. The particulars of their semantic failures pinpoint an old debate between lovers. What one calls freedom, the other calls fear; what one senses as the other's need to travel, the other recognizes as her own ambivalent fear of being bored if she stays—in short, the familiar passion vs. comfort dichotomy now slightly elaborated as fear of intimacy vs. risk of commitment. In language that might have been Robin's in *Nightwood* when she first began her night wanderings, "I" insists on her faithfulness: "I keep coming back to you. Every-time I leave, you say you know I won't return: I do. I come and come again to you. . . . When will you believe these words and maps, these anecdotes are what I give, the way I'm trying to ask you, let me stay?" (31–32). But "you" insists that "stay" means something different in "I"'s language. She recognizes: *This is not what sustains her here. To keep her I must send her out. She is not happy still* (32). Ultimately (or at least for a moment) "I" accedes to "you"'s reading: "You insist that I'd get bored; you're right. You tell me you'd get irritated; you're right. The fact is we are different. Our union is a sharp specific point, the few words we've translated, the tiny border crossed" (33).

And so "I" leaves, but her ambivalence about her freedom marks the end of the story. She finds herself constantly circling back toward "you," wanting "a miracle. I want you to find me. I keep looking back, in rearview mirrors, over my shoulder, through fog" (33). In the story, just as will be the case in *Written on the Body,* comfort never gets fully tested. "I" says she wants to stay, wants to be found, fears being alone, but finally agrees to go.

While "I" and "you" are together, "I" comes to believe that "language is the only thing that lies" (32). Not surprisingly, the nonverbal but expressive sexual body becomes the route of their communicating. The first mention of libidinal desire comes in the context of not speaking: "Sometimes I look up a word you don't say, but just a word I'm thinking. I want to know how you'd think this feeling if you were thinking it yourself. Such as Desire, Longing, Want, Desire. I don't ask you" (26). Their similar needs bridge their linguistic problems: "The difficulty, I decide, is just in language, the time it takes to find things in Berlitz. I know, *I know,* that in your country, as in mine, our needs come from our bodies. In your country, as in mine, surely your countrymen all need the same, to eat and sleep and love" (28). They try to exchange anatomical names ("You give me the etymology of elbow . . . I tell you mouth and breast and thigh") and end by doubling meaning ("Your foreign tongue is mine" [29]). Language about the body becomes language of the body, and they "take each other to new countries neither of us has been to before. . . . There are no maps" (29).

What's more, the lovemaking scene suggests not simply that they share the same desires, but that the bodies with which they express them are alike: "One of our hands is in one of our thighs. One of our tongues is on one of our breasts. . . . One of our hands is in one of our thighs. One of us breathes and one of us breathes" (30). Though conceivably these bodies might be differently sexed, the parts named, the repetition of "one," and the concluding doubling all read as similarity rather than difference, especially in a story that so foregrounds ways in which difference can traverse a ground of resemblance.

Crucially, however, "Isle of Skye" not only recognizes that difference produces desire between like lovers, but acknowledges discursively what *Nightwood* per-forms: differences are difficult. "*Loving difference causes pain. We love what is differ-ent to possess it, to be whole. We want to be everything. The problem is, we can't. The problem is, the differences are different. Water and flame, brilliance and night, longing and fulfillment of desire. What keeps us moving is what keeps us sad, what keeps us moving is the want to be unforeign, whole"* (32). Paradoxically, the passage suggests that loving difference to enable wholeness requires continually moving from one lover to the next, toward an ever-elusive completion. For that very reason, the gesture toward stable subjectivity on which the closure of *The Terrible Girls* will come to depend is never quite final; the trace of this passage in "Isle of Skye" prevents the wholeness that the recovery of "I"'s heart otherwise declares. In the story's erotics, "I"'s recognition that "differences are different" complicates what I have called the dichotomy between passion and comfort. It may be that tension is more sustaining than stasis, that difference produces desire in theory, but too much tension, too many specific differences, drive lovers apart. At the story's end, they have separated, yet "I" still longs to be followed, to be found.

In taking up difference/sameness as a discourse, "Isle of Skye" offers cartography as a trope for the way in which erotics between women create new landscapes. Lovemaking becomes travel to "new countries" where there are no maps. Absence of maps not only in this story but in *Written on the Body* and other fictions of erotics between women marks unknown erotic territory and speaks to the seduction of the untraveled as well as to the lack of guidance from previous travelers.[10] In this story, maps and mapping belong to the rhetoric of traveler and home, foreign and native, your country and mine that shapes the narration. Such figures work against the putative sameness of the lovers' bodies by emphasizing the difference of their origins. One shows the other a map, but it is only a "colored page" to the lover who stays home. She in turn walks the traveler around the local countryside, but it is foggy, so her lover must depend on her descriptions to know what's there. "I'd know more of a different thing if you'd shown me a map" (27). One knows by mapping, the other by walking. The difference between reading codes and sensing the landscape marks them but also makes them mutually (in)dependent. They know where they are by their own epistemologies, but they count on each other for interpreting the foreign.

Unfortunately, interpretation through language fails them. But when they make love there are no maps for the new country they enter. The connection between the maps and sex as an unknown country seems at first to be a later version of Nora's plaint that in loving Robin there are no rules to go by, and an earlier version of *Written on the Body*'s directions for making a new country: "Louise, in this single bed . . . I will find a map as likely as any treasure hunt. I will explore you and mine you and you will redraw me according to your will. We shall cross one another's boundaries and make ourselves one nation" (20). But historical context intervenes in these superficial similarities. In the 1930s when *Nightwood* appeared, there well may have been no, or at least fewer, rules to go by in an erotics between women. At least in the literature of Barnes's moment—the literature of Woolf and Stein and Hall—sexual exchanges were often coded or indirect. Fifty years later, emotional, sexual, and political communities defined variously by crossings of nation, region, class, race, and gender have established specific cultural locations often held together/bound by rules of dress, performance, etiquette, and actions.[11] So when "Isle of Skye" and *Written on the Body* trope the unknown, the unmapped, the new "nation" of two lovers, they reach to escape the rules now so much a part of urban sexual communities. They look (back) to undiscovered territories, ever the gesture of the romance, to locate erotics between women in an old tradition of "newness."

The story's last paragraph returns to the cartographic trope not as the chart for a new erotic territory, but as a mark of difference: "I'm lost in a city whose name you can't pronounce; I think it's my own. Your country's maps spell this name differently. Will you recognize the post mark? Will you recognize my hand? Who'll translate the maps for us? Do you know this means I love you? Do you know this means I love you?" (34). While in the presence of her lover, "I" acknowledges her lover's contention that "I" needs to travel to prevent boredom. Now, in separation, she imagines "you" getting mail she has sent and longs for her. Though "Isle of Skye" narrates seemingly mutual acts of separation, the closing returns "I"'s ambivalence. Her desire to be asked to stay alternates with her need to explore, an uncertainty "you" engages to ensure her own sense that sending her lover away will also guarantee her return. At the same time, "I"'s ambivalence produces safety. She doesn't have to struggle with the risks of intimacy and of difficult differences because finally, she's only a tourist in her lover's "country." By acceding to "you"'s reading of her interiority, she aids in sustaining an erotic connection between them.

V. "Junk Mail": "Excess without reason"

In the following story, "Junk Mail," "I" has no such ambivalence in the context of separation. In fact, "I" and "you" may well not be the same pair of lovers as in "Isle of Skye," but "I" again speaks of loss from a place of separation. Whatever gains she has had in relation to "you" are past before the story begins. Loss produces not even the potential for poignant longing; instead, "I"'s obsession with the missing "you" drives her to "excess without reason" (36) in fantasies of dismemberment. "Junk Mail" proceeds by a series of displacements in a kind of dream logic. "I" is alone, "you" having left, implying that she needed more space. "I" gets junk mail; she imagines returning some of it to a company executive who's trying to sell her something with it; he metamorphoses into the lover ("I see his collar is loose. Like yours. . . . I think he's you. I see his nice brown eyes. He is" [37]). Then she imagines that the junk mail contains a secret message from "you"; she decides to turn the tables and send the message back to "you," but shifts again and imagines sending her bodily self as a message, first as a letter, then as a package. The plain brown package becomes a jack-in-the-box tin container for her body, which she imagines as wound so tightly by "you" that it explodes into body parts. In the next phantasmic scene, she begins to get packages in the mail—"you" is returning her body parts. She is inundated with parts of herself. She tries escaping to an island, but the packaged parts keep coming, dropped, she imagines, by "you" from a plane. The story ends:

> I just keep stacking boxes [of her own body parts] up. They keep arriving, constant, steady, always a surprise, day after day, each hour, every time I blink or try to breathe, just when I think I know they will, just when I think you've sent me back, just when I think there can't be any more, when I think you'll do this to me forever, when I think, just when I think—. (45)

The repetition of "think" at the end suggests the story as a parable of obsessive memory. Mikkel Borch-Jacobsen reiterates Freud's point that in fantasy the subject is always representing itself in the fantasy "characters" (1982, 44).[12] In Brown's story, memory works in much the same way, so that what is imagined in the return of "I"'s body parts is her self-in-her-memories of "you." Too much thought about an absent lover who is a present fiction produced by the remembering self results in an inundating excess of self. That is, since the lover is a phantasm created by "I," obsessive phantasmatic production multiplies the producing subject. But in "Junk Mail" such multiplication is also made specific to an erotics between women by the mechanisms of projective identification at work between like lovers, as Beverly Burch argues in *On Intimate Terms*. When "I" obsesses on the loss of "you," she imagines her by projecting parts of herself; thus it is not surprising that what returns to her are those packages of body parts. It's not only that memory is always a fiction implicating the fiction maker, but that the specific fiction created about a like other projects affects of the self onto the other; hence the rain of body parts signs not just obsessive memory but the endless return of the-self-in-the-other. Their similarities are morphological, so what returns are the parts of the body.

The story offers its own judgment of obsession for a lover lost when it says about junk mail: "It's not just the excess that makes it bad, but excess without reason" (36). Memories such as "I"'s are excessive not only in their unceasingness, but also in their account of "I"'s tie to "you." That the excess is imaged in the continuing shower of "I"'s body parts testifies first to the dynamic begun in "The Dark House." In that story "I"'s abjection before a more powerful "you" is initially eroticized and retrospectively critiqued, though it might be argued that even her critique calls on the erotics of power exchange: "I should have slapped you. I should have done you with a power drill, but I just sat there" (9). In "Junk Mail" the fantasy of the exploding jack-in-the-box eroticizes a similar extremity of power difference. "You" has an excess of control, but "I" puts herself in the box willingly. "You" winds her tightly; "I" explodes into parts. "I"'s act of placing herself completely in her lover's control undoes them: "This is too much even for you. You realize, at last, that you don't want this. You truly want to send me back" (40).

The inundation of body parts that follows emphasizes the danger of giving oneself away too freely. But in its own way it too is a vision of excess so that the affective narrative conveyed by the trope of an exploding body followed by a rain of body parts threatens to overwhelm the discursive presentation of control as destroying the relationship.[13] On the one hand, "I" imagines plausibly that too much control helps drive "you" away; after all, invariant positions of more and less power can be a paralyzing stasis. On the other, "I"'s fantasy continues to require an unending overflow of images signaling excess, so that what is denied in the explanatory discourse is multiplied in the narrative telling.

At the same time, the excess characterizes the particular pain of loss that accompanies the disappearance of a lover who resembles the self. Like Nora's narrative, "I"'s story resonates and revises classic psychoanalytic texts on loss, of which Freud's "Mourning and Melancholia" (1917) is perhaps the most famous.

VI. Freud's Knot: "Narcissistic Identification"

Freud argues in "Mourning and Melancholia" that loss of a lover occasions depression (melancholia) because such a loss also involves a loss of self. Especially in cases of "narcissistic object choice," the libido withdraws from the lost object to the ego when the relationship ends, and substitutes identification with the object for the former erotic cathexis of it. What was a conflict between the lost object and the ego becomes instead a split between the ego as a critical agent (elsewhere in Freud, the ego ideal and finally, in part, the superego) and the ego "as altered by identification." This shift accounts for the mechanism of depressive self-reproach in which the "critical agent" torments the part of the ego that identifies with the lost love object.

In "Junk Mail" the self-reproach is imaged in "I"'s graphic fantasies of her exploding body and cascading body parts. As it follows from the likeness of the lovers' bodies in "Isle of Skye," and in keeping with Freud's observation that "the ego is first and foremost a bodily ego" (1923, 26), the pain of losing "you" is intensified because in losing the lover, parts of the self are also lost; that is, the erotic connection to the lost like-self involves a partial identification with it, condensed in the image of the return of body parts which belong at once to "I" and to "you." "I"'s anger at being left returns as fantasies of "I"'s mutilated self. In its figuring of the exploded body, Brown's story seems commensurate with Freud's story of self-reproach, but the exploding body trope does not mark the story as portraying a specifically lesbian erotic. In its obsessive memories and fantasied attempts to reach "you," however, "Junk Mail" recasts Freud's version of depression to comment more directly on erotics between women.

"Mourning and Melancholia" knots itself around the problem of what it terms "narcissistic identification," and opens questions of the relation of identification to desire—a relation central to an erotics between women in the *Nightwood* tradition. In discussing *Nightwood,* I distinguished between narcissism as self-absorption ("'Robin can't "put herself in another's place," she herself is the only "position"'" (*NW* 146), and as relational connection in which "sameness" is disrupted by figures of difference in nonidentical resemblance. This distinction between *resemblance* in fictional figuring of erotics between women and *self-enclosure* of a singular subject is related to Freud's distinction between narcissism and narcissistic identification, but too often in everyday, nontechnical usage the dif-

ference between the self-absorption of secondary narcissism and the self-exten-
sion of narcissistic object choice is lost. "Junk Mail," like *Nightwood*, theorizes
"sameness" as a connection of resemblance and difference between lovers rather
than as singular self-enclosure; the story also offers a construction of desire and
identification that departs from Freud's usual insistence that the two work separately or sequentially, rather than together or simultaneously. In order to read
Brown's story, with its like lovers, as a further recasting of narcissistic identification in "Mourning and Melancholia," I turn briefly to psychoanalytic discussions
of "identification" in the context of desire.

The earliest discussion of identification in Freud occurs in *The Interpretation of
Dreams,* in which he discusses hysterical identification: He explains that the
ability for hysterics to "express in their symptoms not only their own experiences
but those of a large number of other people" is a feature not of imitation but of
identification, of putting one's self in another's place because one has an unconscious "inference" that she has the same underlying cause or situation as the one
with the symptom. "It expresses a resemblance and is derived from a common
element which remains in the unconscious" (149). Then, significantly, he goes
on to connect identification with the sexual: "Identification is most frequently
used in hysteria to express a common *sexual* element. A hysterical woman identifies herself in her symptoms most readily—though not exclusively—with people with whom she has had sexual relations or with people who have had sexual
relations with the same people as herself. Linguistic usage takes this into account,
for two lovers, are spoken of as being 'one'" (150).[14]

Freud's later formulations, however, explicitly separate identification from
desire, and these texts are frequently cited in discussion on the topic. In *Group
Psychology and the Analysis of the Ego* (1921), which followed "Mourning and
Melancholia," Freud introduces the chapter titled "identification" by saying
that he was explicitly looking for nonsexual emotional ties to account for the
binding together of groups.[15] In *The Ego and the Id* (1923), his main interest is
in the formation of the ego, especially as it relates to family romance, so that
identification with one parent plays against desire for the other. In these discussions, Freud poses identification and libidinal desire as separate from each
other. "Identification" begins with (the boy's) identification with the father,
later described as "a direct and immediate identification." Because (in the "positive" Oedipus) it does not arise from an earlier libidinal object-cathexis, it is
completely separate from desire, which is the pre-Oedipal form of the relation
to the mother. Instead, it is a form of model after an ideal in which he wants
"to grow like him and be like him, and take his place everywhere" (1921, 105).
Other forms of identification involve its becoming "in a regressive way. . . . a
substitute for a libidinal object tie, . . . by means of introjection of the object
into the ego" (this is the form that identification takes in melancholia), and its
arising "with any new perception of a common quality shared with some other
person who is not an object of the sexual instinct" (1921, 107–108). In thus
divorcing desire from identification, Freud would appear to have repudiated

the foundational connection he posited between them in *The Interpretation of Dreams*. His later formations of identification suggest that it either runs parallel to object cathexis, replaces it, or denies it.[16]

The extended discussion of identification in "Mourning and Melancholia" (1917), with which I began my reading of loss and identification in "Junk Mail," is a transitional one in Freud's writing. It occupies a position between the early connection of sexual longing to identification in the discussion in *The Interpretation of Dreams* of hysterical identification, and the separation of the sexual from identification in the later essays.[17] I do not mean to suggest, by discussing identification's relation to desire in Freud chronologically, that his writing on these topics (or others, for that matter) is neatly developmental. Rather, the linkage of identification and desire in Freud's writing seems contingent on the topic being addressed. The two are no more intrinsically bound than, say, sexual aim and sexual object, but neither are they intrinsically separate. In *Group Psychology and the Analysis of the Ego,* for example, where his topic is in part the military, he recognizes homosociality, but not homoeroticism. His separation of identification and desire in the essay may also be historically contingent on attitudes toward homosexuality. "Mourning and Melancholia" resonates with "Junk Mail" and the story that follows it in *The Terrible Girls,* "Forgiveness," both because loss and depression are its principal topics, and because it knits "identification" to "narcissism" in what I have referred to as the "knot" of narcissistic identification in melancholia.

In "Mourning and Melancholia," Freud's theory of identification is premised on a reading of the depression that follows a lover's departure: He observes that depression exhibits itself not in anger but in self-reproach, which suggests to him the introjection of the lost object by the ego. He notices that the object of the cathexis is easily let go, and no new lover is taken. He concludes that by introjecting the object back into the ego, the object is preserved in an identificatory relation that also alters the ego. For the remainder of the essay, Freud is less interested in the present condition of the ego than in undetermined preconditions of ego identification. Following Otto Rank, he argues that because the subject first has a "strong fixation" on the object, then easily gives it up in narcissistic withdrawal, it must have been a narcissistic object choice in the first place. But he admits in a similar summary in *The Ego and the Id* that "the exact nature of this substitution [of identification for libidinal object choice] is as yet unknown to us," and that admission may account for Freud's opacity on the role of narcissistic identification (29). In order to explain why the libido doesn't find another object and reverts instead to altered self-enclosure, he argues that the object choice must be a narcissistic one. This would seem to suggest that analytic object choice never resulted in depression, but always found another object. It also implicates narcissistic object choice in the regression to self-enclosure, as he says later in the essay: "Melancholia, therefore, borrows some of its features from mourning, and the others from the process of regression from narcissistic object-choice to narcissism" (250).

Therein lies the knot: one withdraws to narcissism and introjects the object narcissistically, and at the same time one withdraws to narcissism because one loves by narcissistic choice. Is the identification narcissistic because it operates out of narcissistic object choice, or is it narcissistic because the libido withdraws into the self? In other words, is it the choice of object that makes the identification narcissistic or the self-enclosing process of withdrawal? In subsequent accounts of identification in melancholia, Freud does not mention the condition of narcissistic object choice. In *Group Psychology,* in the section titled "Identification," he reiterates that the shadow of the object has fallen on the ego as a way of explaining how the ego comes to rage against itself. In *The Ego and the Id* he says only that in melancholia the ego is altered by the setting up of the object choice within the ego. In both of these later essays Freud is concerned how the shift from desire to identification operates in ego formation. In "Mourning and Melancholia" he admits that the role of narcissistic object choice in depression "has unfortunately not yet been confirmed by observation" (250).

VII. "Junk Mail": "I know it's you, my darling . . . delivering back the parts of me to me"

The erotics of "Junk Mail" suggest that "narcissistic object choice," which my reading of Nora's narrative refigures as double subjectivity, intensifies the affects of loss and precipitates not inward withdrawal but outward action. At the same time, "Junk Mail" resists the characterization of narcissistic object choice in Freud's account of depression following loss, and specifies how identification and desire may coexist.

In the story, the loss of the lover entails also a partial loss of the self—when "you" disappears, parts of the narrator go with her. But the identification is not complete. "I" does not "put herself in the place of the other" entirely; she imagines standing on the island and being showered with her body parts. "I" *is* "you," but only in part, a troping that returns the notion of resemblance as both sameness *and* difference. Desire is the given context for the story—desire for a lover now intensified by loss. And, as "Isle of Skye" suggests, difference both determines the desire and causes the separation. "I" desires the return of her lover, as her earlier obsessive fantasized attempts to reach her suggest. In "Junk Mail," then, the lost object is partially equated with a loss of self, but this identification of the self with the other, desired self neither parallels nor substitutes desire for identification, but rather coexists with it. It is identification in the context of desire.

In Freud's terms this relation cannot be read as hysterical identification because, although "I" identifies with her lost lover through the dismembered body as symptom, she expresses, rather than represses, her desire for "you." Nor does the story involve the complete withdrawal of the libido into the ego and the giving up of the object, which characterizes melancholia in Freud. It is also not an easily abandoned object which in "Mourning and Melancholia" leads Freud to posit a narcissistic object choice, the loss of which results in the substitution of narcissistic identification for erotic cathexis. Instead "you" persists in "I"'s endless reimaginings of her. Nor, finally, is their relation a regression to "original" (primary) narcissism in which identification and incorporation precede ("is a preliminary stage of") object choice (1917, 249). "Junk Mail" figures a fully object-oriented desire and a partial identification, rather than a totalizing incorporation. The extremity of its tropes stresses the play of sameness and difference.

"I"'s fantasies are, however, marked by ambivalence not unlike that described in "Mourning and Melancholia," in which ambivalence at the loss of a lover through neglect or disappointment is characterized by "opposed feelings of love and hate" (251). Both "Isle of Skye" and "Junk Mail" figure "I"'s ambivalence toward "you" and their relation. In "Isle of Skye," the oscillation is not between love and hate for a lover, but between "I"'s traveling on her own and staying with her lover. The narrator wants both to leave and to be asked to stay, to travel and to be found, to be independent and to be followed. But in "Junk Mail," the ambivalence is directed toward the lost lover rather than toward their relationship. "I" first wants to get rid of her junk mail by sending it back. But in imagining how she returns her mail, she also attempts to reach the lover who has left; tropologically, each move turns into an excess that turns back on itself so that "I'm going to play your own trick back on you. I'm going to send [junk mail] back to you" becomes successively: I send myself back to you; you begin to send myself back to me; I find myself on an island showered by my returning body parts. Lack of response from "you" is a gap that "I" fills with increasingly abject imaginings. Hers is an ambivalence that results in self-torment by way of imagining self-dismemberment.

The following story, "Forgiveness," continues both the tropes and the ambivalence of "Junk Mail." In reading it, I want to take up another, quite different, use of "identification"—that between reader and character(s) in the story—as well as to suggest how the story both ends the triadic meditation on erotics between women begun in "Isle of Skye" and sets the stage for the rest of the narrative of loss and recovery that began with the first story, "The Dark House." In narrating her subsequent encounters with Lady Bountiful, "I" denies the self-enclosure predicted by "Mourning and Melancholia" and suggests instead the endurance of the erotic ambivalence that connects her to her lost object of desire.

VIII. Identification in Reading

As I've outlined, in psychoanalytic discourses "identification" has several specific, sometimes shifting functions. In addition to the knot of narcissistic identification in "Mourning and Melancholia" and Freud's own changing account of the relation between identification and desire, post-Freudian theorists such as Melanie Klein and lesbian psychotherapists such as Beverly Burch detail versions of projective identification. But the nonspecialized use of the term occurs frequently in conversations among readers of narrative (both visual and verbal) to describe their own captations, as in "I really identified with character X in the novel." In her discussion of filmic narratives, de Lauretis is careful to separate the theoretical constructs of spectator theory from the actual responses of audience members. The closest, though still inexact, equivalent in literary study, reader-response theory, also now most often recognizes this difference.[18] Though the position of the lesbian spectator has been theorized and critiqued, there are still few discussions of the specifically lesbian reader.[19]

Both the frame-tale of *The Terrible Girls,* where "I" and "you" are portrayed as women in thrall, and the intervening trio of stories, where the positions of power between the women are increasingly demarcated and separate, raise the issue of "identifying with." It's an issue not only for readers who might name their identity position "lesbian," but also for others with psychosocial investments in erotics between women. The operative question does not contrast readings of women with men, of straight heterosexuals with queers, or even of heterosexual women with self-identified lesbians. Rather, it asks how readers drawn to erotics between women read and "identify with" the emotional-sexual positions of power and exchange between women sketched by the stories. And it asks whether such readerly identifications, which are also productive performances of textual erotics between women, can be theorized.

Traditional reader-response criticism might answer the questions of readerly identification by suggesting how textual positions make themselves available to be "filled" by "the reader," variously defined as "ideal," "intended," or "implied," to name only three such theorized readers. Indeed, absent empirical studies of readers reading, such an appeal to the text seems reasonable. But delineating such "positions" by noting textual aporias to be filled is itself an act of reading subject to individual reading performances. Readers make texts out of their own psychic investments, with all the attendant individual and social complexities those investments involve, so theorizing across them creates at best a fiction and at worst a projection of false universality that is especially offensive in the often intimate context of an erotics between women. Whether theoretically positing a "reader" or "readers" is a productive fiction, enabling diverse readers to position their own readings in agreement or disagreement, is a question that continues to be debated, not just in the context of reading but in all constructs that risk generalizing, especially generalizing some culturally specified version of "the dominant," at the price of specific "nondominant" others. That is to say—in all theory.

Jean Kennard's early study "Ourself behind Ourself: A Theory for Lesbian Readers" (1986) provides one such theory and is useful as an intervention for self-defined lesbian readers into classic (nonlesbian) texts. Drawing on the work of gestalt therapist Joseph Zinker, she proposes "polar reading," in which the reader "leans into" a character, finds a point of commonality, and lets her identification with that difference coexist as a way toward foregrounding her own "opposite" position. She adopts these "psychological" suggestions to critical method, then discusses both Woolf and Rich as critical readers of texts. But even in the case of Rich, in which a "self-identified" lesbian reads "another woman poet she sees as woman-identified" [Emily Dickinson] (75), Kennard stresses the points at which Rich differentiates her own ideas from Dickinson's as she reads them. For a reader interested in the emotional and sexual exchanges between women in a text, such a polar methodology has limitations. In fiction (and Kennard notes that part of the difference between Woolf's reading of Defoe and Rich's of Dickinson may result from the difference between reading fiction and poetry), readers, whether they read purely for pleasure or in preparation for critical argument, often find themselves reading with, rather than against, the text, filling gaps in the narrative with their own highly individual desires, memories, and fantasies. Only partially realized, these traces may direct identification with one position over another, though that identification is likely to be just as unstable, partial, and contingent as theories of ego formation via identification suggest.[20]

This desire to "read with," to find oneself in the text, is determined in part by the relative paucity of texts that sketch dynamics of affect in the context of women's sexual exchange. In turn, this same readerly desire may produce frustration with texts outside classic realism and account for the historical neglect and mixed reviews of fictions in the *Nightwood* tradition. On the one hand, such fictions address taboo sexual topics; on the other, they are more formally experimental and thus "harder" to read; their characters don't lend themselves easily to nonproblematic, empathetic, conscious "identifying with."

I have asserted that one "finds oneself" reading in a direction outlined by the text, but it's worth asking what "self" one "finds," especially when one might want to resist rather than engage with loss, obsession, power differences, and other potentially painful affects of the *Nightwood* tradition. Such a question resonates with cultural and historical particularity; the critical moment of Kennard's essay (1986) provides the context in which it functions as a commentary on lesbian reading. She reads against Judith Fetterley's well-known "resisting reader" as a position for women and cites the phenomenological position of Iser, and the ego psychology of Holland. The "self," in these texts, written at the height of interest in "reader-response criticism" from the mid-seventies to the early eighties, is usually transcendent, unified, and coherent. Holland, for example, speaks of an "unchanging inner core of continuity" with an "identity theme" that works itself out in readings which find textual unity by way of the reader's own identity themes (1976, 338).

In recent years, the coherent "self" of reader-response criticisms has been superseded by the contingent "subject" of poststructuralist discourse. It has been superseded, that is, within the academy where multiple and often contradictory identifications have displaced a singular identity, and where politico-theoretical critique of the unified and transparent self is commonplace. Yet outside the academy, and perhaps sometimes inside it, too, readers continue to speak as if they mean something when they "identify" with an idea, a position, a fictional character. A theory of reading still requires accounting for textual directions and readerly input no matter what the content and tradition of the work. I think of the language of the text as a performance script, a set not of instructions but of possibilities, that is filled in by individual performers who draw consciously and unconsciously on their own socially inflected histories and fantasies, both personal and cultural. Different performers read and enact fictions differently, but under the constraints provided by the text—its language, its narrative structure, its generic conventions—all of which influence the performances, but do not determine them.[21] Since subjectivity itself is multiple, that is, since it involves varying contingent and often contradictory identifications and positionings, the "self" one "finds" in "identifying with" may well be partial, split, surprising, disturbing.

IX. "Forgiveness": Performing Identifications

In "Forgiveness," the story that follows "Junk Mail" in *The Terrible Girls,* for example, there are (at least) two identificatory positions—"I" and "you"; many readers interested in an erotics between women will not see themselves and their self-identified investments located in either of these positions, especially given the imbalance of power with which the story begins and the violence of the cliché that it literalizes. For those drawn to identify, however, "I" 's position would seem the most open to an empathetic reading, simply by virtue of its being in a first-person voice. That is, the entire narration is "I" 's meditation on her relation with "you," so that, like Robin's in *Nightwood,* "you" 's is not a position of represented interiority. To read with the "I" of the text may be to "put yourself in the place of"—to use one of Freud's definitions of identification, and the one that is implied by nonspecialized discourse—the position most fully and directly represented. "Forgiveness" reads like a parable in which the "old saying" "I'd give my right arm for you" is made literal in a gesture of pleasing the lover. Because the narrative is retrospective, the extremity of "I" 's gesture in hacking off her arm carries with it the hindsight of self-knowledge. To identify with "I" is to recognize with her that too much gift of self in love maintains a dramatic imbalance of power that may produce the pleasure of masochism (and) or the helplessness of self-destruction. To identify with "you," who has no voice except in her representation by "I," produces a quite different reading of their erotics, one in which "I" 's self-mutilation is itself an expression of power and her closed narration a mark of narcissistic self-promotion. Both of these positions (and undoubtedly others as well) are open to and produced by readers with differing psychic investments in the relation of power dynamics to an erotics between women.

"I" gives up her right arm because she doesn't want to "be made a liar of," and believes "you" needs it or she wouldn't have asked. She learns to do things with one arm, but can sleep with "you" only when her stump doesn't bleed, and doesn't speak about her injury because she doesn't want "you" to feel bad. "You" leaves anyway, and "I" begins the search for her lost arm, which "you" has had bronzed for the mantlepiece, but has taken with her. Unlike the "I" of "Junk Mail," who never acknowledges that her fantasy of the metamorphosing mail is a search for the lost lover, "I" wonders if her search through pawn shops for her lost arm isn't also a search for "you." Mid-narrative, "you" returns without the arm, and "I" recognizes that she's taught herself "about the strength of having only one" (51) but doesn't tell her lover. Instead, she asks "you" why she did it. "You" apologizes, says she's changed, and asks forgiveness, but "I" is unable to tell her that "you can't re-do a thing that's been undone" (53). The last long sentence of the story captures something of its tone:

> And then I thought, but this was only half a thought, that even if you had changed, no *really* changed, truly and at last, and even if you knew me better than I know myself, and even if I'm better off than I've ever been, and even if this was the only way we could have gotten to this special place where we are now, and even if there's a reason, darling, something bigger than both of us, and even if all these even if's are true, that I would never believe you again, never forget what I know of you, never forget what you've done to me, what you will do, I'll never believe the myth of forgiveness between us. (53)

By the end of the story, "I" has not regained her arm, but she has recovered some agency in her recognition that even though they might go on together in the "special place" wrought by the closeness of their seeming reconciliation, she will never again believe in "you" in quite the same way. For the reader invested in the rhetoric of recovery, "I"'s closing meditation, together with the retrospective narration and the self-ironizing enacted in making literal a cliché, ends the story—and the triad—on an "up" note. "I" no longer seems to be someone who would give her right arm or misplace her trust in a lover who abuses her (permitted) control. I say "permitted" because part of the dynamic begun in "The Dark House" and underlying both "Junk Mail" and "Forgiveness" is "I"'s attraction to a lover who exercises control over her.

In narrating retrospectively a fiction of their dynamics, "I"'s story is divided between the narrating "I" who no longer believes in the myth of forgiveness and the narrated "I" who is subject to "you"'s demands for sacrifice as a mark of love. The last scene of "Forgiveness" makes use of this split "I." The narrator describes a scene in which "you" cries, whispers like a little girl, looks with her "big, sweet, pretty brown eyes," and asks to be held, all the while never responding to "I"'s need to know why she demanded her arm, then left and returned without it. The narrated "I" complies, holds her, rocks her, and watches her while she sleeps. In so doing, she appears to accede to "you"'s performance as naughty child. In the final passage quoted above, however, the interior narrating voice declares that the dynamic between them has shifted. In whatever other ways "I" continues to enact their previous positions of power difference, she declares to herself and the reader her greater independence.

Or at least she makes such a declaration to the reader who empathizes with her position. What of the reader who performs against the grain of the text and puts herself in "you"'s position? Such a one has many more gaps to fill, since "you" is present only as a fiction of the narrating "I." But the second reader might point out just such a fiction and argue that what "I" sees as "you"'s demand that she give her right arm for her is instead "I"'s narcissistic self-enclosure, her need for self-sacrifice as a means of control. In such a reading, a power dynamic is still operative, but now it is "I" who controls through excessive giving of herself as a means to capture "you" by guilt. This reading takes its cues from the few representations of "you" that the narrator offers; at one point the lovers debate the source of "I"'s mutilation:

> But I guess after a while it started bothering you, because one day when I was washing out the sheets I'd bloodied the night before, you said, You sleep too restless. I don't like it when your bleeding wakes me up. I think you're sick. I think it's sick to cut off your own arm.
>   I looked at you, your sweet brown eyes, innocent as a puppy. But you cut it off, I said. You did it. You didn't blink. You asked me for it, so I said OK.
>   Don't try to make me feel guilty, you said, your pretty brown eyes looking at me. It was your arm. (48–49)

The passage, with its two versions of how "I" lost her arm, stands in for two of the versions of the power dynamics that differently invested readers might produce in their identificatory readings. "You" never hears "I"'s final meditation declaring that she can never be so vulnerable again. This private insight remains unshared with "you," who seems to retain such outward signs of her power as her demand to be held, to be comforted. Though "I"'s version would seem to capture more readers through conventions of narratorial authority, "you"'s position is sketched sufficiently enough that it offers an alternative reading script. For the reader who identifies with "you," the story may well be a frustrating, even irritating, one.

"Forgiveness" opens positions named not only "I" and "you" but also "we," and in so doing suggests another version of double subjectivity that complicates the one present in *Nightwood*. I have suggested that in such declarations as "'she is myself,'" Nora's narrative implies not a self-enclosing narcissism but a relation of resemblance in which figures of difference disrupt the rhetoric of identity. In "Junk Mail" "I"'s identification with "you" functions literally in part(s), rather than in toto; "you" is a desired object whose loss is all the more intense because "I" imagines her as part of herself, an investment of "you" with subjectivity. This partial identification continues explicitly in "Forgiveness," since "I"'s search for her lost arm is also a search for "you." Even previous to the search, however, their double subjectivity is marked by a playful and ironic "we":

> The night you took it, I dreamt of arms. I slept on the couch in the den because I was still bleeding, even through the bandages, and I knew I'd stir during the night and need to put on more bandages and *we* didn't want me to wake you up."

And later,

> "I learned to do things differently. To button my shirts, to screw and unscrew the toothpaste cap, to tie my shoes. *We* didn't think of this." (47–48, emphases mine)

The retrospective hindsight that produces "I"'s self-critical irony at once acknowledges the structure and problem of their doubled subject. "One cannot stir without the other," so to speak, and in retrospect, "I" realizes the destructiveness of a "we" in which one subject nearly subsumes the other. "Nearly" is crucial; in keeping with the partial identification implied by the lost arm/lost lover, "I"'s subjugation to "you"'s desires is also not complete. She survives her willing complicity in a "we" where she has little power, and becomes instead the agentic narrator of the stories that follow.

In addition to the deconstructing of "we," evidenced also in the sentences above by the repeating first-person pronoun which precedes the eventual singular "we," double subjectivity appears in "I"'s narration in the form of her fantasies. This structure is not unique to narratives of lesbian erotics, but it heightens those more specific instances of subject doubling. Both "Junk Mail" and "Forgiveness," like *Nightwood* earlier and *Written on the Body* later, feature, as I have said, first-person narrators presenting their erotic dynamics in retrospect so that the lover is a fiction of memory or of fantasy under the conditions of loss. As such, the lover is both object of the narrator's erotic longing and subject of her own narrative actions as the narrator imagines them. Thus these novels present narrators creating for their lovers little fictions in which the object stars as subject and the narrating lover becomes the object.[22] In "Junk Mail" "I" imagines "you" winding her up until she blows apart. In "Forgiveness," "I" decides that the loss of her arm is a "test" that "you" has set for her: "And then I thought how, if you were testing me, you must be watching me, to see if I was passing. So I started acting out my life for you" (50). She goes on to make her lover the subject of a gaze for which she is the object. In so doing, "I" is subject as the constructor of the fantasy, and "you" is subject of the fantasy she constructs. In the context of "I"'s identificatory vision of "you" as part of herself, and her recognition of her dangerous participation in "we," her fantasy of "you" as subject intensifies the double subjectivity of lesbian erotics. *The Terrible Girls* maintains the double subjectivity of an erotics between women, but critiques it by writing it as dangerous to the narrator's ultimate survival. The novel continues the Barnes paradigm but strenuously resists its structuring of subjectivity.

The fantasy (*of* which her lover is object, and *in* which, the subject) is a "butch bottom's" fantasy of living up to expectations culturally determined by the dual positions, "butch" and "bottom." Her performance is coded butch by its gestural codes of masculinity acted by a female body: "I whistled with bravado, jaunted, rather than walked. I had a confident swagger. I slapped friendly pawnshop keepers on their shoulders and told them jokes" (50). Her performance as butch requires only her own sense of herself; that is, she enacts a singular identity position.[23] But hers is also a bottom's enactment, by which term I mean to extend the usual designation of a literal sexual position to an emotional one, in which, in this fantasy scenario, the lover-as-top calls the shots by being the fantasied tester/watcher. When "you" returns, they act out their butch-femme positions: "You leaned into me and pulled my arm around you and ran your pretty fingers down the solid muscle in my sleeve. Just hold me, darling, you said. Just hold me again." Like *Nightwood*'s palimpsest, gender layers with nurturing, and a moment later "I" becomes the caretaker: "You made me rock you and I did and then you cried yourself to sleep as innocent as a baby. When you were asleep I walked you to the bedroom and put you to bed. You slept. I watched you all night" (52).

All of which is not to say that femmes cannot be muscled or that butches usually do the nurturing. Or that any fiction necessarily demands reading in butch-femme terms. Cross-identifications, here written as shifts away from the expectations created by butch-femme scripts influential between the time of *Nightwood* and *The Terrible Girls,* are a mark of recent fictional women's erotics. Nora's position as nurturer is a stable one in *Nightwood,* although her gendered position isn't emphasized. But the logic of butch-femme roles constructed by such essentialized masculine/feminine positions as those of Stephen and Mary in *The Well of Loneliness* remains a powerful model well into the 1960s, as Lillian Faderman points out (1991, 173). Fictional representations such as Hall's, together with rules of bar cultures in specific communities captured differently in, for example, *Zami, Boots of Leather, Slippers of Gold,* and *Stone Butch Blues,* present contemporary fiction with a backdrop against which butch-femme positions can be played out.

In "Forgiveness," posing "I" as a butch one minute and a nurturer the next complicates any easy substitution of "butch" for "masculine." At the same time, it counters a stereotype often seen in lesbian fiction of the butch who needs to be nurtured, versions of *Nightwood*'s Robin as both boy and child. "Top" and "bottom" enter a discourse of erotics between women initially through representations of s/m sexualities, but the dynamics encoded in them play out not only in the "everyday life" of heterosexuals, as Lynn Chancer (1992) argues, but in that of same-sex couples as well.[24] Casting "Forgiveness" in these configurations emphasizes the sexual dimension implicit in a story where the narrator says nothing about what happens in bed. Unlike "butch," "top" and "bottom" function in relation to each other because they bear the trace of their origins in a discourse of sexual exchange. They suggest another kind of emotional power dynamic, one marked not by play on culturally (re)scripted roles, but by ungendered, non-"parental" positions of control. As "I" tells her story, she notes her muscled body and masculine bravado even as she records her recognition that "you"'s control over her is finally unacceptable. In her narrated fiction of past acts and her fantasy of being watched, "I" sounds like a butch bottom; in her role as retrospective narrator, she maintains her butchness, but issues of top/bottom drop out because hers is finally a discourse of identity rather than of acts. She narrates with hindsight from a singular subject position.

The loosely connected narrative of "I" and "you," in which events matter much less than lyric meditations on difference, loss, and obsession, ends with "I"'s knowledge that forgiveness is only a myth. Read as a triad that interrupts the plot events of *The Terrible Girls,* "Isle of Skye," "Junk Mail," and "Forgiveness" set out an erotics between women that moves from seduction through excess to the beginnings of recovery. For those readers identifying in whole or, more likely, in part with "I," the recognition that she narrates from a position of greater insight at the conclusion of the triad carries over to the resumption of the frame narrative that began in "The Dark House." The next story, "Lady Bountiful and the Underground Resistance," begins "I"'s ultimately successful struggle to regain the heart that she has given the lover who then betrays her to stay in the dark house with someone else. Lady Bountiful stands in both for that original lover and for "you" of the triad. Like the lost arm, "I"'s heart is literally missing and turns up in the final story, "The Ruined City," to be restored to her through the loving help of "she."

The final scene closes the novel-in-stories with the happy ending that often operates in contemporary lesbian fiction as a "felt cultural norm."[25] To the extent that *The Terrible Girls* scripts a tale in which "I" ends up with "she" who completes her, it participates in a tradition associated not, of course, with Barnes, but with lesbian romance. This script can be read for the pleasures of closure, if not exactly for the mimesis of classic realism.[26] Bonnie Zimmerman says in her book on lesbian fiction of the seventies and eighties: "Lesbian writers often want to give their readers the happy endings denied us in real life, and so write upbeat romances and domestic comedies (comic in the sense that they lead to happy, harmonious endings)" (106). Certainly some readers do ask for happy endings. Joke Hermes, in an article about sexuality in lesbian romances, criticizes the ending of well-known Naiad writer Katherine V. Forrest's *Emergence of Green* because it isn't happy enough. The women end up as a couple, but agree "to stay together for the time being." Hermes complains, "What kind of romance is that?" and proposes a more definitive happy ending of her own (1992, 61–62). *The Terrible Girls* meets the romance reader's demand for a happy ending because "you" has been left behind and "she" and "I" are together.

The details of the last scene—its lyricism, its mysticism, and its celebration of wholeness—speak also to the reader invested in the "recovery" of "I," because the frame-tale sets up a sui generis *Bildungsroman* as well as a romance. In the frame, "I"'s retrospective stories take her from being "the coffee-cart girl" living on the hope of an ever-deferred love in "The Dark House" through the loss of her heart to Lady Bountiful, to regaining her heart and ending with a new, more giving, lover in "The Ruined City":

> I heard the moving of her hands, the mystery of her patient preparations.
> She said, Believe this telling of the tongue:
>
> > *There is a sundering of blood*
> > *There is the carrying of loss.*
> > *There is the burial in earth.*
> > *There is the waiting in the dark.*
> >
> > *There is the laying on of hands.*
> > *There is the opening of flesh.*

> *There is the light within the body.*
> *There is the resurrected heart.*

And though my eyes were closed and though it was the starless night, I sensed a
light over me, right where she was, but in that light was a loss of light, a shadow,
over me. . . . There was something against my body, there was an opening, a
blaze, there was the heart. (136)

"She" functions as the means to "I"'s wholeness. The making of a unified subjectivity rather than the consummation of a long-sought love completes the
frame-tale. "She"'s ritual of restoration, the mystical opening of one lover by the
other, honors the body and allows "I" to become the knowing narrator of her
recovery from a controlling obsession.

How then can reviewers compare *The Terrible Girls* to Djuna Barnes's fiction?
First, I would argue that the last story, especially in its ending, recalls by reversal
Nightwood's last chapter. In Barnes's "The Possessed," Robin arrives with Jenny
in New York, only to flee both lover and city, and find herself in Nora's ruined
country chapel, where lights burn on a makeshift altar. Nora discovers her there,
but their reunion is never fully complete. Brown's "The Ruined City" begins
with a *fait accompli:* "I" already has her new lover; they reverse the direction of
Robin's singular wanderings in the woods by going together from the country,
where "I" rediscovers, then leaves, "you," to a ruined shack in the ravaged city.
There "she" restores "I"'s lost heart. The mystical language of restoration—"the
light within the body," the "resurrected heart"—echoes *Nightwood*'s emphasis on
the mystic light running the length of the chapel door, and the candles burning
before a Madonna. Their flickerings, however, illuminate Nora's way to Robin
for nought. Unlike the lovers in *Nightwood,* "I" and "she" arrive together at the
ruins; "she"'s healing incantation replaces Robin's "obscene and touching laughter" as the last sounds of the novel.

But the rewriting of *Nightwood*'s conclusion alone does not determine the
place of *The Terrible Girls* in a Barnes genealogy. Finally, and perhaps more
perversely, I would point to (and here I mean to speak for readers who prefer
their endings a little less neat) the triadic narrative of affect, which not only
interrupts the fairy-tale, lesbian-feminist frame, but shadows its completion as
well. In the affective narrative, *The Terrible Girls* takes as its text, produces as its
text, the dynamics of loss and obsessive love that give one lover power over the
other. The interpolated stories, "Isle of Skye," "Junk Mail," and "Forgiveness,"
meditate on difference grounded in like bodies and criticize a connection between lovers that demands giving away too much of one's self. That criticism
separates *The Terrible Girls* from *Nightwood,* but the violence of Brown's metaphors remains as least as vivid as the eventual wholeness imaged in the language.
"I" regains her heart at the story's close, but her sleeve still hangs empty. She's
found a new lover, but the ambivalence of "I" in "The Isle of Skye" lingers in the
performance of the text. After all, it's not just the heart that makes "I" seem

complete: "What keeps us moving is the want to be unforeign, whole," and there's no telling when she might be moving on again (32).

In writing loss, *The Terrible Girls* scripts the often unscripted nuances of power that complicate emotional exchanges between women lovers; in so writing, like *Nightwood* before it and *Written on the Body* after, it teases to invite. The novel's nonlinear story and interplay between frame-tale and affective narrative ensure enactments by readers, but do not guarantee either the shape of those enactments or the positions of the readers. Only the play of memory and the investments of desire can do that: readers, like writers, are lovers too.

NOTES

INTRODUCTION

1. For an account of seduction as "preserved—transformed/translated in transference," see Cummings 1991, esp. 58–95. She reads transference as psychoanalysis itself: "a distinctly unsettling exchange in which founder and disciple, analyst and analysand . . . seduce and are seduced by the other person, site, and/or unconscious scene" (59). In her discussion of pedagogy, Felman (1982a) draws on Lacan's insistence that transference is love directed toward knowledge, a formulation that is literally specified in Harris's relation to Barnes. Although my contexts and formulations are quite different, I have been influenced by Felman's accounts of literary, philosophical, and pedagogical seduction (1982a, 1983) and by what I would term her erotics of reading Woolf, Rich, and de Beauvoir (1993, esp. 1–19, 121–51). See also the discussion of transference in psychoanalysis and literature in Brooks 1987.

Reading with and against transference as authorial influence, represented especially by the work of Harold Bloom, was an influential methodology in feminist literary criticism of the seventies. See, for example, Gilbert and Gubar 1979 and Kolodny 1985 (1980). For a contemporary lesbian novel that might be read as playing with transference-as-seduction in its critique of psychoanalysis, see Schulman 1992.

2. The debates about what any given speaker might mean by using "lesbian" as an identifier or how "lesbian" might function in any given text are too numerous to summarize. The current debates around whether a rubric such as "queer" may decrease the visibility of self-identified lesbians and elide specific oppressions of institutionalized sexism, racism, and classism provide one starting place. See, for example, de Lauretis 1991c; Solomon 1992; Castle 1993, 1–20; Martin 1992, 117; Davy 1993, 78. What is required is clarity about how "lesbian" circulates in the particular text at hand, a clarity I try to provide in the following discussion of my usage in the context of Barnes and Harris.

3. Barney's circle included, among others, expatriate American and British women writers and artists Radclyffe Hall, Una Troubridge, Romaine Brooks, Dolly Wilde, Janet Flanner, and Solita Solano.

4. I do not mean to imply, however, that Harris's own relation to lesbian-feminism was an uncomplicated one. In the late 1970s, she gave presentations at the Modern Language Association annual meetings in which she argued that "lesbian sensibility" was present not just in writing by some self-identified lesbians, but in some distinctly self-identified heterosexual male writers (e.g., Nabokov, Dostoevsky) as well. What's more, she suggested that some texts often thought of as integral to the lesbian canon (e.g., Jane Rule's *Desert of the Heart*) were about lesbianism but lacked lesbian sensibility because they eschewed "Romantic temperament: a love affair with freaks and monsters; a loathing of both mother and father (unless changed into gothic forms); sexual fascination with the 'underdog' (which has nothing to do with class consciousness)" (Harris 1979, 25). Her tongue-in-cheek, deliberately provocative pronouncements succeeded in angering some of her audience. See, for example, Klepfisz 1979. In one such MLA presentation, Harris referred to herself as "the Death's Head at the Feast of Love. The Tipper-over of the Apple Cart. The Fly in the Syrup" (1979, 25). For a brief chronology of lesbian studies and the formulation of lesbian feminism as it began in the late sixties and extended beyond as a theoretical idea as well as a lived practice, see Stimpson 1990, 378 (in Jay and Glasgow); for a contemporary recollection of earlier lesbian-feminism from a Canadian perspective, see Kiss & Tell 1994.

5. The famous quote about "just loving Thelma" is undated by Barnes's biographer; he suggests that their relationship lasted from 1922 to 1931 (Field 1983, 37). The second quote comes in a 1936 letter to Ottoline Morrell (Broe 1991, 53). The pain of loss on Thelma's part is still palpable more than thirty years after they parted. She writes in a 1969 letter to Barnes: "darling, should have sent the photographs earlier, but anything to do with us bothers me, the pain is so unequal that i just naturally avoid it when possible . . . i love you as always" (ibid.).

6. For sexology and lesbian construction in 1928, see, among others, Faderman 1986; Chauncey 1982–83; Newton 1984; Vincinus 1993.

7. I agree with Susan Lanser that it is difficult not to read *Ladies Almanack*, especially in its hilarious portrayal of Dame Musset, as a response to *The Well of Loneliness* and to Stephen Gordon as invert. For an interesting reading of *Ladies Almanack* as a document of queer recruitment, see Kent 1993.

8. "Universalizing" is, however, a highly charged term. Wittig writes about a universalizing point of view as a challenge to sex/gender categories and as an entrée into praising Barnes and Proust as lesbian/gay writers who universalize queer perspectives. She does not suggest that these perspectives are somehow then to speak for all versions of minority sexual difference, or to cover over other varieties of difference, such as racial or class inscriptions, that might also mark minority texts. Hers is not an argument for a transcending of difference, but a praising of sexual minority writers who "change the textual reality" within which their writing exists by making one version of nondominant sexuality the operative textual norm.

9. See, for another example of making erotics between women "the norm," Jane Marcus's reading of *A Room of One's Own* in the context of *The Well of Loneliness*. Marcus argues convincingly that Woolf's ellipses as well as her rhetorical strategies more generally encode female desire and assert as the norm that " 'women like women.' " Though the essay does not discuss Barnes, it uses a quote from *Ladies Almanack* as one of its opening epigrams (Marcus 1987, 169).

10. This is not to say that Barnes's presentation of "a girl's girl" is always celebratory. Indeed, it is troubled especially by questions of reproductive (im)possibilities for women together and satirizes scenes of what the sympathetic 1990s reader recognizes as "dyke drama," complete with romantic clichés and broken hearts. For a less sympathetic reading of *Ladies Almanack* arguing that Barnes attacks the character and morals of Natalie Barney and her coterie because her less comfortable economic circumstances made her an "outsider," see Jay 1990. Harris, too, is keenly aware of her class difference from many of the women of Barney's circle. She describes herself as "peasantmade" and "sweaty with lower-class need" in recognizing that many of her "ancestors" of Paris were "rich or nearly rich" (Harris 1973, 78).

11. Though rhetorically I group these texts as "1990s novels," and though such a grouping is accurate in terms of their publication dates, I should note that Harris's novel *Lover* was first published in 1976; it was reissued in 1993 with a lengthy new introduction and commentary by Harris that makes it in many ways a "new" text. Winterson's *Written on the Body* was published in 1992, *The Passion* in 1987. Brown's *The Terrible Girls* appeared in 1990, though several of the "stories" that form it as a "novel-in-stories" appeared separately during the 1980s.

12. Harris's earlier novels are *Catching Saradove* (1969) and *Confessions of Cherubino* (1972). The latter might also be cast in the Barnes tradition, but in the tradition of *Nightwood* rather than of *Ladies Almanack*. Like *Nightwood*, it is a story of painful love between women. The anti-erotic dynamics of its retrospective narrative may be a consequence of its telling: the reluctant object of desire, rather than the subject who continues to desire even after her separation from her desired object, narrates most of the novel.

13. I read Marcus 1987 as observing a similar textual topping when she comments that Woolf's sexual jokes in *A Room of One's Own* might be meant "to show Radclyffe Hall a trick or two" (169).

14. For Freud's specifications of the psychoanalytic relations among resistance, repetition, and transference, see Freud 1914a ("Remembering, Repeating and Working-Through [Further Recommendations in the Technique of Psycho-Analysis II]") and 1915b ("Observations on Transference-Love [Further Recommendations on the Technique of Psycho-Analysis III]").

15. The world of the sexual subversives largely ignores the homosex/heterosex binary that constructs it (and vice versa), but the threat of intrusion is present throughout the novel in the shape of a sinister male stranger across the lake from the lovers. There are also references to male violence against women throughout; in her "Introduction," Harris, without recanting, situates this thread of the novel in its historical context and cites Solanas's S.C.U.M. Manifesto as a more daring version of *Lover*'s "stab at man-hating." 1990s readers who associate lesbian-feminism not only with "man-hating" but with an avoidance of such acts as cross-dressing, quick sex for pleasure, and butch/femme roles will find *Lover* a correction to current monolithic constructions of lesbian-feminism of the 1970s. For a cogent corrective to the tendency among some 1990s commentators to construct "lesbian-feminism" as a monolith, see Martin 1992, 117.

16. Louise Fishman is an "out" abstract expressionist painter whose most recent solo exhibit was at the Robert Miller Gallery in New York in 1993. In a recent interview she describes her coming out in the 1950s (discovering painting allowed her to recover from the disappointing discovery that after high school there was nowhere for her to play varsity sports), and her sense that "Abstract Expressionist work was an appropriate language for me as a queer. It was a hidden language, on the radical fringe, a language appropriate to being separate" (1994, 59–60). For a review of Fishman's recent work, see Seidel 1993. In a 1994 *Artforum* series in which writers were invited to "discuss a contemporary work that has special significance for them," Harris writes about Fishman: "Louise and I met in 1973 and became lovers. I wrote a novel, *Lover*, about the redemptive power of her painting on my writing. She had saved my work from the clutches of 'beauty.' I thanked her by rewarding her with my thirty-year-old saint in the clutches of her hair shirt. Then the sex stopped and we got serious" (1994, 75).

17. These erotics, in which Harris explicitly addresses Fishman, also replicate Barnes; Lanser (1992) notes that *Ladies Almanack* was originally written in part to amuse Barnes's lover, Thelma Wood. Lanser also writes about *Almanack*'s "evasive and devious" narrative voice: "Each reader, then, will have to construct it (as, of course, we construct all texts) after his or her desire" (xvi, xxxiv). Jane Marcus (1987), too, discusses the seduction of the woman reader by the woman writer. She uses *sapphistry* to name the rhetorical operations at work in such seductions. Though our critical emphases differ, her discussion of collaboration between woman writer and reader informs mine.

18. My thanks to Natasha Meden for assistance in translation.

19. Brossard also notes that Causse was a translator of *Ladies Almanack* (1981, 203).

20. In addition to *A Lover's Discourse,* Brossard's work obviously recalls such texts as *The Pleasure of the Text* and Barthes's passing comments on reading in *Sade/Fourier/Loyola,* and various essays of the early and mid-1970s collected in *The Rustle of Language.* Alice Parker also notes the Brossard/Barthes conjunction (1990, 318).

21. The "discreet but discernible gay specificity of Barthes's texts," including *A Lover's Discourse* with its alternating masculine and feminine pronouns, is elegantly laid out in Miller 1992, esp. 16. Miller's account lovingly performs its own erotics of reading. See Meese 1992 for a work of critical commentary that is at the same time an explicitly lesbian erotics of reading. Meese also comments on Barnes's textual connections to Brossard and Causse (43).

22. In addition to Brossard, Barthes, and Marcus, whose readings of textual desire, desire in reading, and narrative seduction are particularly resonant with mine because cast explicitly (Marcus and Brossard) or partially (Barthes) in a same-sex context, see also, among others, Kristeva 1980, 119; Brooks 1984 and 1987; Chambers 1984; de Lauretis 1984.

De Lauretis's classic essay "Desire in Narrative" (1984) crucially critiques seduction's role in the construction of gendered subjectivity in narratives from Oedipus to Hitchcock. The essay includes a reading of Oedipal constructions of desire in Barthes and Robert Scholes. Brooks's masculinist use of Freud in accounting for plotting in part as a desire moving toward a (delayed) end is open to a similar critique (1984, 111). His sense that "in the notion of forepleasure there lurks . . . the possibility of the polymorphous perverse . . . the possibility of a text that would delay, displace and deviate terminal discharge," and that the erotics of such a textual form might be called "'clock-teasing'" participates in a dominant discourse of male sexuality. (It should be noted, however, that female ejaculation and "cock-teasing" also circulate in some 1990s subcultural discourses of lesbian sexuality [see, for example, among others, fictions in *On Our Backs* or some videos by Femme Fatale], and that "forepleasure" and delayed gratification are not necessarily gender-specific, though public discourse often treats them as if they were.) The complicated nonlinear narrative of *Lover* exceeds even Brooks's reference to the polymorphous perverse and makes "forepleasure" practically beside the point.

Chambers (1984) argues for an exchange between narrator and narratee/reader in which the narrator gives up information in exchange for the reader's attention, while the narratee diverts attention from other possible objects of interest in exchange for information. He refers to this exchange as "the 'art' of seduction" when the "'art story'" (e.g., Balzac's "Sarrasine," Nerval's "Sylvie") produces readerly attention at the same time that narrative authority based on providing information is being dissipated in the very act of exercising that authority (51). *Lover*'s seduction of the reader depends especially on its nonnarrative form, multiple tellers, and contingent characters; Harris's introduction also makes specific and personal the novel's goal of seducing Fishman, so that as a reading text *Lover* has a personal cast absent from Chambers's more abstract formulations.

23. For a selected list of critical readings of *Well,* see Faderman 1994a, 251. In addition, see Newton, who, in a reading contextualized by the development of the "New Woman" born, as Hall and Barnes were, in the late nineteenth century, and by the sexological discourses of the same period, argues that Stephen Gordon's male body drag was a route to claiming her full sexuality in a period that foreclosed most other such routes. Martha Vicinus points out, however, that the styles of Barney, Colette, and others of their circles did provide such alternatives (445). Other particularly important readings of *The Well* include Marcus (1987), who provides a historical context for Hall's obscenity trial as well as arguing for *The Well*'s influence on *A Room of One's Own;* Stimpson (1982), who analyzes its structural logic and cites it as a founding text for the lesbian tradition of "damnation"; and de Lauretis (1994), who includes an extensive reading of Stephen before the mirror as a "perverse" enactment of Lacan's mirror stage. In her argument about lesbian sexuality, she reads Stephen's masculinity as a fetish signifying desire "for the (lost) female body" (209–13, 239–43, esp. 240). That *Well* continues to be a critical touchstone for critics is evident in Findlay 1994, where she asserts that additional research might suggest the extent to which *Well* posed more of a threat to "the straight literary establishment than it did to romantic friends, passionate spinsters, and other antecedents to modern lesbians" (3); and in Barale 1991, a reading of the shifting cover art on mainstream editions of *Well*. She argues that each of these covers finds a way to inscribe heterosexuality on the lesbian textual body.

24. For how *Well* has influenced lesbian negative self-perception, see, among others, Kitzinger 1987, 120–21; Faderman 1981, 322–23; Cook 1979; O'Rourke 1989, 90–142. But not every reader found the constructions negative; Faderman observes: "Radclyffe Hall was, in fact, so influential among some young American lesbians that she was referred to as 'Our Matron Saint' in a postwar article that suggested that the 'inelegant word *butch*' be replaced by the word 'Clyffe' in honor of Radclyffe Hall" (1991, 173). Kennedy and Davis testify to the identification with Stephen Gordon of butches participating in bar life (1993, 328).

25. I mean to refer here to *Nightwood*'s obscurity from the general reading public. It has always had its share of critical admirers and has been singled out by writers for special praise, as I note in the first chapter. The publication of *Silence and Power* (Broe 1991), an anthology reevaluating Barnes's work; the Barnes centennial conference held at the University of Maryland in 1992, and the resulting special issue of *Review of Contemporary Fiction* (Fall 1993), which was listed as a *VLS* "Lit Hit"; and the various projects redefining modernism undertaken by such critics as Gilbert, Gubar, Benstock, Stimpson, and Marcus have provided new contexts in which to situate Barnes's work. Increasingly, I believe work in queer theory and in gay and lesbian studies will augment the literary scholarship on Barnes (see, for example, de Lauretis 1988, Jay 1990; Meese 1992).

26. Harris's reference to "Jaws" (she is referring especially to the film of that title) places Robin in what Harris delineates in her essay as the tradition of the lesbian as monster, by which she has in mind not only an outsider to various cultures of domination, but also "a creature of tooth and claw, of passion and purpose: unassimilable, awesome, dangerous, different: distinguished" (8).

27. Indeed, recent theorists of lesbian sexuality have carefully acknowledged their own investments in reading and constructing arguments. In *The Practice of Love*, de Lauretis points throughout her text (but as she says, "discreetly") to the ways in which her theoretical speculations and textual readings "follow the yellow brick road of my own fantasies, the less-than-royal road of my personal and experiential history" (xiv). Roof writes: "Even if I don't know precisely what a lesbian is, I look for the lesbian in the text, for what happens rhetorically to eroticized relations among women, finding, perhaps narcissistically, their catalytic function in feminist theories of writing and reading. I begin with this perspective probably because reading, even academic reading, is stimulated, at least for me, by a libidinous urge connected both to a sexual practice and to the shape of my own desire" (1991, 120).

28. Zimmerman goes on to discuss both Wittig and Harris as exceptions to this tendency.

29. For ways in which other lesbian *topoi* mark different "traditions," see, for example, SDiane Bogus's study of the "'Queen B'/Queen Bulldagger" figure in African-American culture. For a personal account of living a life that extends and exceeds the tradition outlined in Bogus, see Omosupe 1991. For a discussion of *topoi* in recent Black British lesbian writing, see Pilgrim. For recent collections of short writing from various ethnicities from which other lesbian *topoi* might be read, see, among others, McKinley and DeLaney 1995; Chin et al. 1993; Ratti 1993; Lim-Hing 1994; Trujillo 1991; Silvera 1991.

30. For a useful discussion of lesbian literary traditions that stresses the multiplicity of such "traditions" just as I emphasize that the erotics I construct are only one of many such constructions given the differences—personal, but also institutional racial, economic, and national differences—that contribute to erotic exchanges between lovers, see Abraham 1990, esp. 271.

PART ONE: DJUNA BARNES

1. Obviously other erotic positions constructed by familial discourse are open to women as lovers. Note, for example, the proliferation of "Daddy stories" in contemporary writers such as Pat Califia. See, too, in *Nightwood*, Matthew O'Connor's desire to be some good man's wife.

2. Some writers object to the term "erotic". Hoagland 1988, e.g., argues that it is too marked by "homopatriarchal greco-christian tradition" (165).

3. In the twentieth-century United States, lesbian representations and the lived experiences they refer to and produce have often rested in part on sameness and difference. Bonnie Zimmerman's and Lillian Faderman's historical accounts describe the varying oppressions, suppressions, and even celebrations of differences along a heterosexual/homosexual binary. But they also consider similarity and difference among lesbians. Zim-

merman, e.g., makes clear that what she calls "the myths of origin" for lesbian-feminist fiction often stress sisterhood and mutual collectivity, partially as a reaction against earlier fictive portrayals of difference. But at the same time, Zimmerman and many other commentators argue that difference in lesbian relations creates "a gap in which lies lesbian desire" (Zimmerman 1990, esp. 113; Faderman 1991). For other discussions of the role of difference in lesbian sexual connections, see, e.g., Loulan 1990; Hamer 1990; Moraga 1983, 126; Anzaldúa 1990. For a consideration of lesbian difference in the context of recent French thinking (especially that of Monique Wittig and Jacques Derrida), see Meese 1990, esp. 80–82. For a discussion of likeness in lesbian literary representations, see McNaron 1993. For sameness in lesbian narrative theory, see Farwell 1990.

4. Critical discussions about the rhetorical efficacy of "queer theory," as a term now standardly invoked to mean various antifoundational inquiries stressing intersections and boundary crossings between and among marginalized sexualities and positions of race, class, and gender, continue unabated. As "theory," these inquiries criticize stable identities ("lesbian," "gay," "bisexual," "transsexual," "heterosexual") and instead emphasize provisional identifications and shifting erotic and emotional investments. They resonate with recent feminist poststructuralist articulations of difference and domination (understood both psychoanalytically and socially) at the same time that they reclaim and assert the power of radical sexual "otherness." But as I suggested earlier ("Introduction," note 3), some theorists have asked whether the rubric is always as inclusive as it claims. A sampling of recent books employing "queer" in their titles demonstrates the differing constructions of the term. Higgins's *A Queer Reader* (1994) is restricted by its subtitle: *A Compendium of Quotes by and about Gay Men throughout the Ages*; Alan Sinfield in *Cultural Politics—Queer Reading*, a book largely concerned with gay white men, says that he used "queer" in his title "only after considerable hesitation," fearing that "on the one hand, it may be too limiting—yielding up too easily the aspiration to hold a politics of class, race, and ethnicity alongside a politics of gender and sexuality. On the other, it may be over-ambitious" (x). The introduction to *Queer Looks* (Gever, Greyson, and Parmar 1993) takes it for granted that its readers will understand the term without elaborating its parameters; for good measure, the book's subtitle is *Perspectives on Lesbian and Gay Film and Video*. Alexander Doty, in the introduction to his book *Making Things Perfectly Queer*, worries that his essays don't sufficiently discuss bisexuality; he adds a brief footnote to suggest how mass culture theory might take bisexuality into account. The fluidity of sexual desire across gender and sex (but not race) makes *Nightwood* an arguably queer text; I read only the erotics between Nora and Robin as Nora relates them. For a more extended discussion of queer theory, its relation to lesbian and gay studies, and the importance of racial difference in an understanding of queer sexuality, see de Lauretis 1991c; for queer theory as an emerging field of academic study, see Warner 1992; for queer theory as an intervention into identity politics, see Duggan 1992 and Stein 1992; for a critique of the essays in Stein that construct a monolith of lesbian-feminism, see Rycenga 1994; for a discussion of the controversies surrounding the use of "queer" as inclusive across race and gender, see Solomon 1992.

5. Faderman's 1994 canonizing anthology, *Chloe plus Olivia*, places an excerpt from *Nightwood* in the section titled "Carnivorous Flowers: The Literature of Exotic and Evil Lesbians," a category which also includes a section from Jewelle Gomez's very different work, *The Gilda Stories*, because of its vampire thematics. Although Faderman writes that Barnes continues "the literary legacy of the tormenting and tormented lesbian," she also has said in an interview that she loves the image of the "carnivorous flower," so perhaps her category title is more tongue-in-cheek than it might first appear to be (Faderman 1994b, 25).

6. For an account of lesbian fictional representations that traces the lesbian-feminist response to earlier negative portrayals, see Zimmerman 1990, esp. 120–63.

7. Brossard 1990, 41–66; Wittig 1983; Escomel and Pelletier 1988, 76; Harris 1973; Lynch 1990, 45. Except for Lynch, these writers have done work that is, like *Nightwood*,

linguistically "experimental," which no doubt in part accounts for their praise of Barnes's writing.

8. Though Nora's narrative does not usually figure power differences of race and class, some of *Nightwood*'s other narratives and representations have occasioned important analyses of these issues, especially of the novel's writing of Jewishness. See, e.g., Abraham 1991; Marcus 1991; Levine and Urquilla 1993, particularly essays by Meryl Altman and Karen Kaivola. For recent writing on constructions of whiteness and white privilege as vital to the understanding of racial oppression, see, among others, Morrison 1992; hooks 1992; Ware 1992; Frankenberg 1993.

9. Two excellent sources for study of Barnes are Levine and Urquilla 1993 and Broe 1991. See readings of *Nightwood* by Lee (207–18), Marcus (221–50), and Abraham (252–68). See Broe 1989 for a discussion of Barnes's family dynamics. For other recent feminist readings of *Nightwood*, which take directions other than my own, see Benstock 1986, 230–67; Gerstenberger 1989; Gilbert and Gubar 1989, 358–62; and Kaivola 1991, 59–100. For another critic "following Djuna" ("I wrote her a letter once, and I know someone who left roses on her doorstep") who comments on *Nightwood* as a lesbian text, see Meese 1992 (esp. 62).

10. For an account of how retelling desire works in psychoanalysis, see Cummings 1991, 4–8.

11. For my reading of how even the novel's extravagant language cannot save Nora and stave off Matthew's despair, see Allen 1978.

12. There are several narratives in the novel in addition to Nora's, all of them arguably queer in that they stress fluidity of desire, especially in the cases of Matthew, Robin, and Jenny.

13. For attraction between characters who do not know each other as a lesbian fictional convention, see Wilson 1991, 203.

14. *Spillway* includes *Nightwood*. For an extended discussion of Wittig's uses of "the category of sex," see Butler 1990, 111–28.

15. Note that Butler does not take "sexed bodies" as a stable given any more than she does "gender." My discussion emphasizes gender performance in *Nightwood* as a discursive location.

16. See, e.g., Hollibaugh and Moraga 1983; Case 1989; Hamer 1990; Ardill and O'Sullivan 1990; Brown 1990; de Lauretis 1991a and 1994, 257–97; Roof 1991, 244–53; Butler 1991, 25; Garber 1992, 147–48; Nestle 1992; Burana, Roxxie, and Due, 1994. In popular culture, see attention to gender play in the 1990s issues of *On Our Backs* (San Francisco) and the videotapes advertised there. For a commentary on this attention, see Lamos 1994.

17. Cross-dressing is a prominent feature of other characters in the novel besides Robin, however. Matthew, who calls himself "a boy . . . who am the last woman left in the world, though I am the bearded lady" (100), appears in one scene in rouge and curls; when alive, Robin's mother-in-law has the bearing of a general in leather. For some 1990s readers, cross-dressing, like the sexual fluidity of the characters, also marks *Nightwood* as a queer text. For transvestism and the importance of sexualities beyond the heterosexual/homosexual binary, see Fuss 1991. See also Garber 1992; Herrmann 1992.

18. As I specify above (n. 1), Hoagland would not use "erotics" as a description appropriate for lesbian relations of any kind.

19. For an example of sexology's treatment, see Ellis 1937, 206–208. For a more contemporary version, see Siegel 1988, 15–23.

20. In an interesting essay that, like my discussion, sees narcissism not as pathological but as "the source of a critical [homosexual] potential," Michael Warner (1990) argues further that the heterosexual pathologizing of queer narcissism "allows the constitution of heterosexuality as such" (206, 202).

21. Indeed, many later references in Freud do authorize "narcissism" as pejorative, and narcissistic object choice as a feature of homosexuality, e.g., the case of Schreber (1911) and

"Psychogenesis" (1920b). For a reading of the narcissistic woman as shadowed by the female invert on whom "the fiction of the narcissist as woman" depends, see Lynda Hart's reading of Wedekind's *Pandora's Box*. Hart notes that the invert, the Countess Geschwitz, was the first representative of a homosexual woman on the European stage (1994, 48–50). For an embracing of the enhancing possibilities of psychoanalytically specific narcissism in the context of lesbian sexuality, see de Lauretis's discussion of "mutual narcissistic empowerment" (1994, 264).

22. For a different reading of lesbian subjectivity, see Engelbrecht 1990.

23. I share Esther Newton's belief that some of Freud's concepts "begin to explain sexual desire, at least as it operates in our culture" (Newton 1984, 571). For a full study of the construction of lesbian sexuality in the context of Freud and of other fictions of psychoanalysis, see de Lauretis 1994. For another use of Freud in a reading of *Nightwood*, see Marcus 1991.

24. Irigaray 1985a refers often to the economy of the Same both directly and indirectly in her reading of Freud; see esp. 26, 32–34. Although some of Irigaray's work, notably 1985b, 205–18, might be used in thinking about lesbian sexuality, her more recent essays suggest that she is most interested in theorizing workable heterosexual relations. For such an argument, see Grosz 1988; de Lauretis 1990; and Jagose 1992. De Lauretis 1988 extends Irigaray's distinction between homosexuality and "hommosexuality" (the economy of the Same) in an interesting discussion of lesbian theory, criticism, and film. She is helpful in explaining what may be confusing to readers newly approaching Irigaray: 'The Same' in Irigaray refers to the appropriation of women by a male economy, not "sameness" between lovers of the same sex (156).

25. For the historical turn from "inversion" to "homosexuality" that is marked in the earlier and later dates of these Freud writings, see Halperin 1990, 15–18.

26. For an essay using "On Narcissism" to argue that "femininity" and "the female homosexual" are always definitionally heterosexual in psychoanalysis, see Storr 1993.

27. The absence of the mother and her subjectivity in Freud has been noted by many feminist critics of psychoanalysis, but it is particularly striking in his accounts of sexuality because the narrative is so often focused on the (bisexual) infant and the (male) child. See especially Sprengnether 1990.

28. For critics attending to identification in Freud in the context of lesbian relations, see, e.g., Silverman 1988, 149–54; de Lauretis 1991a and 1994, 180–90; Roof 1991, 174–215; Butler 1993, 95–11; Fuss 1993.

29. I capitalize "Mother" to mark it as a culturally constructed ideological position.

30. The specificity of *Nightwood*'s maternal discourse as white, though racially unmarked, is clear when compared to ideologies of motherhood in other ethnic groups. See, e.g., by contrast, work on African-American motherhood in Davis 1983, 7–18; Spillers 1987; Carby 1987, 20–39.

31. The persistence of Nora's desire in *Nightwood* might also serve as an intervention in "Mourning and Melancholia" (Freud 1917), an essay which I take up in relation to *The Terrible Girls* in Part Three.

32. I borrow the description "spectral" from Sprengnether 1990, 5; for her this term retains its full etymological implications so that it suggests spectacle, something suspicious, a phantom.

33. For a full delineation of the difference between mothering as "institution" and as "experience," see Rich 1976.

34. As in "The Grande Malade," actual parents are absent from the story proper. Barnes saved parental confrontation for *Ryder* and *The Antiphon*.

PART TWO: JEANETTE WINTERSON

1. In fact, Winterson points to Woolf, Calvino, and Shakespeare as her literary predecessors in Constantine and Scott 1990 (25–26).

2. The treatment of Jewishness in *Written on the Body* has not yet been debated as it has in the case of *Nightwood*. But several reviewers find it problematic, as I do. One of the most negative of the British reviewers, A. N. Wilson, notes that "the routine anti-Semitism about Elgin's family is squirm-making" (1992, 34). Valerie Miner, who also doesn't like the novel much, writes, "The clever cleverness is self-defeating and s/he caricatures people who are fat, Jewish, anarchist, Australian" (1993, 21). Sarah Schulman, who says, "For the first 100 pages this is a simple, wonderful book about love," later adds a telling parenthetical comment: "The woman the Narrator loves, named Louise, leaves her stereotypic, despicable Jewish husband (unfortunately described in clichés of hunger for gold, overactive intellect, and chicken soup)" (1993, 20). I argue that clichés of love are consciously deployed in the novel to call attention to ideologies of expectation. But the use of stereotypic ethnic clichés does not seem similarly deconstructed.

3. See Allen and Howard 1990 for an empirical study of readers who felt the need to sex an initially unspecified narrator. In reading Jayne Anne Phillips's story "Home," from her collection *Black Tickets,* most readers in the study assumed at first that the teller, who is a daughter narrating a story about the effect of her heterosexual love affair on her relationship to her mother, was a man. One reader's comments testify to the "naturalization" of dominant-culture sex and sexuality: "At first I thought she was a guy. When it started with Jason and a homosexual relationship, it just didn't sound right, [and] I had to reorganize everything in my mind that happened" (544). The reviewers of *Written on the Body,* familiar with Winterson as an "out" writer, often assumed a female narrator who had both male and female lovers; in our study we did not specify either the sex or the sexuality of the story's author. Obviously received knowledge about the author plays a large role in producing readerly assumptions.

4. Her second book, a growing-up novel set during Noah's preparations for the biblical flood, was for a time omitted altogether from her list of published works (Petro 1993, 113). In the front pages of her most recent fiction, *Art and Lies,* Winterson lists *Boating* separately from her fiction, under the category of "comic book." One reviewer who especially dislikes *Written on the Body,* partially because its narrator is "a strutting, self-advertising dyke," finds *Boating* her best work (A. N. Wilson 1992, 34).

5. *Written on the Body* won the 1994 *Lambda Book Report* Prize for best lesbian novel of the year; while such an award does not make the sex of the narrator a certainty, it suggests how many readers assume that possibility. What seems more interesting than definitive sexual casting is the textual function of narrative ambiguity in the novel, as I will argue.

6. Chapter 2 of *Risk and Blame* is reprinted in *Daedalus* 1990. The issue provides examples from a variety of contemporary disciplines and discourses not included in my brief list of how risk has come to signify danger.

7. References to and accounts of the "sex wars" are by now well known and too numerous to list individually. Often, they begin with detailing the controversies over the presence of "sex radicals" at the 1982 Barnard Conference, "Towards a Politics of Sexuality." The volume of papers that came from that conference remains crucial for work on women's sexual practices (Vance 1984). For a summary of the debates to the mid-eighties, see Rich 1986. For an early, often overlooked "roundtable" on gay and lesbian s/m, see Young et al. 1978. The still-classic anti-s/m volume is Linden et al. 1982. For recent theorizing of lesbian s/m in psychoanalytic contexts, see Adams 1989, whose attempts to separate economies of s/m lesbian practices from other versions of erotics between women too easily discounts the gender and power enactments of such erotics; Meese 1992, 103–25; Creet 1991; Modleski 1991, 152–60; for more general commentaries, see Merck 1993, who comments on Creet, Adams, and Modleski (236–66); and Stein 1993. For a recent account of connections between s/m representations and censorship (in Canada), see Kiss & Tell 1994. For recent discussions of s/m practices in heterosexual contexts, see Williams 1989; Chancer 1992; and Mistress Vena 1993.

8. In a recent interview, Amber Hollibaugh makes a similar point that lesbians, just by being visible, "take a risk." At the same time her comments imply without saying so directly that taking this risk also puts "the social contract" at risk: "'The place where lesbians are brave is that we've taken a risk that few women have been willing to take—to announce that we are sexual people on our own terms and that we will find the partners we want and negotiate that living reality every day of our lives'" (Goldstein 1994, 43).

9. Califia's reviewers and commentators occasionally name risk explicitly in passing as a given in the erotic exchanges she invents; Randy Turoff refers to "that risky dance, the one which incorporates the power struggle between restraint and indulgence, need and denial, flickers on the page like a jagged flame," in her largely positive review of *Melting Point* (1994, 22). In an essay critical of Califia, Gabriele Griffin says of Califia's comment that writing about safe sex is not sexy, "This suggests the importance of the notion of risk that can be involved in sexuality as a significant aspect of 'the sexy' but it also highlights how difficult it is to re-vision sexual practice and cultural attitudes towards the erotic" (1993, 153). For a commentary on Califia in which the author acknowledges her own ambivalence toward her subject matter, see Dolan 1993, 183–86.

10. "Psychology" in Douglas usually means versions of cognitive psychology. Throughout *Risk and Blame*, Douglas is particularly critical of psychology for attempting to bring "objectivity" to risk analysis without taking cultural bias into account. Such a criticism is part of what she acknowledges in her introduction as "a complaint of inhospitality against the social sciences" (1992, ix). Not surprisingly, she does not take up psychoanalytic discourses at all.

11. As readers familiar with *The Passion* will recognize, what follows is not a reading of the whole novel, but a theorizing of its erotics between women as it emerges in the (relatively few) interactions between Villanelle and the Queen of Spades. The novel also takes up, among other things, discourses of war, unrequited heterosexual desire, and further understandings of "passion."

12. As a participant in the novel's anti-war discourse, Henri criticizes rather than supports ideologies of winning and losing.

13. Critical interest in cross-dressing and drag increased dramatically with the organizing of lesbian/gay/queer studies in academia. Readers should consult Garber 1992, though as her book makes clear, "transvestism" as a category extends well beyond queer erotic contexts. For cross-dressing in recent lesbian fiction, see Herrmann 1992. What is especially important about cross-dressing for my argument about Winterson is its function in *The Passion* as an erotic game rather than as an economic necessity, a figuring of stable desire, or an outward expression of psychic body-sex. I mean to emphasize the liminality, the possibility of transgression, and the uncertainty of knowing in the service of the erotic dynamics.

14. In her brief discussion of *The Passion* (in an essay focused primarily on reading *Oranges* and *Sexing the Cherry*), Laura Doan sees Villanelle's cross-dressing as an exploration of fictional multiple identity in keeping with Doan's positioning of Winterson as a lesbian feminist postmodernist (1994, 148). De Lauretis reads the webbed feet as a tongue-in-cheek spoof of the theory of sexual difference. Because they substitute for the penis as a marker of male privilege, they also may be read as a figure of fetishism when the Queen of Spades says, "let me stroke your feet" (private communication).

15. For a related contemporary fictional working through of heterosexual desire and homosexual possibility, see Acker 1986.

16. Zimmerman also comments on Rich's revision of Tristan and Iseult in arguing that lesbian romance codes are often "congruent" with those of illicit heterosexuality" (1990, 78–79).

17. I am grateful to Kate Cummings for pointing out the relevance of this text for my reading of Freud.

18. Freud differentiates fear (*Furcht*) from anxiety (*Angst*) in *Beyond the Pleasure Principle* by specifying that fear requires a definite object, while anxiety describes a condi-

tion of expecting or preparing for danger, even though it may be an unknown one. Laplanche and Pontalis are careful to point out, however, that "the contrast frequently made between *fear,* which is said to have a specific object, and *anxiety,* defined by the absence of any object, does not correspond precisely with Freudian distinctions" (379). Their caveat may result from the greater importance and complexity of Freud's earlier and later theories of anxiety, which make the term, unlike "fear," harder to define briefly. In any case, Winterson's use of "fear" more closely approximates Freud's "anxiety" in its affective role.

19. That stereotypes often construct black (and frequently also white working-class) women as strong rather than vulnerable marks *The Passion* as a text imbued, like *Nightwood,* with whiteness as an invisible racial category.

20. For a reading of lesbian fiction of the 1950s, see Weir and Wilson 1992.

21. In unmarried heterosexual couples, the rules of marriage are also suspended, though I would argue that traces of those conventions are still at play. Convention for gay male couples often includes mutual permission for sexual encounters outside the committed couple. In the mid-1990s, at least in the Anglo-American context, coupling as the norm for women together cannot be assumed as easily as it could be even ten years ago, though it remains the dominant mode of relationship. The hegemony in some lesbian cultures of long-term couples is evident in Joan Nestle's critique of it in *A Restricted Country.*

22. Connections between women and interpersonal relational dynamics have been argued by many feminist theorists, but are probably most associated with the early feminist work of Gilligan and Chodorow.

23. For an extended discussion of the conflict between commitment and "casual love" in one lesbian community, see Kennedy and Davis 1993, 231–77. For a critique of opting for long-term comfort or for romance over hot sex of the moment, see, among others, Califia 1994.

24. This is not to suggest that specific lesbian or queer communities are without unstated but often persuasive "rules" about how to behave in a "relationship." But they lack the juridical force of heterosexual marriage conventions.

25. Winterson's foregrounding of cliché brings to mind Barnes's satire in *Ladies Almanack* of how a "Maid goes at a Maid":

> Nay——I cannot write it! It is worse than this! More dripping, more lush, more lavender, more mid-mauve, more honeyed, more Flower casting, more Cherub-bound, more downpouring, more saccharine, more lamentable, more gruesomely unmindful of Reason, Sense, to say nothing of Humor. . . . And yet! (46)

Like Winterson's treatment of the "saggy armchair of cliché," the passage wittily addresses the excess of romance. But Barnes's making fun is more ambivalent. The closing "And yet!" undercuts the satire on the linguistic excesses of romance.

26. I thank Teresa de Lauretis for suggesting to me how Winterson's conclusion parallels Barnes's.

27. For a reading of mirroring in *Desert of the Heart,* see Spraggs 1992.

28. The tropic body discourse almost inevitably situates the novel in the age of AIDS. Queer reviewers were divided about whether the novel can be read as alluding indirectly to AIDS. D'Adesky (*Out*) says that AIDS "remains a social subtext" but quotes British writer Cherry Smyth as complaining, "'It makes me feel as if the lover can't contemplate the horror of living with a loved one who's dying'" (1993, 39). Sarah Schulman says that Winterson never makes the connection with AIDS in writing about leukemia (1993, 20).

29. Teresa de Lauretis suggests that this tattooed "L" might well refer to "Lesbian" in addition to "Louise" (private communication).

30. It is difficult in reading *Written on the Body* not also to hear echoes of Wittig's *The Lesbian Body* (1975), a set of poems that might be seen as an intertexual bridge between Winterson and Barnes. (Wittig, as I note in Part One, has translated Barnes into French

and made her work a focus of theorizing a lesbian/"universal" point of view [Wittig 1983]). Wittig writes in her introduction, "To recite one's own body, to recite the body of the other, is to recite the words of which the book is made up" (10). Like the body meditations in *Written*, which "recite the body" of Louise and of "I," the poems of *The Lesbian Body* figure loss, incorporation, and (sometimes) violent destruction of the body so that it might be reconstructed in an Amazonian future. Wittig offers lists of parts of the body printed entirely in block letters; Winterson begins the anatomy book meditations with descriptions of the body also in block letters. Wittig's text centers the body in sex, Winterson's in death, Barnes's in both, though in *Nightwood* the sex is implicit and the body is not "recited." Wittig's several references to the lesbian as monster also bring to mind Bertha Harris's later description of the lesbian/monster as "a creature of . . . passion and purpose: unassimilable, awesome, dangerous, different: distinguished" (1977, 8).

31. Laplanche and Pontalis point out that Freud never published an extended study of projection. Their reading brings together a number of scattered references in a helpful attempt to (re)construct the metapsychology of projection in various Freud texts (1973, 349–56). Klein's emphasis on identification in projection is not to say that identification in Klein as in Freud cannot also be a defense.

32. For another reading of the negativity of projection, see Lacan 1977, "Agressivity in psychoanalysis." For an argument for the rereading of Klein in contemporary theoretical contexts, and for a helpful reading of Klein's relation to the psychoanalytic concept of negation, see Rose 1993, 137–90.

33. Rose names Kristeva as the contemporary French theorist most influenced by Klein (1993, 179 n. 11). For references to other contemporary analysts taking similar positions, see Burch 1993, 67; and Segal and Bell 1991.

PART THREE: REBECCA BROWN

1. In *TLS*, Sue Roe describes *The Terrible Girls* as "a powerful account of erotic love which exchanges the comforts of illusion for more complex and less certain reward. In the process, Brown also challenges our understanding of the ways in which language may be re-sculpted to admit the most unsettling and most vital forms of human contact" (1990, 1359); another British reviewer writes, "*The Terrible Girls* . . . comes from one of the fiercest, most potent, original writers around" (Gilbert 1990, 32). Brown's first review in the *New York Times Book Review* (of her collection *Annie Oakley's Girl*) begins, "A strange and wonderful first-person voice emerges from the stories of Rebecca Brown, who strips her language of convention to lay bare the ferocious rituals of love and need" (Boaz 1993, 18); *Annie* was a Quality Book Club selection in its New Voices series. In addition to *The Terrible Girls* and *Annie Oakley's Girl*, Brown is the author of two earlier novels, *The Haunted House* and *The Children's Crusade* (both published in the U.S. by Seal Press). Her newest novel, *The Gifts of the Body*, focuses on home care of AIDS patients. It won the Fisk Fiction Prize from the *Boston Book Review* in 1995 and is scheduled for translation into Danish and Norwegian.

2. *The Passion* will also use the trope of the (literally) lost heart recovered with the help of a third person.

3. I argue that "you" "becomes" Lady Bountiful, but the connection is never directly explicit in the text. The order of the stories' composition supports my decision to discuss the three interpolated stories as a separate narrative of affect; "Isle of Skye," "Junk Mail," and "Forgiveness" were written and separately published before *The Terrible Girls* appeared as a "novel-in-stories." In fact, that designation was given to the book only in its second printing. The frame-tale stories that open and close the collection were the last to be composed (Rebecca Brown, private communication).

4. The violence of dismemberment in Brown's text, like the meditations on parts of the body in Winterson, recalls Wittig's *The Lesbian Body*.

5. The use of sex-unspecified narrators is popular in novels that may be read as involving erotics between women. See, for example, the pronoun play of June Arnold's *The Cook and the Carpenter,* written before Brown's stories, and not only *Written on the Body* but also, and to different effect, Sarah Schulman's *Empathy,* written after.

6. In their survey of the psychoanalytic literature from Freud forward, O'Connor and Ryan (1993) make depressingly clear the extent to which psychoanalysis pathologizes lesbian relations.

7. Citizens' Alliance of Washington, Initiative 610, Section 5. The measure further specifies that "the gender that is established at the conception of all persons is the only and natural gender of that person for the duration of their life." This language was intended to make certain that transgendered persons were included in the same non-protected class as lesbians and gays.

8. For an early and still influential discussion arguing the necessity of understanding differences among women as well as any woman's multiple and contradictory identifications, see de Lauretis 1986. As a theorist, de Lauretis has been especially attentive to sexuality as a marker of difference among women.

9. O'Connor and Ryan 1993 confirms in its overview that psychoanalytic discourse as well as subcultural toss-offs makes these three tropes central to etiologies of lesbianism.

10. Examples of the "new territory" trope include, among others, such poems in *Dream of a Common Language* as "Transcendental Etude" and "Twenty-One Love Poems" and Daphne Marlatt's novel *Ana Historic.*

11. For a foregrounding of one such rule, see the fantasy scene in Rose Troche's 1994 film, *Go Fish,* sending up one lesbian community's rules about not sleeping with men. The offender imagines being menacingly surrounded by threatening dykes who tell her she's not a "real lesbian" because she extended her sexual preference too far. The scene parodies stable identities and the idea of a mythic "lesbian police," but at the same time the parody speaks to the discursive fear both of such policing and of bisexual choice.

12. Freud asserts in *The Interpretation of Dreams* that the ego of the dreamer "lies concealed by identification behind" the appearance of others in dreams (1900, 323).

13. For a discussion of "excess" in the specifically sexual dynamics of women's erotics, see Meese 1992, 106–15.

14. For a discussion of some of Freud's texts on hysterical identification, including the butcher's wife dream, see Adams 1993. With a focus on bisexuality, she argues that hysterical identification involves identification with both the woman's and the man's position, and that these oscillating places cannot be "fixed" in an Oedipal resolution. Unlike mine, her attention is to acts rather than to object choice. Freud's thinking on the ego ideal in the last section of "On Narcissism" and its extension in "Mourning and Melancholia" suggest some other possibilities for identification in the context of the sexual.

15. Though for the "importance of [male] homosexuality in the structure of groups," see Freud 1914b ("On Narcissism"), editors note 1, 101.

16. Identification is crucial in the formation of the ego, as both *Group Psychology* and *The Ego and the Id* argue, but I am most interested in its role in nonfamilial libidinal relations. See, among others, Butler 1993, 94–119, and Borch-Jacobsen 1982, 173–85, for debates over the process of identifications in ego formation.

17. Other relevant references to identification occur more briefly but significantly in a 1910 note added to *Three Essays,* and in *Leonardo* (1910). Conversations with Kate Cummings have been helpful in my discussion of identification and its relation to desire in Freud.

18. For a summary of the position of reader-response critics and the construction of the reader, see Mailloux, 192–207.

19. For delineations of a lesbian spectator position, see, among others, White 1991; Traub 1991; Johnson 1993; Mayne 1993, 157–72; de Lauretis 1994, 81–148.

20. See, for example, de Lauretis, who notes that contradictions between subjectivity and "subjecthood," that is, between "fantasmatic configuration[s]" and locations in social

relations, may produce contradictory spectorial identifications (1994, 123–30, esp. 129). See also n. 16 above.

21. My position is thus related both to Rosenblatt's "transaction" and to Iser's "aesthetic response." I prefer to think of "scripts" and "performers"; these terms privilege conscious and unconscious investments of readers more obviously than does Iser's phenomenological conception of "the implied reader," with its privileging of the text as a set of "instructions" constraining the reader (Iser 1978, ix–xii). Helen Taylor's description of reading captures not only the idea of process, but also that of exchange: "The process of reading itself is not an abstraction between a fixed book and a generalised universal reader, rather it is an *exchange,* a relationship between an active, critical reader, with all her educational, social and cultural baggage of experience, and a text, with all its literary historical and cultural references, not to mention the ways it has been produced, packaged and marketed" (1989, 66). I would add to her list of "baggage of experience" the reader's affective experiences.

22. For a related, though by no means identical, filmic fantasy with the object starring as subject, see Sheila McLaughlin's *She Must Be Seeing Things* (1987) and de Lauretis's discussion of it in *The Practice of Love* (1994, esp. 123, 142).

23. Femme performance, because it more nearly coincides with heterosexual versions of femininity, is not as obviously marked an identity position when acted solo, without the presence of butch difference.

24. Laura Antoniou, author of the Leatherwomen series of dyke erotica, makes a similar point: "Every human interaction is based on power-exchange. There will almost always be a dominant partner—acknowledged or not. It may be who always picks the restaurant, or it may be the one who knows all along which restaurant they will go to" (1994, 19).

25. I borrow this term from Gayatri Spivak (1992, 800), who uses it in a quite different context.

26. The final story, "The Ruined City," with its parable of a parched urban area ravaged by selfishness and neglect, also opens itself to performance by readers interested in the politics of ecofeminism.

WORKS CITED

Abraham, Julie. 1990. "History as Explanation: Writing about Lesbian Writing or 'Are Girls Necessary?'" In *Left Politics and the Literary Profession,* ed. Lennard J. Davis and M. Bella Mirabella, 254–83. New York: Columbia University Press.

———. 1991. "'Women, Remember You': Djuna Barnes and History." In *Silence and Power,* ed. Mary Lynn Broe, 252–68. Carbondale: Southern Illinois University Press.

Acker, Kathy. 1986. *Don Quixote.* New York: Grove Press.

Adams, Parveen. 1989. "Of Female Bondage." In *Between Feminism and Psychoanalysis,* ed. Teresa Brennan, 247–65. New York: Routledge.

———. 1993. "Per Os(cillation)." In *Male Trouble,* ed. Constance Penley and Sharon Willis, 3–25. Minneapolis: University of Minnesota Press.

Aguilar–San Juan, Karin. "Landmarks in Literature by Asian-American Lesbians." *Signs* 18 (Summer): 936–43.

Allen, Carolyn. 1978. "'Dressing the Unknowable in the Garments of the Known': The Style of Djuna Barnes' *Nightwood.*" In *Women's Language and Style,* ed. Douglas Buturff and Edmund Epstein, 106–18. Akron: L&S Books.

Allen, Carolyn, and Judith A. Howard. 1990. "The Gendered Context of Reading." *Gender and Society* 4 (4): 534–51.

Allen, Jeffner, ed. 1990. *Lesbian Philosophies and Cultures.* Albany: State University of New York Press.

Antoniou, Laura. 1994. Interview in *Girlfriends* 1 (November/December): 18–19.

Anzaldúa, Gloria. 1990. "She Ate Horses." In *Lesbian Philosophies and Cultures,* ed. Jeffner Allen, 371–88. Albany: State University of New York Press.

Ardill, Susan, and Sue O'Sullivan. 1990. "Butch/Femme Obsessions." *Feminist Review* 34: 79–85.

Arnold, June. 1973. *The Cook and the Carpenter.* Plainfield, V.t: Daughters, Inc.

Barale, Michele Aina. 1991. "Below the Belt: (Un)Covering *The Well of Loneliness.*" In *Inside/Out,* ed. Diana Fuss, 235–57. New York: Routledge.

Barnes, Djuna. (1925a) 1962. "Cassation." In *Selected Works of Djuna Barnes,* 12–20. New York: Farrar, Strauss and Cudahy. First published as "A Little Girl Tells a Story to a Lady," in *Contact Collection of Contemporary Writers,* 1–10. Paris: Three Mountains Press.

———. (1925b) 1962. "The Grande Malade." In *Selected Works of Djuna Barnes,* 21–28. New York: Farrar, Strauss and Cudahy. First published as "The Little Girl Continues," *This Quarter* 1:195–202.

———. 1927. "Dusie." In *American Esoterica,* 75–82. New York: Macy-Masius.

———. (1928) 1972. *Ladies Almanack.* New York: Harper and Row.

———. (1928) 1979. *Ryder.* New York: St Martin's Press.

———. (1936) 1961. *Nightwood.* New York: New Directions.

———. 1962. *Selected Works of Djuna Barnes.* New York: Farrar, Straus and Cudahy.

Barthes, Roland. 1974. *S/Z.* Trans. Richard Miller. New York: Hill and Wang.

———. 1975. *The Pleasure of the Text.* Trans. Richard Miller. New York: Hill and Wang.

———. 1976. *Sade/Fourier/Loyola.* Trans. Richard Miller. New York: Hill and Wang.

———. 1978. *A Lover's Discourse.* Trans. Richard Howard. New York: Hill and Wang.

———. 1989 (1986). *The Rustle of Language.* Trans. Richard Howard. Berkeley: University of California Press.

Batsleer, Janet; Tony Davies; Rebecca O'Rourke; and Chris Weedon. 1985. *Rewriting English*. London: Methuen.

Benstock, Shari. 1986. *Women of the Left Bank*. Austin: University of Texas Press.

Birtha, Becky. 1987. *Lover's Choice*. Seattle: Seal Press.

Bloom, Harold. 1973. *The Anxiety of Influence: A Theory of Poetry*. New York: Oxford University Press.

———. 1975. *A Map of Misreading*. New York: Oxford University Press.

Boaz, Amy. 1993. Review of *Annie Oakley's Girl* by Rebecca Brown. *New York Times Book Review*, 1 August 1993, 18.

Bogus, SDiane. 1990. "The 'Queen B' Figure in Black Literature." In *Lesbian Texts and Contexts*, ed. Karla Jay and Joanne Glasgow, 275–90. New York: New York University Press.

Borch-Jacobsen, Mikkel. 1982. *The Freudian Subject*. Trans. Catherine Porter. Stanford: Stanford University Press.

Bowles, Jane. (1966) 1978. *My Sister's Hand in Mine: An Expanded Edition of the Collected Works of Jane Bowles*. New York: Ecco Press.

Broe, Mary Lynne. 1989. "My Art Belongs to Daddy: Incest as Exile, The Textual Economics of Hayford Hall." In *Women's Writing in Exile*, ed. Mary Lynn Broe and Angela Ingram, 41–86. Chapel Hill: University of North Carolina Press.

———, ed. 1991. *Silence and Power: A Reevaluation of Djuna Barnes*. Carbondale: Southern Illinois University Press.

Brooks, Peter. 1984. *Reading for the Plot*. New York: Random House.

———. 1987. "The Idea of a Psychoanalytic Literary Criticism." In *Discourses in Psychoanalysis and Literature*, ed. Shlomith Rimmon-Kenan, 1–18. London: Methuen.

Brossard, Nicole. 1981. "Djuna Barnes: De Profil Moderne." In *Mon Héroïne*, 189–214. Montreal: Les éditions du remue-ménage.

———. 1986. *Lovhers*. Trans. Barbara Godard. Montreal: Guernica. French edition (*Amantes*) 1980.

———. 1990. *Picture Theory*. Trans. Barbara Godard. New York: Roof Books.

Brown, Jan. 1990. "Sex, Lies & Penetration." *Out/look* (Winter): 30–34.

Brown, Rebecca. 1986. *The Haunted House*. Seattle: Seal Press.

———. 1989. *The Children's Crusade*. Seattle: Seal Press.

———. 1990. *The Terrible Girls*. San Francisco: City Lights Books.

———. 1993. *Annie Oakley's Girl*. San Francisco: City Lights Books.

———. 1994. *The Gifts of the Body*. New York: Harper Collins.

Brown, Ritamae. 1973. *Rubyfruit Jungle*. Plainfield, Vt.: Daughters, Inc.

Burana, Lily; Roxxie; and Linnea Due, eds. 1994. *Dagger: On Butch Women*. Pittsburgh: Cleis Press.

Burch, Beverly. 1993. *On Intimate Terms: The Psychology of Difference in Lesbian Relationships*. Urbana: University of Illinois Press.

Bush, Catherine. 1993. "Jeanette Winterson." *Bomb* (Spring): 55–58.

Butler, Judith. 1990. *Gender Trouble: Feminism and the Subversion of Identity*. New York: Routledge.

———. 1991. "Imitation and Gender Insubordination." In *Inside/Out: Lesbian Theories, Gay Theories*, ed. Diana Fuss, 13–31. New York: Routledge.

———. 1993. *Bodies That Matter*. New York: Routledge.

Califia, Pat. 1988. *Macho Sluts*. Boston: Alyson Publications.

———. 1993. *Melting Point*. Boston: Alyson Publications.

———. 1994. "*Un*Monogamy: Loving Tricks and Tricking Lovers." In Califia, *Public Sex*, 199–204. Pittsburgh: Cleis Press.

Carby, Hazel. 1987. *Reconstructing Womanhood*. New York: Oxford University Press.

Case, Sue-Ellen. 1989. "Towards a Butch-Femme Aesthetic." *Discourse* 11 (1): 55–73.

Castle, Terry. 1993. *The Apparitional Lesbian: Female Homosexuality and Modern Culture.* New York: Columbia University Press.

Chambers, Ross. 1984. *Story and Situation.* Minneapolis: University of Minnesota Press.

Chancer, Lynn. 1992. *Sadomasochism in Everyday Life: The Dynamics of Power and Powerlessness.* New Brunswick, N.J.: Rutgers University Press.

Chauncey, George. 1982–83. "From Sexual Inversion to Homosexuality: Medicine and the Changing Conceptualization of Female Deviance." *Salmagundi* 58–59 (Fall–Winter): 114–46.

Chin, Curtis; Gayatri Gopinath; Joo-Hyun Kang; and Alvin Realuyo, eds. 1993. *Witness Aloud: Lesbian, Gay and Bisexual Asian/Pacific American Writing.* Special issue of the *APA Journal* 2 (Spring/Summer).

Chodorow, Nancy. 1978. *The Reproduction of Mothering.* Berkeley: University of California Press.

Clarke, Cheryl. 1993. *Experimental Love.* Ithaca: Firebrand Books.

Constantine, Lynne M., and Suzanne Scott. 1990. "Belles Lettres Interview with Jeanette Winterson." *Belles Lettres* 5 (4): 24–26.

Cook, Blanche Wiesen. 1979. "'Women Alone Stir My Imagination': Lesbianism and the Cultural Tradition." *Signs* 2 (Summer): 719–20.

Creet, Julia. 1991. "Daughter of the Movement: The Psychodynamics of Lesbian S/M Fantasy." *Differences* 3 (Summer): 135–59.

Cummings, Katherine. 1991. *Telling Tales: The Hysteric's Seduction in Fiction and Theory.* Stanford: Stanford University Press.

D'Adesky, Anne-Christine. 1993. "Still Life with Winterson." *Out* (Feb./March): 33–39.

Daedalus (1990). Special issue on "risk." 119: 4.

Davis, Angela. 1983. *Women, Race, and Class.* New York: Vintage.

Davy, Kate. 1993. "From *Lady Dick* to Ladylike: The Work of Holly Hughes." In *Acting Out: Feminist Performances,* ed. Lynda Hart and Peggy Phelan, 55–84. Ann Arbor: University of Michigan Press.

De Lauretis, Teresa. 1984. "Desire in Narrative." In de Lauretis, *Alice Doesn't,* 103–57. Bloomington: Indiana University Press.

——. 1986. "Feminist Studies/Critical Studies: Issues, Terms, and Contexts." In *Feminist Studies/Critical Studies,* ed. Teresa de Lauretis, 1–19. Bloomington: Indiana University Press.

——. 1987. *Technologies of Gender.* Bloomington: Indiana University Press.

——. 1988. "Sexual Indifference and Lesbian Representation." *Theatre Journal* 40 (2): 155–77.

—— 1990. "The Practice of Sexual Difference and Feminist Thought In Italy: An Introductory Essay." Introduction to *Sexual Difference: A Theory of Social-Symbolic Practice* by the Milan Women's Bookstore Collective, trans. Patricia Cicogna and Teresa de Lauretis. Bloomington: Indiana University Press.

——. 1991a. "Film and the Visible." In *How Do I Look?,* ed. Bad Object-Choices, 225–64. Seattle: Bay Press.

——. 1991b. "Perverse Desire: The Lure of the Mannish Lesbian." *Australian Feminist Studies* 13 (Autumn): 15–26.

——. 1991c. "Queer Theory: Lesbian and Gay Sexualities—An Introduction." *Differences* 3 (2): iii–xvii.

—— 1994. *The Practice of Love: Lesbian Sexuality and Perverse Desire.* Bloomington: Indiana University Press.

DeLombard, Jeannine. 1995. "Balancing the Books." *Out* 18 (Dec./Jan.): 72–75, 134–35.

DeLynn, Jane. 1990. *Don Juan in the Village.* New York: Ballantine Books.

De Rougemont, Denis. (1940) 1956. *Love in the Western World.* New York: Schocken Books.

Deutsch, Helene. 1944. *The Psychology of Women.* New York: Grune and Stratton.

Doan, Laura. 1994. "Jeanette Winterson's Sexing the Postmodern." In *The Lesbian Postmodern,* ed. Laura Doan, 137–55. New York: Columbia University Press.

Dolan, Jill. 1993. *Presence and Desire: Essays on Gender, Sexuality, Performance.* Ann Arbor: University of Michigan Press.

Doty, Alexander. 1993. *Making Things Perfectly Queer.* Minneapolis: University of Minnesota Press.

Douglas, Mary. 1992. *Risk and Blame.* New York: Routledge.

Duchartre, Pierre, and René Saulnier. 1926. *L'imagerie populaire.* Paris: Librairie de France.

Duggan, Lisa. 1992. "Making It Perfectly Queer." *Socialist Review* 22 (1): 11–31.

Edelman, Lee. 1994. *Homographesis: Essays in Gay Literary and Cultural Theory.* New York: Routledge.

Ellis, Havelock. 1937. *Studies in the Psychology of Sex.* Vol. 4. New York: Random House.

Engelbrecht, Penelope. 1990. "'Lifting Belly Is a Language': The Postmodern Lesbian Subject." *Feminist Studies* 16 (Spring): 85–114.

Escomel, Gloria, and Francine Pelletier. 1988. "Michèle Causse: For a Sea of Women. Interview in *La Vie en Rose,* July/August 1986." Trans. Lise Weill. *Trivia* 13 (Fall): 74–78.

Ewald, François. 1993. "Two Infinities of Risk." In *The Politics of Everyday Fear,* ed. Brian Massumi, 221–28. Minneapolis: University of Minnesota Press.

Faderman, Lillian. 1981. *Surpassing the Love of Men.* New York: William Morrow.

——. 1986. "Love between Women in 1928: Why Progressivism Is Not Always Progress." In *Historical, Literary, and Erotic Aspects of Lesbianism,* ed. Monika Kehoe, 23–42. New York: Harrington Park Press.

——. 1991. *Odd Girls and Twilight Lovers.* New York: Columbia University Press.

——. 1994a. *Chloe plus Olivia: An Anthology of Lesbian Literature from the Seventeenth Century to the Present.* New York: Viking.

——. 1994b. "The SGN Interview: Lillian Faderman, part 2." By Frederic Kahler. *Seattle Gay News,* 28 October 1994, 25, 32.

Fallon, Mary. 1989. *Working Hot.* Melbourne: Sybylla Co-operative.

Farwell, Marilyn. 1990. "Heterosexual Plots and Lesbian Subtexts: Toward a Theory of Lesbian Narrative Space." In *Lesbian Texts and Contexts,* ed. Karla Jay and Joanne Glasgow, 91–103. New York: New York University Press.

Feinberg, Leslie. 1993. *Stone Butch Blues.* Ithaca: Firebrand Books.

Felman, Shoshana. 1982a. "Psychoanalysis and Education: Teaching Terminable and Interminable." *Yale French Studies* 63: 21–44.

——. 1982b. "To Open the Question." In *Literature and Psychoanalysis,* ed. Shoshana Felman, 5–10. Baltimore: Johns Hopkins University Press.

——. 1983. *The Literary Speech Act: Don Juan with J. L. Austin, or Seduction in Two Languages.* Trans. Catherine Porter. Ithaca: Cornell University Press.

——. 1993. *What Does a Woman Want: Reading and Sexual Difference.* Baltimore: Johns Hopkins University Press.

Fetterley, Judith. 1978. *The Resisting Reader: A Feminist Approach to American Fiction.* Bloomington: Indiana University Press.

Field, Andrew. 1983. *Djuna: The Life and Times of Djuna Barnes.* New York: G. P. Putnam's.

Findlay, Heather. 1994. Review of *The Lesbian Heresy* by Sheila Jeffreys. *The Lesbian Review of Books* 1 (2): 3.

Fishman, Louise. 1994. "Art after Stonewall: Twelve Artists Interviewed—Louise Fishman." *Art in America* 82 (6): 59–60.

Forrest, Katherine V. 1987. *Murder at the Nightwood Bar.* Tallahassee, Fla.: Naiad Press.

Foster, Jeannette. 1975. *Sex Variant Women in Literature.* New York: Vantage Press, 1956. Reprint, Baltimore: Diana Press.

Frankenberg, Ruth. 1993. *White Women, Race Matters: The Social Construction of Whiteness.* Minneapolis: University of Minnesota Press.

Freud, Sigmund. 1953–74. *Standard Edition of the Complete Psychological Works*. Ed. and trans. James Strachey. 24 vols. London: Hogarth Press.

——. 1895. "On the Grounds for Detaching a Particular Syndrome from Neurasthenia." In *Standard Edition*, vol. 3, 87–117.

——. 1900. *The Interpretation of Dreams*. In *Standard Edition*, vol. 4.

——. 1905. *Three Essays on the Theory of Sexuality*. In *Standard Edition*, vol .7, 135–243.

——. 1910. *Leonardo da Vinci and a Memory of His Childhood*. In *Standard Edition*, vol. 9, 63–137.

——. 1911. "Psycho-Analytic Notes on an Autobiographical Account of a Case of Paranoia (Dementia Paranoides)." In *Standard Edition*, vol. 12, 3–82.

——. 1914a. "Remembering, Repeating and Working-Through (Further Recommendations on the Technique of Psycho-Analysis II)." In *Standard Edition*, vol. 12, 145–56.

——. 1914b. "On Narcissism." In *Standard Edition*, vol. 14, 73–102.

——. 1915a. "Instincts and Their Vicissitudes." In *Standard Edition*, vol. 14, 109–40.

——. 1915b. "Observations on Transference-Love (Further Recommendations on the Technique of Psycho-Analysis III)." In *Standard Edition*, vol. 12, 157–71.

——. 1917. "Mourning and Melancholia." In *Standard Edition*, vol. 14, 243–58.

——. 1920a. "Beyond the Pleasure Principle." In *Standard Edition*, vol. 8, 1–64.

——. 1920b. "The Psychogenesis of a Case of Homosexuality in a Woman." In *Standard Edition*, vol. 18, 147–72.

——. 1921. *Group Psychology and the Analysis of the Ego*. In *Standard Edition*, vol. 8, 65–143.

——. 1923. *The Ego and the Id*. In *Standard Edition*, vol. 19, 3–66.

——. 1926. *Inhibitions, Symptoms and Anxiety*. In *Standard Edition*, vol. 20, 75–175.

——. 1933. *New Introductory Lectures on Psycho-Analysis*. Lecture XXXIII, "Femininity." In *Standard Edition*, vol. 22, 112–35.

——. 1985. *The Complete Letters of Sigmund Freud to Wilhelm Fliess, 1887–1904*. Trans. and ed. Jeffrey Masson. Cambridge: Harvard University Press.

Frye, Marilyn. 1990. "Lesbian 'Sex.'" In *Lesbian Philosophies and Cultures*, ed. Jeffner Allen, 305–15. Albany: State University of New York Press.

Fuss, Diana. 1991. "Inside/Out." In *Inside/Out: Lesbian Theories, Gay Theories*, ed. Diana Fuss, 1–10. New York: Routledge.

——. 1993. "Freud's Fallen Women: Identification, Desire, and 'A Case of Homosexuality in a Woman.'" In *Fear of a Queer Planet*, ed. Michael Warner, 42–68. Minneapolis: University of Minnesota Press.

Garber, Marjorie. 1992. *Vested Interests: Cross-Dressing and Cultural Anxiety*. New York: Columbia University Press.

Gerstenberger, Donna. 1989. "The Radical Narrative of Djuna Barnes's *Nightwood*." In *Breaking the Sequence: Women's Experimental Fiction*, ed. Ellen Friedman and Miriam Fuchs, 129–39. Princeton: Princeton University Press.

Gever, Martha; John Greyson; and Pratibha Parmar. 1993. *Queer Looks: Perspectives on Lesbian and Gay Film and Video*. New York: Routledge.

Gilbert, Harriett. "Flaying Alive." *The Listener*, 9 August 1990, 32.

Gilbert, Sandra, and Susan Gubar. 1979. *The Madwoman in the Attic*. New Haven: Yale University Press.

——. 1989. *No Man's Land: The Place of the Woman Writer in the Twentieth Century*. Vol. 2, *Sexchanges*. New Haven: Yale University Press.

Gilligan, Carol. 1982. *In a Different Voice: A Psychological Theory of Women's Development*. Cambridge: Harvard University Press.

Goldstein, Nancy. 1994. "Trading Shame for Power: Amber Hollibaugh and the Lesbian AIDS Project." *Deneuve* (July/August): 42–43.

Gomez, Jewelle. 1991. *The Gilda Stories*. Ithaca: Firebrand Books.

Gonnard, Catherine. 1987. "Interview with Michèle Causse: Catherine Gonnard in *Lesbia*." Trans. Lise Weil. *Trivia* 14 (Spring): 59–65.

Griffin, Gabriele. 1993. *Heavenly Love? Lesbian Images in Twentieth-Century Women's Writing*. Manchester: Manchester University Press.

Grosz, Elizabeth. 1988. "The Hetero and the Homo: The Sexual Ethics of Luce Irigaray." *Gay Information* 17–18: 37–44.

Hacker, Marilyn. 1986. *Love, Death and the Changing of the Seasons*. New York: Arbor House.

Hall, Radclyffe. (1928) 1950. *The Well of Loneliness*. New York: Pocket Books.

Halperin, David. 1990. *One Hundred Years of Homosexuality and Other Essays on Greek Love*. New York: Routledge.

Hamer, Diane. 1990. "Significant Others: Lesbianism and Psychoanalytic Theory." *Feminist Review* 34 (Spring): 134–51.

Harris, Bertha. 1969. *Catching Saradove*. New York: Harcourt Brace.

———. 1972. *Confessions of Cherubino*. New York: Harcourt Brace.

———. 1973. "The More Profound Nationality of Their Lesbianism: Lesbian Society in Paris in the 1920s." In *Amazon Expedition*, ed. Phyllis Birkby, Bertha Harris, Jill Johnston, Esther Newton, and Jane O'Wyatt, 77–88. Washington, N.J.: Times Change Press.

———. 1976. *Lover*. Plainfield, Vt.: Daughters, Inc.

———. 1977. "What We Mean to Say: Notes toward Defining the Nature of Lesbian Literature." *Heresies* (Fall): 5–8.

———. 1979. "Melancholia, and Why It Feels Good." *Sinister Wisdom* 9 (Spring): 24–26.

———. 1993. *Lover*. Reprint with a foreword by Karla Jay and a new introduction by Harris. New York: New York University Press. Original ed., Plainfield, Vt.: Daughters, Inc., 1976.

———. 1994. "Louise Fishman: *Valles Marineris, 1992*." *Artforum* 32 (9): 74–75, 119.

Hart, Lynda. 1994. *Fatal Women: Lesbian Sexuality and the Mark of Aggression*. Princeton: Princeton University Press.

Hayes, John Charles. 1990. *The Tradition of Prejudice versus the Principle of Equality: Homosexuals and Heightened Equal Protection Scrutiny after Bowers v. Hardwick*, 31 B.C.L. Rev. 375, 388–89. Quoted in Carl F. Stychin, "Inside and Out of the Military," *Law & Sexuality* (1993), vol. 3: 27–43.

Hermes, Joke. 1992. "Sexuality in Lesbian Romance." *Feminist Review* 42 (Autumn): 49–66.

Herrmann, Anne. 1992. "Imitations of Marriage: Crossdressed Couples in Contemporary Lesbian Fiction." *Feminist Studies* 18 (3): 609–24.

Higgins, Patrick, ed. 1994. *A Queer Reader: A Compendium of Quotes by and about Gay Men throughout the Ages*. New York: New Press.

Hoagland, Sarah. 1988. *Lesbian Ethics toward New Values*. Palo Alto: Institute of Lesbian Studies.

———. 1991. "Some Thoughts about 'Caring.'" In *Feminist Ethics*, ed. Claudia Card, 246–63. Lawrence: University of Kansas Press.

Holland, Norman. 1976. "Transactive Criticism: Re-creation through Identity." *Criticism* 18. Quoted in Steven Mailloux, *Interpretive Conventions: The Reader in the Study of American Fiction* (Ithaca: Cornell University Press, 1982), 24.

Hollibaugh, Amber, and Cherrie Moraga. 1983. "What We're Rollin Around in Bed With: Sexual Silences in Feminism." In *Powers of Desire: The Politics of Sexuality*, ed. Ann Snitow, Christine Stansell, and Sharon Thompson, 394–405. New York: Monthly Review Press.

hooks, bell. 1992. "Representations of Whiteness in the Black Imagination." In hooks, *Black Looks: Race and Representation*, 165–88. Boston: South End Press.

Irigaray, Luce. 1981. "And One Doesn't Stir without the Other." Translated and with an introduction by Helene Wenzel. *Signs* 7 (Autumn): 66–79.

———. 1985a. "The Blind Spot of an Old Dream of Symmetry." In Irigaray, *Speculum of the Other Woman*, trans. Gillian Gill, 13–129. Ithaca: Cornell University Press.

———. 1985b. *This Sex Which Is Not One*. Trans. Catherine Porter with Carolyn Burke. Ithaca: Cornell University Press.

Iser, Wolfgang. 1978. *The Act of Reading: A Theory of Aesthetic Response*. Baltimore: Johns Hopkins University Press.

Jagose, Annamarie. 1992. "Irigaray and the Lesbian Body: Remedy and Poison." *Genders* 13 (Spring): 30–42.

Jay, Karla. 1990. "The Outsider among the Expatriates: Djuna Barnes's Satire on the Ladies of the *Almanack*." In *Lesbian Texts and Contexts*, ed. Karla Jay and Joanne Glasgow, 204–16. New York: New York University Press.

Jay, Karla, and Joanne Glasgow, eds. 1990. *Lesbian Texts and Contexts*. New York: New York University Press.

Johnson, Barbara. 1993. "Lesbian Spectacles: Reading *Sula, Passing, Thelma and Louise*, and *The Accused*." In *Media Spectacles*, ed. Marjorie Garber, Jann Matlock, and Rebecca L. Walkowitz, 160–66. New York: Routledge.

Kaivola, Karen. 1991. *All Contraries Confounded: The Lyrical Fiction of Virginia Woolf, Djuna Barnes, and Marguerite Duras*. Iowa City: University of Iowa Press.

Kennard, Jean. 1986. "Ourself behind Ourself: A Theory for Lesbian Readers." In *Gender and Reading*, ed. Elizabeth Flynn and Patrocinio Schweickart, 63–80. Baltimore: Johns Hopkins University Press.

Kennedy, Elizabeth Lapovsky, and Madeline D. Davis. 1993. *Boots of Leather, Slippers of Gold: The History of a Lesbian Community*. New York: Routledge.

Kent, Kathryn R. 1993. "'Lullaby for a Lady': Lesbian Identity in *Ladies Almanack*." *Review of Contemporary Fiction* 13 (3): 89–96.

Kiss & Tell. 1994. *Her Tongue on My Theory*. Vancouver, B.C.: Press Gang Publishers.

Kitzinger, Celia. 1987. *The Social Construction of Lesbianism*. London: Sage.

Klein, Melanie. 1946 (1986). "Notes on Some Schizoid Mechanisms." In *The Selected Melanie Klein*, ed. Juliet Mitchell, 176–200. New York: The Free Press.

Klepfisz, Irena. 1979. "Criticism: Form and Function in Lesbian Literature." *Sinister Wisdom* 9 (Spring): 27–30.

Kolodny, Annette. 1985 (1980). "A Map for Misreading: Gender and the Interpretation of Literary Texts." In *The New Feminist Criticism*, ed. Elaine Showalter, 46–62. New York: Pantheon Books.

Koestenbaum, Wayne. 1993. "The Purple Reign of Bertha Harris." *Village Voice Literary Supplement* 119: 18.

Kristeva, Julia. 1980. *Desire in Language; A Semiotic Approach to Literature and Art,* ed. Leon S. Roudiez, trans. Thomas Gora, Alice Jardine, and Leon S. Roudiez. New York: Columbia University Press.

———. 1986. "Freud and Love: Treatment and Its Discontents." Trans. Leon S. Roudiez. In *The Kristeva Reader*, ed. Toril Moi, 238–71. New York: Columbia University Press.

Lacan, Jacques. 1977. *Ecrits*. Trans. Alan Sheridan. New York: W. W. Norton.

Lamos, Colleen. 1994. "The Lesbian Postmodern Position: *On Our Backs*." In *The Lesbian Postmodern*, ed. Laura Doan, 85–103. New York: Columbia University Press.

Lanser, Susan Sniader. 1991. "Speaking in Tongues: *Ladies Almanack* and the Discourse of Desire." In *Silence and Power,* ed. Mary Lynn Broe, 156–68. Carbondale: Southern Illinois University Press.

———. 1992. Introduction to *Ladies Almanack*. New York: New York University Press.

Laplanche, Jean, and J.-B. Pontalis. 1973. *The Language of Psycho-Analysis*. Trans. Donald Nicholson-Smith. New York: W. W. Norton.

Lee, Judith. 1991. "*Nightwood*: 'The Sweetest Lie.'" In *Silence and Power,* ed. Mary Lynn Broe, 207–18. Carbondale: Southern Illinois University Press.

Levine, Nancy, and Marian Urquilla, eds. 1993. *Review of Contemporary Fiction: Djuna Barnes Centennial Issue*. Naperville, Ill.: Dalkey Archive Press.

Lim-Hing, Sharon, ed. 1994. *The Very Inside: An Anthology of Writing by Asian and Pacific Islander Lesbian and Bisexual Women*. Toronto: Sister Vision Press.

Linden, Robin Ruth; Darlene Pagano; Diana Russell; and Susan Leigh Star, eds. 1982. *Against Sado-Masochism*. East Palo Alto: Frogs in the Well Press.

Lorde, Audre. 1982. *Zami: A New Spelling of My Name*. Trumansburg, N.Y.: Crossing Press.

———. 1985. "Uses of the Erotic: The Erotic as Power." In Lorde, *Sister Outsider*. Trumansburg, N.Y.: Crossing Press.

Loulan, JoAnn (with Sherry Thomas). 1990. *The Lesbian Erotic Dance*. San Francisco: Spinster Book Company.

Lynch, Lee. 1990. "Cruising the Libraries." In *Lesbian Texts and Contexts,* ed. Karla Jay and Joanne Glasgow, 39–48. New York: New York University Press.

McKinley, Catherine, and L. Joyce Delaney, eds. 1995. *Afrekete: An Anthology of Black Lesbian Writing*. New York: Anchor Books.

McNaron, Toni. 1993. "Mirrors and Likeness: A Lesbian Aesthetic in the Making." In *Sexual Practice/Textual Theory,* ed. Susan Wolfe and Julia Penelope. Cambridge, Mass: Basil Blackwell.

Mailloux, Steven. 1982. *Interpretive Conventions: The Reader in the Study of American Fiction*. Ithaca: Cornell University Press.

Marcus, Jane. 1987. *Virginia Woolf and the Languages of Patriarchy*. Bloomington: Indiana University Press.

———. 1991. "Laughing at Leviticus: *Nightwood* as Woman's Circus Epic." In *Silence and Power,* ed. Mary Lynn Broe, 221–50. Carbondale: Southern Illinois University Press.

Marks, Elaine. 1979. "Lesbian Intertextuality." In *Homosexuality and French Literature,* ed. Elaine Marks and George Stambolian, 353–77. Ithaca: Cornell University Press.

Marlatt, Daphne. 1988. *Ana Historic*. Toronto: Coach House Press.

Martin, Biddy. 1992. "Sexual Practice and Changing Lesbian Identities." In *Destabilizing Theory,* ed. Michèle Barrett and Anne Phillips, 93–119. Stanford: Stanford University Press.

Mayne, Judith. 1993. *Cinema and Spectatorship*. New York: Routledge.

Meese, Elizabeth. 1990. "Theorizing Lesbian: Writing—A Love Letter." In *Lesbian Texts and Contexts,* ed. Karla Jay and Joanne Glasgow, 70–87. New York: New York University Press.

———. 1992. *(Sem)Erotics*. New York: New York University Press.

Merck, Mandy. 1993. *Perversions*. New York: Routledge.

Milan Women's Bookstore Collective. 1990. *Sexual Difference: A Theory of Social-Symbolic Practice*. Trans. Patricia Cicogna and Teresa de Lauretis.

Miller, D. A. 1992. *Bringing Out Roland Barthes*. Berkeley: University of California Press.

Miner, Valerie. 1993. "At Her Wit's End." *Women's Review of Books* (May): 21.

Mistress Vena. 1993. "Confessions of a Psycho-Mistress." *Social Text* 37 (Winter): 65–72.

Mitchell, Juliet. 1984. *Women: The Longest Revolution*. New York: Pantheon Books.

———. 1986. "Introduction" to *The Selected Melanie Klein*. New York: Free Press.

Modleski, Tania. 1991. *Feminism without Women: Culture and Criticism in a Postmodern Age*. New York: Routledge.

Moraga, Cherríe. 1983. *Loving in the War Years*. New York: Kitchen Table Press.

Morrison, Toni. 1992. *Playing in the Dark: Whiteness and the Literary Imagination*. Cambridge: Harvard University Press.

Nestle, Joan. 1987. *A Restricted Country*. Ithaca: Firebrand Books.

———. ed. 1992. *The Persistent Desire: A Femme-Butch Reader*. Boston: Alyson Publications.

Newton, Esther. 1984. "The Mythic Mannish Lesbian: Radclyffe Hall and the New Woman." *Signs* 9 (Summer): 557–75.

Nichols, Margaret. 1987. "Lesbian Sexuality: Issues and Developing Theory." In *Lesbian Psychologies: Explorations and Challenges,* ed. the Boston Lesbian Psychologies Collective, 97–125. Urbana: University of Illinois Press.

Nin, Anaïs. 1959. *Cities of the Interior*. Denver: Alan Swallow Press.

O'Connor, Noreen, and Joanna Ryan. 1993. *Wild Desires and Mistaken Identities*. New York: Columbia University Press.

Omosupe, Erua. 1991. "Black/Lesbian/Bulldagger." *Differences* 5 (2): 101–11.

O'Rourke, Rebecca. 1989. *Reflecting on the Well of Loneliness*. London: Routledge.

Palmer, Pauline. 1993. "The Lesbian Thriller: Crimes, Clues and Contradictions." In *Outwrite: Lesbianism and Popular Culture,* ed. Gabriele Griffin, 86–105. London: Pluto Press.

Parker, Alice. 1990. "Nicole Brossard: A Differential Equation of Lesbian Love." In *Lesbian Texts and Contexts,* ed. Karla Jay and Joanne Glasgow, 304–29. New York: New York University Press..

Petro, Pamela. 1993. "A British Original." *Atlantic* (February): 113–15.

Phillips, Jayne Anne. 1979. *Black Tickets*. New York: Dell.

Pilgrim, Anita Naoko. 1995. "A Literary Movement." In *Talking Black: Lesbians of African and Asian Descent Speak Out,* ed. Valerie Mason-John, 151–85. London: Cassell.

Radford, Jean. 1986. *The Progress of Romance: The Politics of Popular Fiction*. London and New York: Routledge & Kegan Paul.

Radway, Janice A. 1984. *Reading the Romance*. Chapel Hill: University of North Carolina Press.

Ratti, Rakesh, ed. 1993. *A Lotus of Another Color: An Unfolding of the South Asian Gay and Lesbian Experience*. Boston: Alyson Press.

Reich, June L. 1992. "Genderfuck: The Law of the Dildo." *Discourse* 15 (Fall): 112–27.

Rich, Adrienne. 1976. *Of Woman Born*. New York: W. W. Norton.

———. 1978. "Twenty-One Love Poems." In *Dream of a Common Language*. New York: W. W. Norton.

Rich, B. Ruby. 1986. "Feminism and Sexuality in the 1980s." *Feminist Studies* 12 (3): 525–61.

Roberts, Michele. 1986. "Write, She Said." In *The Progress of Romance,* ed. Jean Radford, 221–35. London and New York: Routledge and Kegan Paul.

Roe, Sue. 1990. "Under the Scalpel." *TLS* 14–20 (December): 1359.

Roof, Judith. 1991. *A Lure of Knowledge: Lesbian Sexuality and Theory*. New York: Columbia University Press.

Rose, Jacqueline. 1993. *Why War?* London: Blackwell.

Rosenblatt, Louise M. 1978. *The Reader, the Text, the Poem: The Transactional Theory of the Literary Work*. Carbondale: Southern Illinois University Press.

Rubin, Gayle. 1978. "The Traffic in Women: Notes on the 'Political Economy of Sex.'" In *Toward an Anthropology of Women,* ed. Rayna Reiter, 157–210. New York: Monthly Review Press.

Ruehl, Sonja. 1991. "Defining Identities." In *Stolen Glances: Lesbians Take Photographs,* ed. Tessa Boffin and Jean Fraser, 34–41. London: Pandora.

Rule, Jane. 1965. *Desert of the Heart*. Cleveland: World Publishing.

Rycenga, Jennifer. 1994. "Multiple Lesbian Identities." *Lesbian Review of Books* 1 (2): 22.

Sapphire. 1994. *American Dreams*. New York: Serpent's Tail Press.

Schulman, Sarah. 1988. *After Delores*. New York: E. P. Dutton.

———. 1992. *Empathy*. New York: Dutton.

———. 1993. "Guilty with Explanation: Jeanette Winterson's Endearing Book of Love." *Lambda Book Report* (March/April): 20.

Scott, Joan W. 1990. "Deconstructing Equality-versus-Difference: Or, the Uses of Poststructuralist Theory for Feminism." In *Conflicts in Feminism,* ed. Marianne Hirsch and Evelyn Fox Keller, 134–48. New York: Routledge.

Sedgwick, Eve. 1990. *The Epistemology of the Closet*. Berkeley: University of California Press.

Segal, Hanna, and David Bell. 1991. "The Theory of Narcissism in the Work of Freud and Klein." In *Freud's "On Narcissism: An Introduction,"* ed. Joseph Sandler, Ethel Spector Person, and Peter Fonagy, 149–74. New Haven: Yale University Press.

Seidel, Miriam. 1993. "Material Imperatives." *Art in America* 81 (9): 95–96, 98.

Siegel, Elaine. 1988. *Female Homosexuality: Choice without Volition.* Hillsdale, N.J.: The Analytic Press.

Silvera, Makeda, ed. 1991. *Piece of My Heart: A Lesbian of Colour Anthology.* Toronto: Sister Vision Press.

Silverman, Kaja. 1988. *The Acoustic Mirror.* Bloomington: Indiana University Press.

Sinfield, Alan. 1994. *Cultural Politics—Queer Reading.* Philadelphia: University of Pennsylvania Press.

Solomon, Alisa. 1992. "Identity Crisis: Queer Politics in the Age of Possibilities." *Village Voice* 37 (26): 27–29, 33.

Sorel, Barbara. 1990. *Sorel in Love.* New York: Fifth Street Press.

Spillers, Hortense. 1987. "Mama's Baby, Papa's Maybe: An American Grammar Book." *Diacritics* 17 (2): 65–81.

Spivak, Gayatri. 1992. "Acting Bits/Identity Talk." *Critical Inquiry* 18 (Summer): 770–803.

Spraggs, Gillian. 1992. "Hell and the Mirror: A Reading of *Desert of the Heart.*" In *New Lesbian Criticism,* ed. Sally Munt, 115–31. New York: Columbia University Press.

Sprengnether, Madelon. 1990. *The Spectral Mother: Freud, Feminism and Psychoanalysis.* Ithaca: Cornell University Press.

Stein, Arlene. 1992. "Sisters and Queers: The Decentering of Lesbian Feminism." *Socialist Review* 22 (1): 33–55.

——. 1993. "The Year of the Lustful Lesbian." In *Sisters. Sexperts. Queers: Beyond Lesbian Nation,* ed. Arlene Stein, 13–34. New York: Penguin.

Steptoe, Lydia [pseud]. 1994. "Sex Memory." *Venus Infers* 2 (1): 24–37.

Stimpson, Catharine. 1982. "Zero-Degree Deviancy: The Lesbian Novel in English." In *Writing and Sexual Difference,* ed. Elizabeth Abel, 243–59. Chicago: University of Chicago Press.

——. 1990. "Afterword: Lesbian Studies in the 1990s." In *Lesbian Texts and Contexts,* ed. Karla Jay and Joanne Glasgow, 377–82. New York: New York University Press.

——. 1991. Afterword to *Silence and Power,* ed. Mary Lynn Broe, 370–73. Carbondale: Southern Illinois University Press.

Storr, Merl. 1993. "Psychoanalysis and Lesbian Desire: The Trouble with Female Homosexuals." In *Activating Theory,* ed. Joseph Bristow and Angelia R. Wilson, 53–69. London: Lawrence and Wishart.

Taylor, Helen. 1989. "Romantic Readers." In *From My Guy to Sci-Fi: Genre and Women's Writing in the Postmodern World,* ed. Helen Carr, 58–77. London: Pandora.

Traub, Valerie. 1991. "Ambiguities of 'Lesbian' Viewing Pleasure: The (Dis)articulations of *Black Widow.*" In *Body Guards,* ed. Julia Epstein and Kristina Straub, 305–28. New York: Routledge.

Trujillo, Carla, ed. 1991. *Chicana Lesbians: The Girls Our Mothers Warned Us About.* Berkeley: Third Woman Press.

Turoff, Randy. 1994. "The Pleasures of Transgression." *Lesbian Review of Books* 1 (Autumn): 21–22.

Vance, Carole, ed. 1984. *Pleasure and Danger: Exploring Female Sexuality.* New York: Routledge and Kegan Paul, 1984.

Vaux, Anna. 1992. "Body Language." *Times Literary Supplement,* 4 September, 20.

Vicinus, Martha. 1993. "'They Wonder to Which Sex I Belong.'" In *The Lesbian and Gay Studies Reader,* ed. Henry Abelove et al., 432–52. New York: Routledge.

Ware, Vron. 1992. *Beyond the Pale: White Women, Racism and History.* London: Verso.

Warner, Michael. 1990. "Homo-Narcissism; or, Heterosexuality." In *Engendering Men,* ed. Joseph Boone and Michael Cadden, 190–206. New York: Routledge.

——. 1992. "From Queer to Eternity." *Village Voice Literary Supplement* 102: 18–19.

Weber, Samuel. 1982. *The Legend of Freud*. Minneapolis: University of Minnesota Press, 1982.

Weir, Angela, and Elizabeth Wilson. 1992. "The Greyhound Bus Station in the Evolution of Lesbian Popular Culture." In *New Lesbian Criticism*, ed. Sally Munt, 95–113. New York: Columbia University Press.

White, Patricia. 1991. "Female Spectator, Lesbian Specter: *The Haunting*." In *Inside/Out: Lesbian Theories, Gay Theories*, ed. Diana Fuss, 142–72. New York: Routledge.

Williams, Linda. 1989. *Hard Core: Power, Pleasure and the "Frenzy of the Visible."* Berkeley: University of California Press.

Wilson, A. N. 1992. "The Narrator That Dare Not Speak Her Name." *The Spectator*, 19 September, 34.

Wilson, Barbara. 1991. "The Erotic Life of Fictional Characters." In *An Intimate Wilderness: Lesbian Writers on Sexuality*, ed. Judith Barrington, 199–209. Portland, Ore.: Eighth Mountain Press.

Wilson, Elizabeth (with A. Weir). 1986. *Hidden Agendas: Theory, Politics and Experience in the Women's Movement*. London: Tavistock. Quoted in Pauline Palmer, "The Lesbian Thriller: Crimes, Clues and Contradictions," in *Outwrite: Lesbianism and Popular Culture*, ed. Griffin Gabriele, 86–105. London: Pluto Press, 1990.

Winterson, Jeanette. 1985. *Oranges Are Not the Only Fruit*. New York: Atlantic Monthly Press.

——. 1986. *Passion Fruit: Romantic Fiction with a Twist*. London: Pandora.

——. 1987. *The Passion*. New York: Atlantic Monthly Press.

——. 1989. *Sexing the Cherry*. New York: Atlantic Monthly Press.

——. 1992. *Written on the Body*. New York: Random House.

——. 1994. *Art and Lies*. Toronto: Knopf.

Wittig, Monique. 1983. "Point of View: Universal or Particular." *Feminist Issues* 3 (2): 63–69.

Wolff, Charlotte. 1973. *Love between Women*. London: Duckworth.

Woolf, Virginia. (1929) 1957. *A Room of One's Own*. New York: Harcourt, Brace and World.

Young, Ian; John Stoltenberg; Lyn Rosen; and Rose Jordan. 1978. "Forum on Sado-Masochism." In *Lavender Culture*, ed. Karla Jay and Allen Young, 85–118. New York: Harcourt Brace.

Zimmerman, Bonnie. 1990. *The Safe Sea of Women*. Boston: Beacon Press.

INDEX

Abraham, Julie, 5, 115n.30
Acker, Kathy, 120n.15
Adams, Parveen, 119n.7, 123n.14
Affect and women's erotics, 63, 67, 82
Affective exchange between women, 2, 6, 17, 46, 52, 76
Aguilar-San Juan, Karin, 14
AIDS, 50, 51, 52, 121n.28
Altman, Meryl, 117n.8
American Dreams (Sapphire), 18
Antoniou, Laura, 124n.24
Anxiety, 19, 59–62; erotics of, 52, 76; and fear, 120–21n.8; in Freud, 120n.18; and loss, 59–62, 73
Arnold, June, 123n.5

Bad Attitude, 89
Barale, Michele Aina, 114n.23
Barnes, Djuna, 112n.5; biography, 4; family life, 24; literary scholarship on, 115n.25; as "Lydia Steptoe," 1; *Ryder*, 4, 118n.34; *Spillway*, 27, 43. See also *Ladies Almanack; Nightwood;* "Cassation"; "Dusie"; "The Grande Malade"
Barnes tradition. See *Nightwood* literary tradition
Barney, Natalie Clifford, 4, 10, 112n.10
Barthes, Roland, 11, 113nn.20,21; *A Lover's Discourse*, 10
Batsleer, Janet, 69, 70
Birtha, Becky (*Lover's Choice*), 18
Bloom, Harold, 111n.1
Boaz, Amy, 122n.1
Body, language of, 77–80, 87, 91, 121–22n.30
Bogus, SDiane, 115n.29
Borch-Jacobsen, Mikkel, 93
Bowles, Jane, 1
Broe, Mary Lynn, 112n.5; *Silence and Power*, 115n.25
Brooks, Peter, 58, 114n.22
Brooks, Romaine, 10
Brossard, Nicole, 1; *Lovhers*, 10, 11, 23; on *Nightwood*, 10
Brown, Rebecca, 1, 81. See also *The Terrible Girls*
Burch, Beverly, 18, 63, 99; and complementarity, 78; *On Intimate Terms: The Psychology of Difference in Lesbian Relationships*, 78, 94; and projective identification, 76
Bush, Catherine, 49
Butch-femme, 26, 89; butch, 61, 114n.24; femme, 124n.23; as performance, 27; and top/bottom, 105–106
Butler, Judith, 8, 22, 23, 117nn.14,15; on sex and gender, 27

Califia, Pat, 52, 120n.9; *Macho Sluts,* 50–51
"Cassation" (Barnes), 38–41, 42; anticipating *Nightwood,* 39–41; difference-resemblance in, 39; gender reversal in, 38–39; mother-child dynamics of, 40–41; power exchanges in, 39
Causse, Michèle, 1, 10, 23, 33
Chambers, Ross, 114n.22
Chancer, Lynn, 106
Chodorow, Nancy, 39, 121n.22
Clarke, Cheryl (*Experimental Love*), 18
Class differences, 83, 112nn.8,10, 115n.30, 117n.8, 121n.19; and dominant culture, 84–85; and marital status, 64, 79
Cross, Milton, 7
Cross-dressing, 53–59, 117n.17, 120n.13
Cross-identification, 79, 89, 106
Cummings, Katherine, 117n.10, 120n.117, 123n.17

Davis, Madeline D., 114n.24
De Lauretis, Teresa, 14–15, 33, 114nn.22,23, 115n.25, 118nn.23,24, 120n.14; on identification, 123–24n.20; on lesbian sexuality, 3, 21, 22, 28; on multiple identifications, 123n.8; *The Practice of Love*, 3, 115n.27, 124n.22
DeLombard, Jeaninne, 23
DeLynn, Jane, 1, 14
De Rougemont, Denis, 63; *Love in the Western World,* 57–58
Desire, 36; and absence, 29; and deferral, 84–86; and difference, 90, 116n.3; and identification, 19, 32, 34, 82, 95–97, 98–99; and loss, 75, 98; and power, 22; of the reader, 58–59; retrospective, 2, 24–26, 33; and risk, 55, 75; textual, 11, 15, 113n.22; between women, 28, 29, 34, 36, 90. *See also* Difference
Deutsch, Helene, 28
Dickinson, Emily, 101
Difference, 22, 88–90, 123n.8; and desire, 90, 116n.3; as difficult, 91–92; erotics of, 32–33; and otherness, 32, 64; and resemblance, 19–20, 23, 32, 33, 37, 46, 75–80, 82, 87, 89, 96; and "sameness," 22, 27, 95, 115n.3; tensions of, 33. *See also* Difference-sameness; Resemblance; "Sameness" between lovers
Difference-sameness, 27, 41, 43, 87, 88–90, 115–16n.3; and body likeness, 87, 89, 90, 91; and colonization of women, 89; feminist discourses of, 88–89; and homosexuality, 22, 88; poststructural discourses of, 88–89; and sexuality, 32–33; technology of, 88

CAROLYN ALLEN, Associate Professor of English at the University of Washington, has published articles on a variety of twentieth-century writers and on topics in feminism and cultural theory. She is co-editor of *Signs: Journal of Women in Culture and Society.*